enVisionmath 2.0
SCOTT FORESMAN · ADDISON WESLEY

Volume 2 Topics 5–8

Authors

Robert Q. Berry, III
Associate Professor of Mathematics Education, Department of Curriculum, Instruction and Special Education, University of Virginia, Charlottesville, Virginia

Zachary Champagne
Assistant in Research Florida Center for Research in Science, Technology, Engineering, and Mathematics (FCR-STEM) Jacksonville, Florida

Eric Milou
Professor of Mathematics Rowan University, Glassboro, New Jersey

Jane F. Schielack
Professor Emerita, Department of Mathematics Texas A&M University, College Station, Texas

Jonathan A. Wray
Mathematics Instructional Facilitator, Howard County Public Schools, Ellicott City, Maryland

Randall I. Charles
Professor Emeritus Department of Mathematics San Jose State University San Jose, California

Francis (Skip) Fennell
L. Stanley Bowlsbey Professor of Education and Graduate and Professional Studies, McDaniel College Westminster, Maryland

PEARSON

Glenview, Illinois   Boston, Massachusetts   Chandler, Arizona   Hoboken, New Jersey

Mathematician Reviewers

Gary Lippman, Ph.D.
Professor Emeritus
Mathematics and Computer Science
California State University, East Bay
Hayward, California

Karen Edwards, Ph.D.
Mathematics Lecturer
Arlington, MA

PEARSON

ISBN-13:   978-0-328-88191-8
ISBN-10:   0-328-88191-0

11   18

CONTENTS

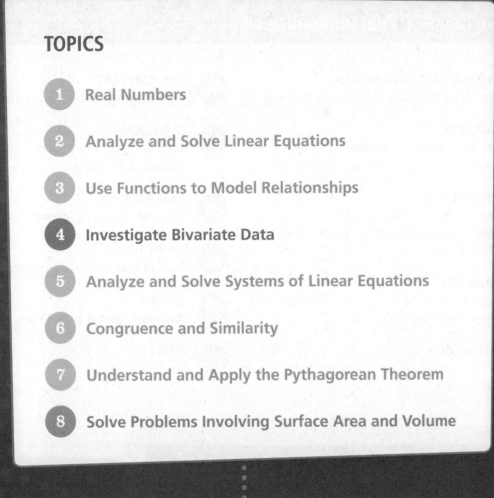

KEY

Major Cluster

Supporting Cluster

Additional Cluster

DIGITAL RESOURCES

🛜 Go Online | **PearsonRealize.com**

👁 INTERACTIVE ANIMATION
Interact with visual learning animations

☝ ACTIVITY
Use with *Solve & Discuss It, Explore It,* and *Explain It* activities and Examples

▶ VIDEOS
Watch clips to support *3-Act Mathematical Modeling* Lessons and *STEM Projects*

✍ PRACTICE
Practice what you've learned and get immediate feedback

⏻ TUTORIALS
Get help from *Virtual Nerd* any time you need it

🔑 KEY CONCEPT
Review important lesson content

A-Z GLOSSARY
Read and listen to English and Spanish definitions

☑ ASSESSMENT
Show what you've learned

🔧 MATH TOOLS
Explore math with digital tools

🎮 GAMES
Play math games to help you learn

📖 ETEXT
Access your book online

PEARSON
realize™
Everything you need for math anytime, anywhere

TOPIC 5

Analyze and Solve Systems of Linear Equations

Congruence and Similarity

TOPIC 7

Understand and Apply the Pythagorean Theorem

TOPIC 8

Solve Problems Involving Surface Area and Volume

COMMON CORE STATE STANDARDS

| MAJOR CLUSTER | SUPPORTING CLUSTER | ADDITIONAL CLUSTER |

Standards for Mathematical Content

THE NUMBER SYSTEM

8.NS.A **Know that there are numbers that are not rational, and approximate them by rational numbers.**

1. Know that numbers that are not rational are called irrational. Understand informally that every number has a decimal expansion; for rational numbers show that the decimal expansion repeats eventually, and convert a decimal expansion which repeats eventually into a rational number.

2. Use rational approximations of irrational numbers to compare the size of irrational numbers, locate them approximately on a number line diagram, and estimate the value of expressions (e.g., π^2).

EXPRESSIONS & EQUATIONS

8.EE.A Work with radicals and integer exponents.

1. Know and apply the properties of integer exponents to generate equivalent numerical expressions.

2. Use square root and cube root symbols to represent solutions to equations of the form $x^2 = p$ and $x^3 = p$, where p is a positive rational number. Evaluate square roots of small perfect squares and cube roots of small perfect cubes. Know that $\sqrt{2}$ is irrational.

3. Use numbers expressed in the form of a single digit times an integer power of 10 to estimate very large or very small quantities, and to express how many times as much one is than the other.

4. Perform operations with numbers expressed in scientific notation, including problems where both decimal and scientific notation are used. Use scientific notation and choose units of appropriate size for measurements of very large or very small quantities (e.g., use millimeters per year for seafloor spreading). Interpret scientific notation that has been generated by technology.

Standards for Mathematical Content

8.EE.B Understand the connections between proportional relationships, lines, and linear equations.

5. Graph proportional relationships, interpreting the unit rate as the slope of the graph. Compare two different proportional relationships represented in different ways.

6. Use similar triangles to explain why the slope m is the same between any two distinct points on a non-vertical line in the coordinate plane; derive the equation $y = mx$ for a line through the origin and the equation $y = mx + b$ for a line intercepting the vertical axis at b.

8.EE.C Analyze and solve linear equations and pairs of simultaneous linear equations.

7. Solve linear equations in one variable.

   a. Give examples of linear equations in one variable with one solution, infinitely many solutions, or no solutions. Show which of these possibilities is the case by successively transforming the given equation into simpler forms, until an equivalent equation of the form $x = a$, $a = a$, or $a = b$ results (where a and b are different numbers).

   b. Solve linear equations with rational number coefficients, including equations whose solutions require expanding expressions using the distributive property and collecting like terms.

8. Analyze and solve pairs of simultaneous linear equations.

   a. Understand that solutions to a system of two linear equations in two variables correspond to points of intersection of their graphs, because points of intersection satisfy both equations simultaneously.

   b. Solve systems of two linear equations in two variables algebraically, and estimate solutions by graphing the equations. Solve simple cases by inspection.

   c. Solve real-world and mathematical problems leading to two linear equations in two variables.

Standards for Mathematical Content

FUNCTIONS

8.F.A Define, evaluate, and compare functions.

1. Understand that a function is a rule that assigns to each input exactly one output. The graph of a function is the set of ordered pairs consisting of an input and the corresponding output.[1]

2. Compare properties of two functions each represented in a different way (algebraically, graphically, numerically in tables, or by verbal descriptions).

3. Interpret the equation $y = mx + b$ as defining a linear function, whose graph is a straight line; give examples of functions that are not linear.

8.F.B Use functions to model relationships between quantities.

4. Construct a function to model a linear relationship between two quantities. Determine the rate of change and initial value of the function from a description of a relationship or from two (x, y) values, including reading these from a table or from a graph. Interpret the rate of change and initial value of a linear function in terms of the situation it models, and in terms of its graph or a table of values.

5. Describe qualitatively the functional relationship between two quantities by analyzing a graph (e.g., where the function is increasing or decreasing, linear or nonlinear). Sketch a graph that exhibits the qualitative features of a function that has been described verbally.

GEOMETRY

8.G.A Understand congruence and similarity using physical models, transparencies, or geometry software.

1. Verify experimentally the properties of rotations, reflections, and translations:

    a. Lines are taken to lines, and line segments to line segments of the same length.

    b. Angles are taken to angles of the same measure.

    c. Parallel lines are taken to parallel lines.

2. Understand that a two-dimensional figure is congruent to another if the second can be obtained from the first by a sequence of rotations, reflections, and translations; given two congruent figures, describe a sequence that exhibits the congruence between them.

3. Describe the effect of dilations, translations, rotations, and reflections on two-dimensional figures using coordinates.

4. Understand that a two-dimensional figure is similar to another if the second can be obtained from the first by a sequence of rotations, reflections, translations, and dilations; given two similar two-dimensional figures, describe a sequence that exhibits the similarity between them.

5. Use informal arguments to establish facts about the angle sum and exterior angle of triangles, about the angles created when parallel lines are cut by a transversal, and the angle-angle criterion for similarity of triangles.

---

[1]Function notation is not required for Grade 8.

Standards for Mathematical Content

● MAJOR CLUSTER
● SUPPORTING CLUSTER
● ADDITIONAL CLUSTER

8.G.B Understand and apply the Pythagorean Theorem.

6. Explain a proof of the Pythagorean Theorem and its converse.

7. Apply the Pythagorean Theorem to determine unknown side lengths in right triangles in real-world and mathematical problems in two and three dimensions.

8. Apply the Pythagorean Theorem to find the distance between two points in a coordinate system.

8.G.C Solve real-world and mathematical problems involving volume of cylinders, cones, and spheres.

9. Know the formulas for the volumes of cones, cylinders, and spheres and use them to solve real-world and mathematical problems.

STATISTICS & PROBABILITY

8.SP.A Investigate patterns of association in bivariate data.

1. Construct and interpret scatter plots for bivariate measurement data to investigate patterns of association between two quantities. Describe patterns such as clustering, outliers, positive or negative association, linear association, and nonlinear association.

2. Know that straight lines are widely used to model relationships between two quantitative variables. For scatter plots that suggest a linear association, informally fit a straight line, and informally assess the model fit by judging the closeness of the data points to the line.

3. Use the equation of a linear model to solve problems in the context of bivariate measurement data, interpreting the slope and intercept.

4. Understand that patterns of association can also be seen in bivariate categorical data by displaying frequencies and relative frequencies in a two-way table. Construct and interpret a two-way table summarizing data on two categorical variables collected from the same subjects. Use relative frequencies calculated for rows or columns to describe possible association between the two variables.

Math Practices and Problem Solving Handbook

CONTENTS

Common Core State Standards
Standards for Mathematical Practice

MP.1 **Make sense of problems and persevere in solving them.**

Mathematically proficient students:
- can explain the meaning of a problem
- look for entry points to begin solving a problem
- analyze givens, constraints, relationships, and goals
- make conjectures about the solution
- plan a solution pathway
- think of similar problems, and try simpler forms of the problem
- evaluate their progress toward a solution and change pathways if necessary
- can explain similarities and differences between different representations
- check their solutions to problems.

MP.2 **Reason abstractly and quantitatively.**

Mathematically proficient students:
- make sense of quantities and their relationships in problem situations:
  - They *decontextualize*—create a coherent representation of a problem situation using numbers, variables, and symbols; and
  - They *contextualize* – attend to the meaning of numbers, variables, and symbols in the problem situation
- know and use different properties of operations to solve problems.

MP.3 **Construct viable arguments and critique the reasoning of others.**

Mathematically proficient students:
- use definitions and problem solutions when constructing arguments
- make conjectures about the solutions to problems
- build a logical progression of statements to support their conjectures and justify their conclusions
- analyze situations and recognize and use counterexamples
- reason inductively about data, making plausible arguments that take into account the context from which the data arose
- listen or read the arguments of others, and decide whether they make sense
- respond to the arguments of others
- compare the effectiveness of two plausible arguments
- distinguish correct logic or reasoning from flawed, and—if there is a flaw in an argument—explain what it is
- ask useful questions to clarify or improve arguments of others.

MP.4 Model with mathematics.

Mathematically proficient students:
- can develop a representation—drawing, diagram, table, graph, expression, equation–to model a problem situation
- make assumptions and approximations to simplify a complicated situation
- identify important quantities in a practical situation and map their relationships using a range of tools
- analyze relationships mathematically to draw conclusions
- interpret mathematical results in the context of the situation and propose improvements to the model as needed.

MP.5 Use appropriate tools strategically.

Mathematically proficient students:
- consider appropriate tools when solving a mathematical problem
- make sound decisions about when each of these tools might be helpful
- identify relevant mathematical resources, and use them to pose or solve problems
- use tools and technology to explore and deepen their understanding of concepts.

MP.6 Attend to precision.

Mathematically proficient students:
- communicate precisely to others
- use clear definitions in discussions with others and in their own reasoning
- state the meaning of the symbols they use
- specify units of measure, and label axes to clarify their correspondence with quantities in a problem
- calculate accurately and efficiently
- express numerical answers with a degree of precision appropriate for the problem context.

MP.7 Look for and make use of structure.

Mathematically proficient students:
- look closely at a problem situation to identify a pattern or structure
- can step back from a solution pathway and shift perspective
- can see complex representations, such as some algebraic expressions, as single objects or as being composed of several objects.

MP.8 Look for and express regularity in repeated reasoning.

Mathematically proficient students:
- notice if calculations are repeated, and look both for general methods and for shortcuts
- maintain oversight of the process as they work to solve a problem, while also attending to the details
- continually evaluate the reasonableness of their intermediate results.

Make sense of problems and persevere in solving them.

Nori, her friend, and her mother bought a baseball game ticket package. The package includes good seats, lunch, and a chance to get autographs from players. The total cost for the three of them is $375. They each paid a $50 deposit. Write an equation that shows how much each of them still owes.

What am I asked to find? An equation that shows how much each of them still owes.

What are the quantities and variables? How do they relate? The cost of the ticket package and the deposit amount are their expenses.

The amount of the deposits is subtracted from the price of the ticket package.

What can I do if I get stuck? I can start subtracting each $50 deposit to find out how much all 3 still owe.

What is a good plan for solving the problem? Define a variable for the unknown and use the quantities I know to write an equation that relates these quantities.

Other questions to consider:

- Have I solved a similar problem before?
- What information is necessary and unnecessary?
- How can I check that my answer makes sense?
- How is my solution pathway the same as or different from my classmate's?

Nori finds out that if 6 people buy the ticket package it only costs $684. Each person still needs to pay a $50 deposit. How does that change the equation? Does each person pay less if 6 people go?

How can I represent this problem situation using numbers, variables, and symbols? I can use the equation I wrote before and change the number of people and the total cost of the ticket package.

What do the numbers, variables, and symbols in the expression or equation mean/represent in the problem situation? $6(p + 50)$ represents the total cost of the package, where p is each person's share.

3-Person Ticket Package

$$3(p + 50) = 375$$
$$3p + 150 = 375$$
$$3p + 150 - 150 = 375 - 150$$
$$3p = 225$$
$$p = 75$$

6-Person Ticket Package

$$6(p + 50) = 684$$
$$6p + 300 = 684$$
$$6p + 300 - 300 = 684 - 300$$
$$6p = 384$$
$$p = 64$$

The 6-person plan is less expensive per person.

Math Practices and Problem Solving Handbook

Michael's class is conducting an experiment by tossing a coin. The table below shows the results of the last 9 tosses.

Michael

Tails has come up 5 times in a row. That means the next toss will land heads up.

Coin Toss

Trial	1	2	3	4	5	6	7	8	9	10
Result	H	T	H	H	T	T	T	T	T	

What assumptions can I make when constructing an argument? A coin can land on heads or tails, so there are two equally likely outcomes.

What questions can I ask to understand other people's thinking? Why does Michael think that the results of the last 5 tosses will affect the outcome of the next coin toss?

What flaw, if any, do I note in his thinking? He thinks that the outcomes of the previous tosses will affect the outcome of the current toss.

How can I justify my conclusions? I can make a diagram to show the possible outcomes.

Other questions to consider:

- How can I determine the accuracy (truth) of my conjectures?
- What arguments can I present to defend my conjectures?
- What conjectures can I make about the solution to the problem?
- Which argument do I find more plausible?

In the next experiment, the class decided to toss two coins at the same time. They wanted to decide whether it is more likely that both coins will show the same side, heads-heads or tails-tails, or more likely that the coins will show one heads and one tails.

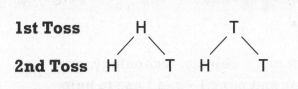

Can I use a drawing, diagram, table, graph, or equation to model the problem? A tree diagram can show the possible outcomes.

1st Toss   H   T

2nd Toss   H   T   H   T

Possible Outcomes: HH, HT, TH, TT

Other questions to consider:

• What representation can I use to show the relationship among quantities or variables?
• How can I make my model better if it doesn't work?
• What assumptions can I make about the problem situation to simplify the problem?
• Does my solution or prediction make sense?
• Is there something I have not considered or forgotten?

Math Practices and Problem Solving Handbook

The Golden Company uses signs in the shape of golden rectangles to advertise its products. In a golden rectangle the length of the longer side is about 1.618 times longer than the shorter side. Draw rectangles to scale to create templates of possible small, medium, and large advertising signs.

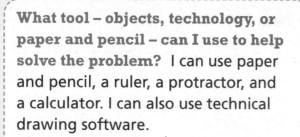

What tool – objects, technology, or paper and pencil – can I use to help solve the problem? I can use paper and pencil, a ruler, a protractor, and a calculator. I can also use technical drawing software.

How can technology help me with a solution strategy? Technical drawing software can help to make the templates more precise and help me develop a variety of templates more efficiently.

Other questions to consider:

- Can I use different tools? Which ones?
- What other resources can I use to help me reach and understand my solution?

MP.6 Attend to precision.

Is my work precise/exact enough?
I am using the appropriate tools to make sure that the dimensions of the templates are precise.

Have I calculated accurately? I draw the the shorter side and then multiply that dimension by 1.618 to determine the length of the longer side.

Other questions to consider:

- Have I stated the meaning of the variables and symbols I am using?
- Have I specified the units of measure I am using?
- Is my work precise/exact enough?
- Did I provide carefully formulated explanations?

Stuart is studying cell division. The table below shows the number of cells after a certain number of divisions. He wants to make a chart that shows drawings of the cell divisions through 10 divisions. Is it reasonable to draw this?

Cell Division

Division	Initial Cell	2	3	4	5	6	7
Number of Cells	1	2	4	8	16	32	64

Can I see a pattern or structure in the problem or solution strategy?
I see that 1 cell becomes 2 cells and 2 cells become 4 cells, and so on.

How can I use the pattern or structure I see to help me solve the problem?
I can write an expression that will show the number of cells after each division.

Other questions to consider:
• Are there attributes in common that help me?
• What patterns in numbers can I see and describe?
• How can I see expressions or equations in different ways?

Cell Division

Do I notice any repeated calculations or steps? Yes; the number of cells after each cell division is the previous number of cells multiplied by 2.

Are there general methods that I can use to solve the problem? I want to show 10 divisions, so I would have to draw 2^{10}, or 1,024 cells. If I try to draw this number of cells on my chart, I could have a really hard time making them fit.

Other questions to consider:

- What can I generalize from one problem to another?
- Can I derive an expression or equation from generalized examples or repeated observations?
- How reasonable are the results that I am getting?

Bar Diagrams with Operations

You can draw bar diagrams to show how quantities are related and to write an equation to solve the problem.

Add To

Result
145.86

x	85.04
Start	Change

The start is unknown, so this is a variable.

Take From

The start is unknown, so this is a variable.

Start
t

2.08417	1.3056
Change	Result

Put Together/Take Apart

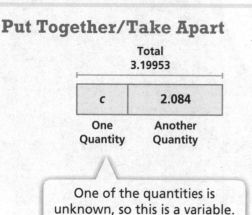

Total
3.19953

c	2.084
One Quantity	Another Quantity

One of the quantities is unknown, so this is a variable.

Compare: Addition and Subtraction

Greater Quantity

14.63	
8.41	m
Lesser Quantity	Difference

The difference is unknown, so this is a variable.

Equal Groups: Multiplication and Division

The number of equal groups is unknown, so this is a variable.

Total
s

$3\frac{2}{5}$	$3\frac{2}{5}$	$3\frac{2}{5}$	$3\frac{2}{5}$

Group Size

Compare: Multiplication and Division

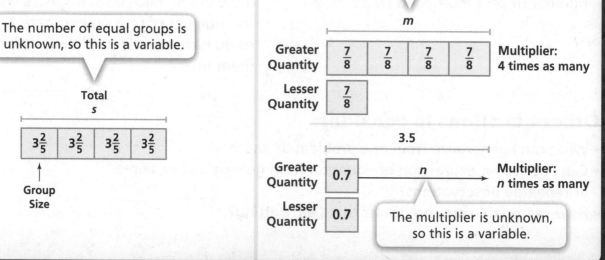

The bigger quantity is unknown, so this is a variable.

m

| Greater Quantity | $\frac{7}{8}$ | $\frac{7}{8}$ | $\frac{7}{8}$ | $\frac{7}{8}$ | Multiplier: 4 times as many |

| Lesser Quantity | $\frac{7}{8}$ |

3.5

| Greater Quantity | 0.7 | n | Multiplier: n times as many |

| Lesser Quantity | 0.7 |

The multiplier is unknown, so this is a variable.

Go Online | PearsonRealize.com

Bar Diagrams in Proportional Reasoning

You can draw bar diagrams to show how quantities are related in proportional relationships.

Ratios and Rates

Draw this bar diagram to show ratios and rates.

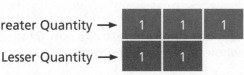

Greater Quantity ➡ | 1 | 1 | 1 |

Lesser Quantity ➡ | 1 | 1 |

This **bar diagram** represents the ratio **3 : 2**.

Greater Quantity Unknown

For every 3 cashews in a snack mix, there are 5 almonds. A package contains 42 cashews. How many almonds are in the same package?

Draw a bar diagram to represent the ratio of cashews to almonds.

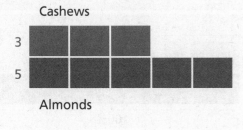

Cashews

3

5

Almonds

Use the same diagram to represent 42 cashews and to determine the number of almonds.

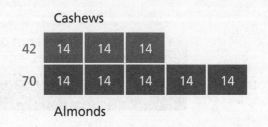

Cashews

42 | 14 | 14 | 14 |

70 | 14 | 14 | 14 | 14 | 14 |

Almonds

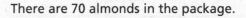

There are 70 almonds in the package.

Math Practices and Problem Solving Handbook BAR DIAGRAMS

Bar Diagrams in Proportional Reasoning

You can draw bar diagrams to show how quantities are related in proportional relationships.

Percents

Draw this bar diagram to show percents.

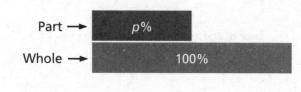

Part → $p\%$

Whole → 100%

This **bar diagram** relates a part to a whole to represent percent.

Part Unknown

A candy company creates batches of colored candies so that, on average, 30% of the candies are orange. About how many orange candies should be included in a batch of 1,500 candies?

Use the bar diagram to write an equation.

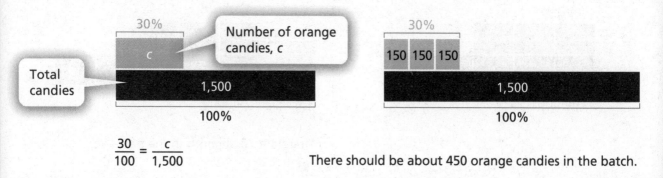

30%

Number of orange candies, c

c

Total candies

1,500

100%

30%

150 150 150

1,500

100%

$$\frac{30}{100} = \frac{c}{1,500}$$

There should be about 450 orange candies in the batch.

Go Online | PearsonRealize.com

Bar Diagrams in Quantitative Reasoning

You can use bar diagrams to solve one-variable equations.

Solve for x: $2x + 5 = 19$

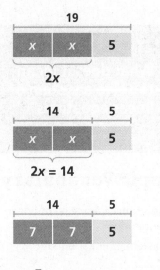

$x = 7$

Solve for y: $4(y - 2) = 24$

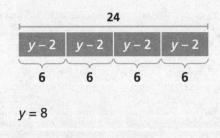

$y = 8$

Solve for m: $4m + 2 = 3m + 4$

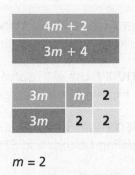

$m = 2$

Andy's brother can spend $80 each month on his cable bill. The local cable company charges a $45 monthly fee for basic cable and $8 per month for each premium channel a customer orders.

How many premium channels can Andy's brother order?

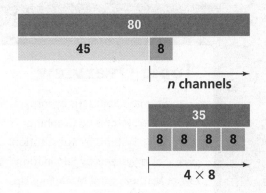

He can order 4 premium channels.

Ella opens a savings account with the $150 she got for her birthday. She plans to deposit $25 each month.

Assuming she does not withdraw any money, how much will she have saved after 2 years?

t, total after 2 years			
150	25	25	25

24 months × $25 = $600

$600 + $150 = $750

She will have saved $750 after 2 years.

TOPIC 5

ANALYZE AND SOLVE SYSTEMS OF LINEAR EQUATIONS

? Topic Essential Question

What does it mean to solve a system of linear equations?

Topic Overview

5-1 Estimate Solutions by Inspection

5-2 Solve Systems by Graphing

5-3 Solve Systems by Substitution

5-4 Solve Systems by Elimination

3-Act Mathematical Modeling: Ups and Downs

Topic Vocabulary

- solution of a system of linear equations
- system of linear equations

Lesson Digital Resources

INTERACTIVE ANIMATION Interact with visual learning animations.

ACTIVITY Use with *Solve & Discuss It, Explore* and *Explain It* activities, and to explore Examp

VIDEOS Watch clips to support *3-Act Mathem Modeling Lessons* and *STEM Projects*.

PRACTICE Practice what you've learned.

 Go online | PearsonRealize.com

Ups and Downs

 Ups and Downs

The express elevators at One World Trade Center in New York are some of the fastest in the world. They can take you 1,280 feet to the observation deck in 60 seconds. That's about 23 miles per hour! Compare that to a typical elevator that travels between 3 and 5 miles per hour. Think about this during the 3-Act Mathematical Modeling lesson.

Additional Digital Resources

 TUTORIALS Get help from *Virtual Nerd*, right when you need it.

 KEY CONCEPT Review important lesson content.

 GLOSSARY Read and listen to English/Spanish definitions.

 ASSESSMENT Show what you've learned.

 MATH TOOLS Explore math with digital tools.

 GAMES Play Math Games to help you learn.

ETEXT Interact with your Student's Edition online.

 VIDEO

Did You Know?

After the Boston Tea Party of 1773, many Americans **switched to drinking coffee** rather than tea because drinking tea was considered unpatriotic.

The United States consumes the most coffee by total weight, but Americans do not drink the most coffee per capita. People in northern European countries like Finland, Norway, and Holland drink more than twice as much coffee as their American counterparts each day.

Although Brazil is the largest coffee-producing nation in the world, Americans combine to drink 0.2% more coffee each year than Brazilians. The third ranked nation for total **coffee consumption**, Germany, consumes approximately 44% as much coffee as either the United States or Brazil.

🫘 **Areas of coffee cultivation**

Tropic of Cancer

Equator

Tropic of Capricorn

In some coffee-producing nations, millions of acres of forest are cleared to make space for coffee farming. **Sustainable farms** grow coffee plants in natural growing conditions without chemicals and with minimal waste.

Coffee beans are actually **seeds** that are harvested from cherries that grow on coffee plants in **tropical climates**.

Your Task: Daily Grind ▶

Coffee roasters create coffee blends by mixing specialty coffees with less expensive coffees in order to create unique coffees, reduce costs, and provide customers with consistent flavor. You and your classmates will explore coffee blends while considering the environmental and economical impact of the coffee trade.

Review What You Know!

Vocabulary

Choose the best term from the box to complete each definition.

linear equation
parallel
slope
y-intercept

1. The value of m in the equation $y = mx + b$ represents the _____.

2. When lines are the same distance apart over their entire lengths, they are _____.

3. The _____ is the value b in the equation $y = mx + b$.

4. A _____ is a relationship between two variables that gives a straight line when graphed.

Identifying Slope and y-Intercept

Identify the slope and the y-intercept of the equation.

5. $y = 2x - 3$

slope = ⬜

y-intercept = ⬜

6. $y = -0.5x + 2.5$

slope = ⬜

y-intercept = ⬜

7. $y - 1 = -x$

slope = ⬜

y-intercept = ⬜

Graphing Linear Equations

Graph the equation.

8. $y = \frac{2}{3}x - 2$

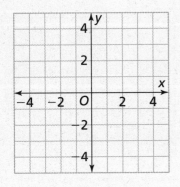

9. $y = -2x + 1$

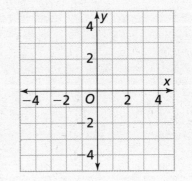

Solving Equations for Variables

Solve the equation for y.

10. $y - x = 5$

11. $y + 0.2x = -4$

12. $-\frac{2}{3}x + y = 8$

Prepare for Reading Success

Before beginning each lesson, preview its content. Write what you already know about the lesson in the second column. Then write a question that you want answered about the lesson in the third column. After the lesson, complete the fourth column with the answer to your question.

Lesson	What I Know	Questions I Have	Answer
5-1			
5-2			
5-3			
5-4			

Go Online | PearsonRealize.com

Solve & Discuss It!

ACTIVITY

Draw three pairs of lines, each showing a different way that two lines can intersect or not intersect. How are these pairs of lines related?

I can...
find the number of solutions of a system of equations by inspecting the equations.

Ⓒ **Common Core Content Standards**
8.EE.C.8b, 8.EE.C.8c

Mathematical Practices
MP.2, MP.3, MP.4, MP.7

Focus on math practices

Look for Relationships Is it possible for any of the pairs of lines drawn to have exactly two points in common? Explain. Ⓒ MP.7

INTERACTIVE ANIMATION   ASS

EXAMPLE 1 **Relate Solutions of Linear Systems**

Scan for
Multimedia

Deanna drew the pairs of lines below.
Each pair of lines represents a *system of linear equations*.
A **system of linear equations** is formed by two or more linear equations that use the same variables.

How can you use the graphs to determine the number of solutions of each system?

Look for Relationships How do the points of intersection of the graphed lines relate to the solutions of the systems of linear equations? © MP.7

The lines intersect at 1 point. This system has 1 solution.

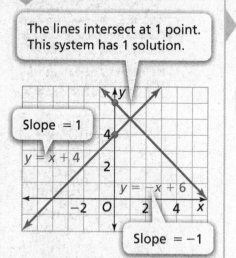

Slope = 1
$y = x + 4$
$y = -x + 6$
Slope = -1

The equations of the linear system
$y = x + 4$
$y = -x + 6$

have different slopes.

The system has *1 solution* (1, 5).

> A **solution of a system of linear equations** is any ordered pair that makes all equations in the system true.

The lines do not intersect; they are parallel. This system has no solution.

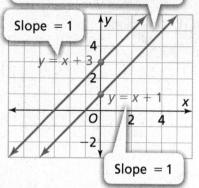

Slope = 1
$y = x + 3$
$y = x + 1$
Slope = 1

The equations of the linear system
$y = x + 3$
$y = x + 1$

have the same slopes and different *y*-intercepts.

The system has *no solution.*

The lines intersect at every point; they are the same line. This system has infinitely many solutions.

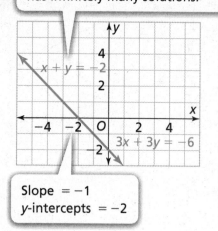

$x + y = -2$
Slope = -1
y-intercepts = -2
$3x + 3y = -6$

The equations of the linear system
$x + y = -2$
$3x + 3y = -6$

have the same slopes and the same *y*-intercepts. They represent the same line.

The system has *infinitely many solutions.*

✓ **Try It!**

How many solutions does this system of equations have? Explain.

The system of equations has ⬚ solution. The equations have

⬚ slopes, so the lines intersect at ⬚ point.

$y = x + 1$
$y = 2x + 2$

Convince Me! The equations of a system have the same slopes. What can you determine about the solution of the system of equations?

Go Online | PearsonRealize.com

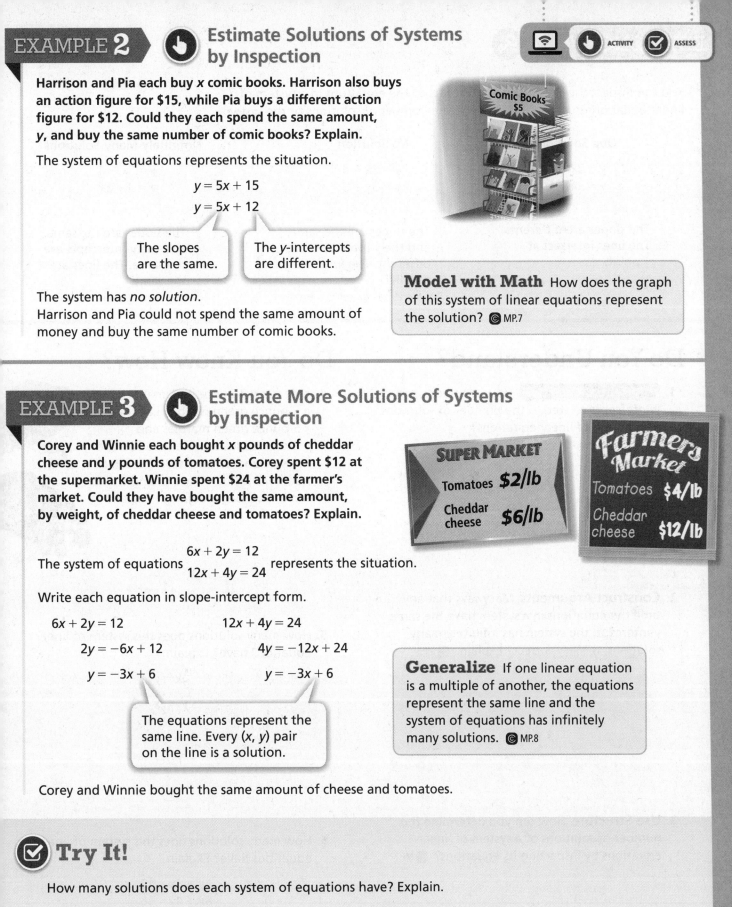

EXAMPLE 2   **Estimate Solutions of Systems by Inspection**

ACTIVITY   ASSESS

Harrison and Pia each buy *x* comic books. Harrison also buys an action figure for $15, while Pia buys a different action figure for $12. Could they each spend the same amount, *y*, and buy the same number of comic books? Explain.

The system of equations represents the situation.

$$y = 5x + 15$$
$$y = 5x + 12$$

The slopes are the same.

The *y*-intercepts are different.

Comic Books
$5

The system has *no solution*.
Harrison and Pia could not spend the same amount of money and buy the same number of comic books.

Model with Math How does the graph of this system of linear equations represent the solution? © MP.7

EXAMPLE 3   **Estimate More Solutions of Systems by Inspection**

Corey and Winnie each bought *x* pounds of cheddar cheese and *y* pounds of tomatoes. Corey spent $12 at the supermarket. Winnie spent $24 at the farmer's market. Could they have bought the same amount, by weight, of cheddar cheese and tomatoes? Explain.

SUPER MARKET

Tomatoes   **$2/lb**

Cheddar cheese   **$6/lb**

Farmers Market

Tomatoes   **$4/lb**

Cheddar cheese   **$12/lb**

The system of equations $\begin{array}{l} 6x + 2y = 12 \\ 12x + 4y = 24 \end{array}$ represents the situation.

Write each equation in slope-intercept form.

$$6x + 2y = 12 \qquad\qquad 12x + 4y = 24$$
$$2y = -6x + 12 \qquad\qquad 4y = -12x + 24$$
$$y = -3x + 6 \qquad\qquad y = -3x + 6$$

The equations represent the same line. Every (*x*, *y*) pair on the line is a solution.

Generalize If one linear equation is a multiple of another, the equations represent the same line and the system of equations has infinitely many solutions. © MP.8

Corey and Winnie bought the same amount of cheese and tomatoes.

✓ Try It!

How many solutions does each system of equations have? Explain.

a. $y = -3x + 5$
    $y = -3x - 5$

b. $y = 3x + 4$
    $5y - 15x - 20 = 0$

You can inspect the slopes and y-intercepts of the equations in a system of linear equations in order to determine the number of solutions of the system.

One Solution	No Solution	Infinitely Many Solutions
$y = 2x + 4$ $y = 3x - 1$	$y = 3x + 4$ $y = 3x + 5$	$y = 3x + 4$ $y = 4 + 3x$
The slopes are different. The lines intersect at 1 point.	The slopes are the same, and the y-intercepts are different. The lines are parallel.	The slopes are the same, and the y-intercepts are the same. The lines are the same.

Do You Understand?

1. **Essential Question** How are slopes and y-intercepts related to the number of solutions of a system of linear equations?

2. **Construct Arguments** Macy says that any time the equations in a system have the same y-intercept, the system has infinitely many solutions. Is Macy correct? Explain. © MP.3

3. **Use Structure** How can you determine the number of solutions of a system of linear equations by inspecting its equations? © MP.7

Do You Know How?

4. Kyle has x 3-ounce blue marbles and a 5-ounce green marble. Lara has x 5-ounce green marbles and a 3-ounce blue marble. Is it possible for Kyle and Lara to have the same number of green marbles and the same total bag weight, y? Explain.

5. How many solutions does this system of linear equations have? Explain.
$$\frac{1}{2}x = y$$
$$y = \frac{1}{2}x + 3$$

6. How many solutions does this system of linear equations have? Explain.
$$3y + 6x = 12$$
$$8x + 4y = 16$$

Practice & Problem Solving ✏️ ⏻

7. **Leveled Practice** Two rovers are exploring a planet. The system of
equations below shows each rover's elevation, y, at time x. What
conclusion can you reach about the system of equations?

Rover A: $y = 1.9x - 8$ **Rover B:** $7y = 13.3x - 56$

The slope for the Rover A equation is ⬚ the
slope for the Rover B equation.

The y-intercepts of the equations are ⬚.

The system of equations has ⬚ solution(s).

8. How many solutions does this system have?

$$y = x - 3$$
$$4x - 10y = 6$$

9. How many solutions does this system have?

$$x + 3y = 0$$
$$12y = -4x$$

10. What can you determine about the solution(s) of
this system?

$$-64x + 96y = 176$$
$$56x - 84y = -147$$

11. Determine whether this system of equations
has one solution, no solution, or infinitely many
solutions.

$$y = 8x + 2$$
$$y = -8x + 2$$

12. **Construct Arguments** Maia says that the two lines in this system of
linear equations are parallel. Is she correct? Explain. © MP.3

$$2x + y = 14$$
$$2y + 4x = 14$$

13. **Reasoning** Describe a situation that can be represented by using this system of
equations. Inspect the system to determine the number of solutions and interpret
the solution within the context of your situation. © MP.2

$$y = 2x + 10$$
$$y = x + 15$$

14. **Look for Relationships** Does this system have one solution, no solutions, or infinitely many solutions? Write another system of equations with the same number of solutions that uses the first equation only. © MP.7

$$12x + 51y = 156$$
$$-8x - 34y = -104$$

15. The equations represent the heights, y, of the flowers, in inches, after x days. What does the y-intercept of each equation represent? Will the flowers ever be the same height? Explain.

$y = 0.7x + 2$

$y = 0.4x + 2$

16. Does this system have one solution, no solution, or an infinite number of solutions?

$$4x + 3y = 8$$
$$8x + 6y = 2$$

17. **Higher Order Thinking** Under what circumstances does the system of equations $Qx + Ry = S$ and $y = Tx + S$ have infinitely many solutions?

© Assessment Practice

18. By inspecting the equations, what can you determine about the solution(s) of this system?

$$12y = 9x + 33$$
$$20y = 15x + 55$$

19. Choose the statement that correctly describes how many solutions there are for this system of equations.

$$y = \frac{2}{3}x + 3$$
$$y = \frac{5}{4}x + 3$$

Ⓐ Infinitely many solutions because the slopes are equal and the y-intercepts are equal

Ⓑ Exactly one solution because the slopes are equal but the y-intercepts are not equal

Ⓒ No solution because the slopes are equal and the y-intercepts are not equal

Ⓓ Exactly one solution because the slopes are not equal

 Go Online | PearsonRealize.com

Explore It!

Beth and Dante pass by the library as they
walk home using separate straight paths.

ACTIVITY

I can...
find the solution to a system of
equations using graphs.

© **Common Core Content Standards**
8.EE.C.8a, 8.EE.C.8c

Mathematical Practices
MP.1, MP.2, MP.6, MP.7

A. Model with Math The point on the graph
represents the location of the library. Draw
and label lines on the graph to show each
possible path to the library. © MP.4

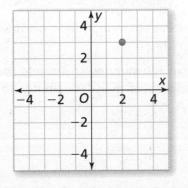

B. Write a system of equations that represents
the paths taken by Beth and Dante.

Focus on math practices

Reasoning What does the point of intersection of the lines represent in the
situation? © MP.2

INTERACTIVE ANIMATION | AS

EXAMPLE 1 👁 **Solve a System by Graphing**

Scan for Multimedia 🅑

Li is choosing a new cell phone plan. How can Li use the graphs of a system of linear equations to determine when the phone plans cost the same? Which plan should Li choose? Explain.

> **Model with Math** You can use the graphs of a system of linear equations to compare the costs of each plan. © MP.4

COMPANY A
20¢/minute
PLUS $75
Unlimited Data 📱

COMPANY B
25¢ Per minute
PLUS **$70**
Unlimited Data

STEP 1 Write a system of equations.

Let $x =$ the number of minutes used each month.

Let $y =$ the total monthly cost of the plan.

Total monthly cost of plan	=	Cost of minutes used	+	Cost for unlimited data
y	=	$0.20x$	+	75
y	=	$0.25x$	+	70

The system of equations is $\begin{array}{l} y = 0.20x + 75 \\ y = 0.25x + 70 \end{array}$.

STEP 2 Graph the system.

The point of intersection, (100, 95), is the solution of the system.

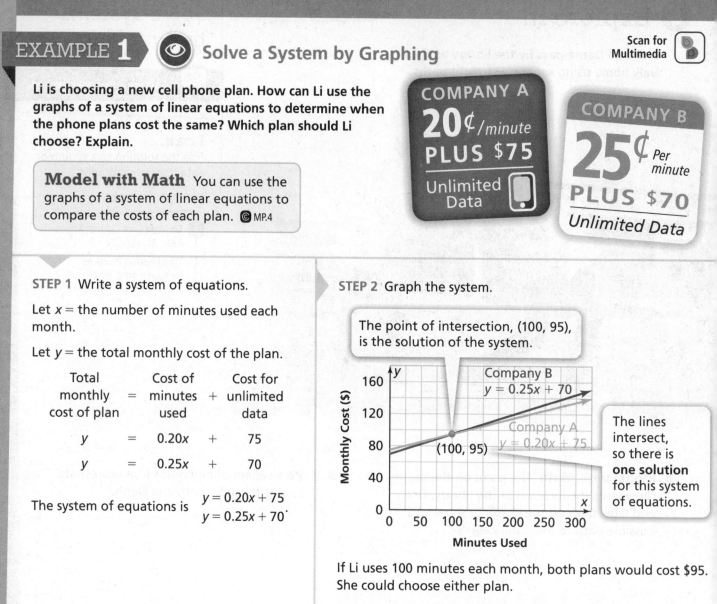

Company B
$y = 0.25x + 70$

Company A
$y = 0.20x + 75$

(100, 95)

The lines intersect, so there is **one solution** for this system of equations.

If Li uses 100 minutes each month, both plans would cost $95. She could choose either plan.

If Li uses fewer than 100 minutes, she should choose Company B. If Li uses more than 100 minutes, she should choose Company A.

✅ **Try It!**

Solve the system by graphing. $\quad y = 3x + 5$
$\qquad\qquad\qquad\qquad\qquad\quad y = 2x + 4$

The solution is the point of intersection (☐ , ☐).

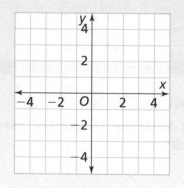

Convince Me! How does the point of intersection of the graphs represent the solution of a system of linear equations?

📶 Go Online | PearsonRealize.com

EXAMPLE 2 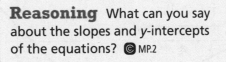 Graph a System of Equations with No Solution

Solve the system.
$$y = x - 4$$
$$2x - 2y = -2$$

Graph the equations of the system to determine the solution.

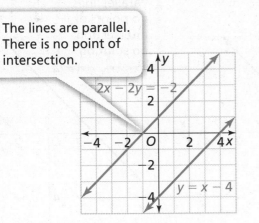

The lines are parallel. There is no point of intersection.

Reasoning What can you say about the slopes and y-intercepts of the equations? © MP.2

There are no (x, y) pairs that make both equations true. The system has no solution.

EXAMPLE 3 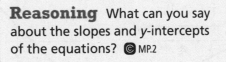 Graph a System of Equations with Infinitely Many Solutions

Solve the system.
$$y = \frac{1}{2}x + 3$$
$$-3x + 6y = 18$$

Graph the equations of the system to determine the solution.

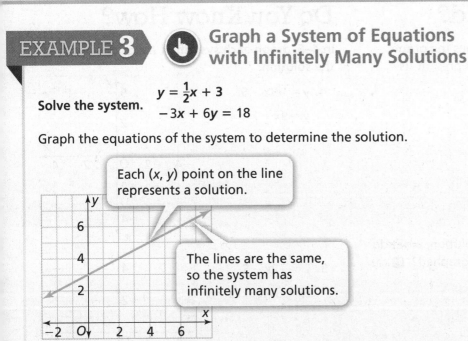

Each (x, y) point on the line represents a solution.

The lines are the same, so the system has infinitely many solutions.

There are an infinite number of (x, y) pairs that make both equations true. The system has infinitely many solutions.

✓ Try It!

Solve each system by graphing. Describe the solutions.

a. $5x + y = -3$
$10x + 2y = -6$

b. $\frac{1}{3}x + y = 7$
$2x + 6y = 12$

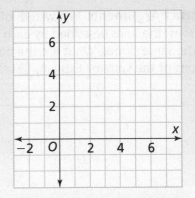

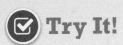

The solution of a system of linear equations is the point of intersection of the lines defined by the equations.

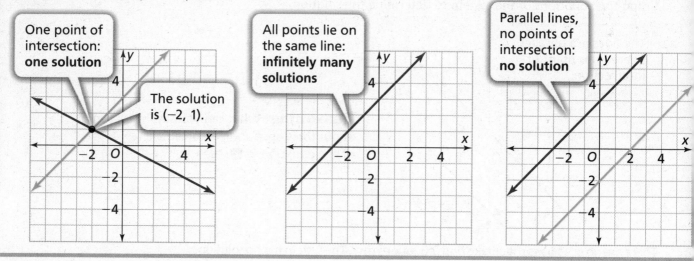

One point of intersection: **one solution**

The solution is (−2, 1).

All points lie on the same line: **infinitely many solutions**

Parallel lines, no points of intersection: **no solution**

Do You Understand?

1. **Essential Question** How does the graph of a system of linear equations represent its solution?

2. **Reasoning** If a system has no solution, what do you know about the lines being graphed? © MP.2

3. **Construct Arguments** In a system of linear equations, the lines described by each equation have the same slopes. What are the possible solutions of the system? Explain. © MP.3

Do You Know How?

In 4–6, graph each system of equations and find the solution.

4. $y = -3x - 5$
   $y = 9x + 7$

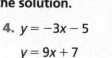
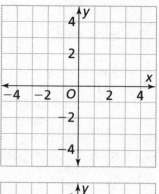

5. $y = -2x - 5$
   $6x + 3y = -15$

6. $y = -4x + 3$
   $8x + 2y = 8$

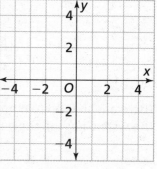
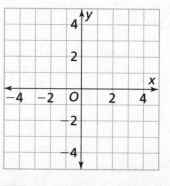

Go Online | PearsonRealize.com

Name: _____

Practice & Problem Solving

In 7 and 8, graph each system of equations to determine the solution.

7. $x + 4y = 8$
   $3x + 4y = 0$

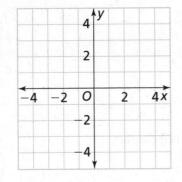

8. $2x - 3y = 6$
   $4x - 6y = 12$

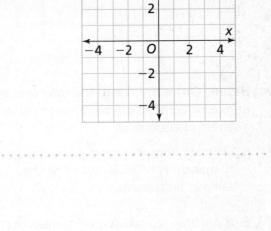

9. The total cost, c, of renting a canoe for n hours can be represented by a system of equations.

   a. Write the system of equations that could be used to find the total cost, c, of renting a canoe for n hours.

   b. Graph the system of equations.

   c. When would the total cost for renting a canoe be the same on both rivers? Explain.

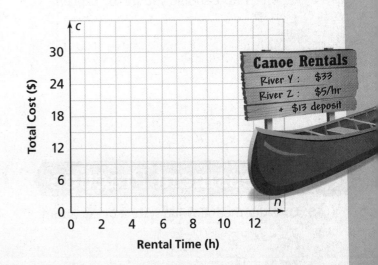

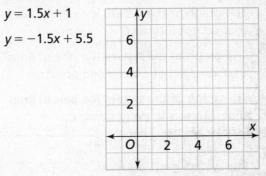

10. Graph the system of equations and determine the solution.

    $x + 2y = 4$
    $4x + 8y = 64$

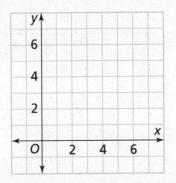

11. Graph the system of equations, then estimate the solution.

    $y = 1.5x + 1$
    $y = -1.5x + 5.5$

In **12** and **13**, graph and determine the solution of the system of equations.

12. $-3y = -9x + 3$

$-6y = -18x - 12$

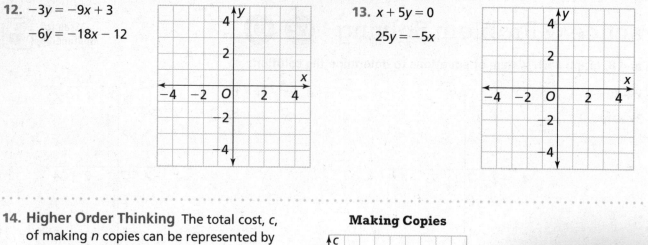

13. $x + 5y = 0$

$25y = -5x$

14. Higher Order Thinking The total cost, c, of making n copies can be represented by a system of equations.

   a. Estimate how many copies you need to make for the total cost to be the same at both stores.

   b. If you have to make a small number of copies, which store should you go to? Explain.

Making Copies

Number of Copies

STORE W

$5

unlimited copies

STORE

20¢/co

+

$2

machi

use

15. Consider the following system of equations.

$y = -3x + 6$

$y = 3x - 12$

PART A

Which of the following statements are true about the system? Select all that apply.

☐ The graph of the system is a pair of lines that do not intersect.

☐ The graph of the system is a pair of lines that intersect at exactly one point.

☐ The graph of the system is a pair of lines that intersect in every point.

☐ The system has no solution.

☐ The system has 1 solution.

☐ The system has infinitely many solutions.

PART B

Graph the system. What is the solution of the system of equations?

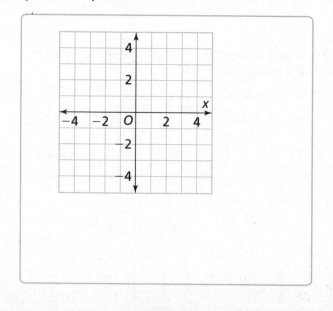

Name: _____

1. **Vocabulary** How can you determine the number of solutions of a system by looking at the equations? *Lesson 5-1*

2. How many solutions does the system of equations have? Explain. *Lesson 5-1*

$2x - 9y = -5$

$4x - 6y = 2$

3. Graph the system of equations and find the solution. *Lesson 5-2*

$y + 1 = 2x$

$y = \frac{1}{2}x + 2$

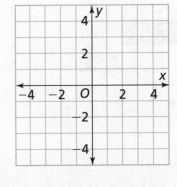

4. One equation in a system is $y = -3x + 7$. Which equation gives the system no solution? *Lesson 5-1*

Ⓐ $y - 7 = -3x$

Ⓒ $y + 3x = 5$

Ⓑ $y = 3x + 5$

Ⓓ $y = \frac{1}{3}x - 7$

5. Finn bought 12 movie tickets. Student tickets cost $4, and adult tickets cost $8. Finn spent a total of $60. Write and graph a system of equations to find the number of student and adult tickets Finn bought. *Lesson 5-2*

Types of Movie Tickets

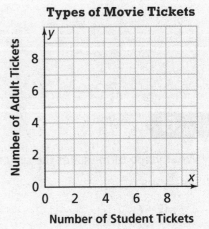

Number of Adult Tickets

Number of Student Tickets

6. What value of m gives the system infinitely many solutions? *Lesson 5-1*

$-x + 4y = 32$

$y = mx + 8$

How well did you do on the mid-topic checkpoint? Fill in the stars.

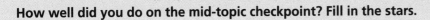

MID-TOPIC PERFORMANCE TASK

Perpendicular lines intersect to form right angles. The system of equations below shows perpendicular lines.

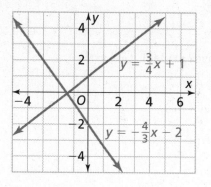

PART A

How many solutions does the system have? Explain.

PART B

Identify the slope and *y*-intercept of each line. What do you notice about the slopes of the lines?

PART C

What value of *m* makes the system show perpendicular lines? Explain.

$y = \frac{1}{2}x + 8$

$y = mx - 6$

Go Online | PearsonRealize.com

Explain It!

ACTIVITY

Jackson needs a taxi to take him to a destination that is a little over 4 miles away. He has a graph that shows the rates for two companies. Jackson says that because the slope of the line that represents the rates for On Time Cabs is less than the slope of the line that represents Speedy Cab Co., the cab ride from On Time Cabs will cost less.

Lesson 5-3
Solve Systems by Substitution

Go Online | PearsonRealize.com

I can...
solve systems of equations using substitution.

Common Core Content Standards
8.EE.C.8b, 8.EE.C.8c

Mathematical Practices
MP.2, MP.3, MP.4, MP.6, MP.7, MP.8

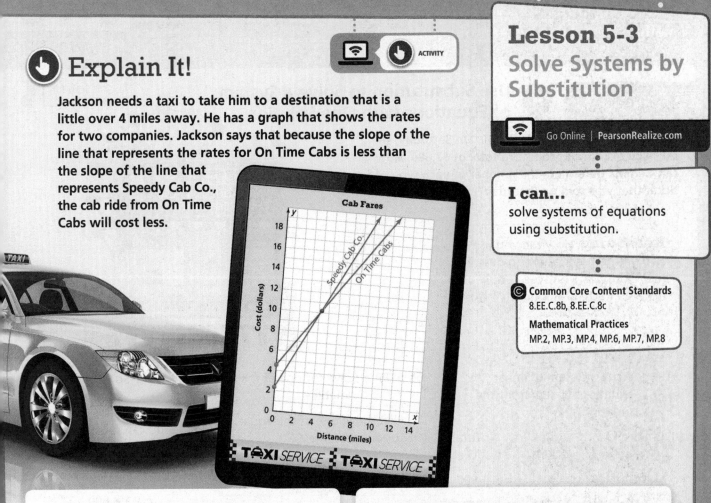

A. Do you agree with Jackson? Explain.

B. Which taxi service company should Jackson call? Explain your reasoning.

Focus on math practices

Be Precise Can you use the graph to determine the exact number of miles for which the cost of the taxi ride will be the same? Explain. MP.6

271

INTERACTIVE ANIMATION   AS.

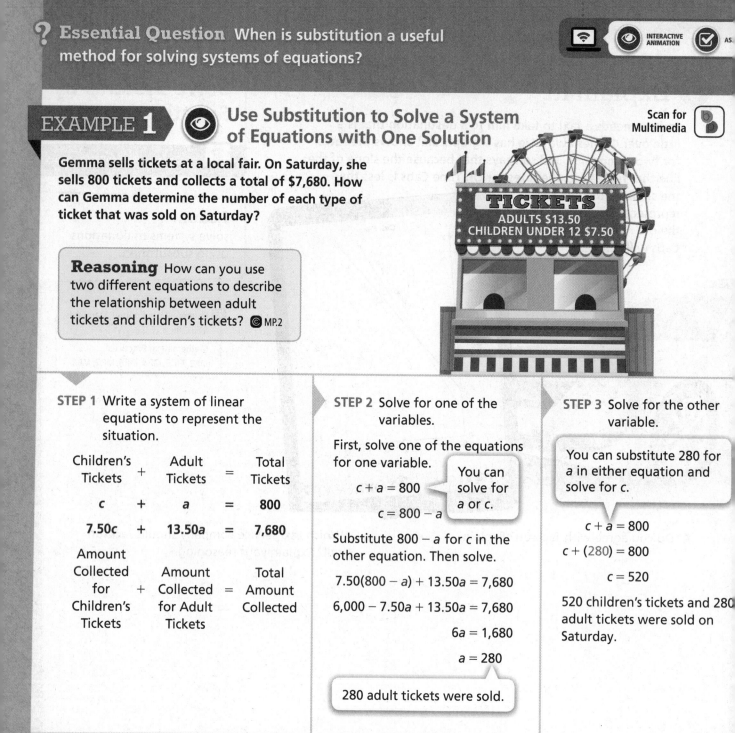

EXAMPLE 1 👁 **Use Substitution to Solve a System of Equations with One Solution**

Scan for Multimedia

Gemma sells tickets at a local fair. On Saturday, she sells 800 tickets and collects a total of $7,680. How can Gemma determine the number of each type of ticket that was sold on Saturday?

Reasoning How can you use two different equations to describe the relationship between adult tickets and children's tickets? © MP.2

TICKETS
ADULTS $13.50
CHILDREN UNDER 12 $7.50

STEP 1 Write a system of linear equations to represent the situation.

Children's Tickets	+	Adult Tickets	=	Total Tickets
c	+	a	=	800
$7.50c$	+	$13.50a$	=	7,680
Amount Collected for Children's Tickets	+	Amount Collected for Adult Tickets	=	Total Amount Collected

STEP 2 Solve for one of the variables.

First, solve one of the equations for one variable.

$c + a = 800$ — You can solve for a or c.
$c = 800 - a$

Substitute $800 - a$ for c in the other equation. Then solve.

$7.50(800 - a) + 13.50a = 7,680$

$6,000 - 7.50a + 13.50a = 7,680$

$6a = 1,680$

$a = 280$

280 adult tickets were sold.

STEP 3 Solve for the other variable.

You can substitute 280 for a in either equation and solve for c.

$c + a = 800$

$c + (280) = 800$

$c = 520$

520 children's tickets and 280 adult tickets were sold on Saturday.

✓ **Try It!**

Brandon took a 50-question exam worth a total of 160 points. There were x two-point questions and y five-point questions. How many of each type of question were on the exam?

$x + y = 50$
$2x + 5y = 160$

Convince Me! How do you know which equation to choose to solve for one of the variables?

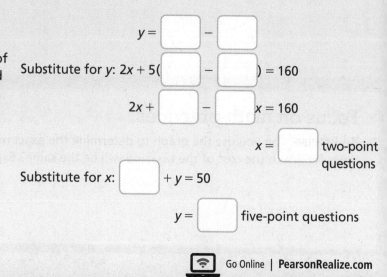

$y = \boxed{} - \boxed{}$

Substitute for y: $2x + 5(\boxed{} - \boxed{}) = 160$

$2x + \boxed{} - \boxed{}x = 160$

$x = \boxed{}$ two-point questions

Substitute for x: $\boxed{} + y = 50$

$y = \boxed{}$ five-point questions

Go Online | PearsonRealize.com

EXAMPLE 2 👆 Use Substitution to Solve a System with No Solution

Seiko takes pottery classes at two different studios. Is there a number of hours for which Seiko's cost is the same at both studios?

STEP 1 Write a system of linear equations to represent the situation. Let x equal the number of hours and y equal Seiko's cost.

$$y = 14x$$
$$y = \frac{1}{2}(28x + 15)$$

STEP 2 Use substitution to solve one of the equations for one variable.

$$14x = \frac{1}{2}(28x + 15)$$

> Substitute 14x for y in the second equation.

$$14x = 14x + 7.50$$
$$0 \neq 7.50$$

The result is not a true statement, so the system has no solution. There is no number of hours for which Seiko's cost is the same at both studios.

EXAMPLE 3 👆 Use Substitution to Solve a System with Infinitely Many Solutions

Solve the system $-2y - x = -84.91$ and $3x + 6y = 254.73$ by using substitution.

STEP 1 Solve one of the equations for one variable.

$$-2y - x = -84.91$$
$$-x = -84.91 + 2y$$
$$x = 84.91 - 2y$$

> **Reasoning** You can use either equation to solve for either variable. How do you decide which equation and which variable to choose? © MP.2

STEP 2 Substitute $84.91 - 2y$ for x in the other equation. Then solve.

$$3(84.91 - 2y) + 6y = 254.73$$
$$254.73 - 6y + 6y = 254.73$$
$$254.73 = 254.73$$

The result is a true statement. This system has infinitely many solutions.

☑ Try It!

Use substitution to solve each system of equations. Explain.

a. $y + \frac{1}{2}x = 3$
$4y + 2x = -6$

b. $y = \frac{1}{4}x - 2$
$8y - 2x = -16$

COMMUNITY POTTERY STUDIO & CLUB
PLEASE COME AND JOIN US
$14 per hour
All clay included
Please come and see us at the Community Hall.

PRIVATE STUDIO CERAMICS
$28 per hour plus $15 for clay
BRING THIS COUPON FOR HALF-OFF THE PRICE ADVERTISED ABOVE.

Systems of linear equations can be solved algebraically. When one of the equations can be easily solved for one of the variables, you can use substitution to solve the system efficiently.

STEP 1 Solve one of the equations for one of the variables. Then substitute the expression into the other equation and solve.

STEP 2 Solve for the other variable using either equation.

Do You Understand?

1. **Essential Question** When is substitution a useful method for solving systems of equations?

2. **Generalize** When using substitution to solve a system of equations, how can you tell when a system has no solution? © MP.8

3. **Construct Arguments** Kavi solved the system of equations as shown. What mistake did Kavi make? What is the correct solution? © MP.3

$$3x + 4y = 33$$
$$2x + y = 17 \quad y = 17 - 2x$$

$$2x + (17 - 2x) = 17$$
$$2x + 17 - 2x = 17$$
$$2x - 2x + 17 = 17$$
$$17 = 17$$

Infinitely many solutions

Do You Know How?

In 4–6, solve each system using substitution.

4. $y = \frac{1}{2}x + 4$

   $x - y = 8$

5. $3.25x - 1.5y = 1.25$

   $13x - 6y = 10$

6. $y - 0.8x = 0.5$

   $5y - 2.5 = 4x$

Name: _____

Practice & Problem Solving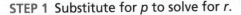

Leveled Practice In 7–9, solve the systems of equations.

7. Pedro has 276 more hits than Ricky. Use substitution to solve the system of equations to find how many hits Pedro, p, and Ricky, r, have each recorded.

$$p + r = 2{,}666$$
$$p = r + 276$$

Teammates Combined Hit Total is 2,666!

Ricky

Pedro

STEP 1 Substitute for p to solve for r.

$$p + r = 2{,}666$$
$$\boxed{} + r = 2{,}666$$
$$\boxed{} + 276 = 2{,}666$$
$$2r = \boxed{}$$
$$r = \boxed{}$$

STEP 2 Substitute for r to solve for p.

$$p = r + 276$$
$$p = \boxed{} + 276$$
$$p = \boxed{}$$

Pedro has $\boxed{}$ hits, and Ricky has $\boxed{}$ hits.

8. $2y + 4.4x = -5$
$y = -2.2x + 4.5$

$$2(-2.2x + \boxed{}) + 4.4x = -5$$
$$-4.4x + \boxed{} + 4.4x = -5$$
$$\boxed{} \neq -5$$

The statement is not true. There is $\boxed{}$ solution.

9. $x + 5y = 0$
$25y = -5x$

$$x = \boxed{}\, y$$
$$25y = -5(\boxed{})$$
$$25y = \boxed{}\, y$$

The statement is true. There are $\boxed{}$ solutions.

10. On a certain hot summer day, 481 people used the public swimming pool. The daily prices are $1.25 for children and $2.25 for adults. The receipts for admission totaled $865.25. How many children and how many adults swam at the public pool that day?

11. Construct Arguments Tim incorrectly says that the solution of the system of equations is $x = -9$, $y = -4$. Ⓒ MP.3

$$6x - 2y = -6$$
$$11 = y - 5x$$

a. What is the correct solution?

b. What error might Tim have made?

12. The number of water bottles, y, filled in x minutes by each of two machines is given by the equations below. Use substitution to determine if there is a point at which the machines will have filled the same number of bottles.

$$160x + 2y = 50$$

$$y + 80x = 50$$

13. a. Use substitution to solve the system below.

$$x = 8y - 4$$
$$x + 8y = 6$$

b. Reasoning Which expression would be easier to substitute into the other equation in order to solve the problem? Explain. Ⓒ MP.2

14. The perimeter of a photo frame is 36 inches. The length is 2 inches greater than the width. What are the dimensions of the frame?

W

$L = W + 2$

15. Higher Order Thinking The members of the city cultural center have decided to put on a play once a night for a week. Their auditorium holds 500 people. By selling tickets, the members would like to raise $2,050 every night to cover all expenses. Let d represent the number of adult tickets sold at $6.50. Let s represent the number of student tickets sold at $3.50 each.

a. If all 500 seats are filled for a performance, how many of each type of ticket must have been sold for the members to raise exactly $2,050?

b. At one performance there were three times as many student tickets sold as adult tickets. If there were 480 tickets sold at that performance, how much below the goal of $2,050 did ticket sales fall?

Ⓒ Assessment Practice

16. What is the solution of the system?

$$y = 145 - 5x$$

$$0.1y + 0.5x = 14.5$$

Ⓐ Infinitely many solutions

Ⓑ (20, 45)

Ⓒ (10, 95)

Ⓓ No solution

17. What is the solution of the system?

$$y = 3x - 10$$

$$3x + 2y = 16$$

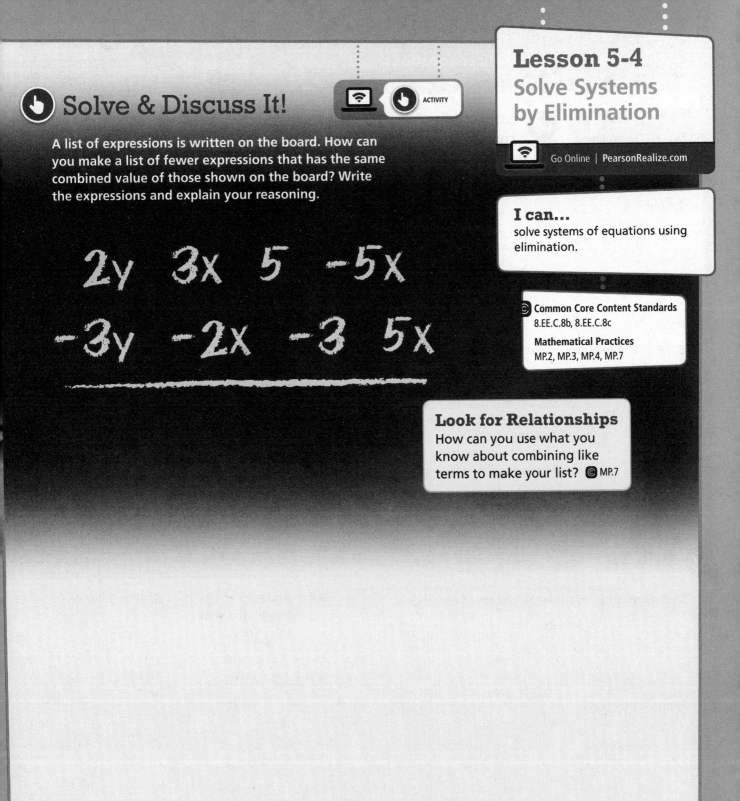
Solve & Discuss It!

A list of expressions is written on the board. How can you make a list of fewer expressions that has the same combined value of those shown on the board? Write the expressions and explain your reasoning.

$$2y \quad 3x \quad 5 \quad -5x$$

$$-3y \quad -2x \quad -3 \quad 5x$$

I can...
solve systems of equations using elimination.

© **Common Core Content Standards**
8.EE.C.8b, 8.EE.C.8c

Mathematical Practices
MP.2, MP.3, MP.4, MP.7

Look for Relationships
How can you use what you know about combining like terms to make your list? © MP.7

Focus on math practices

Reasoning Two expressions have a sum of 0. What must be true of the expressions? © MP.3

? **Essential Question** How are the properties of equality used to solve systems of linear equations?

INTERACTIVE ANIMATION   ASS

EXAMPLE 1 👁 **Solve a System of Equations by Adding**

Scan for Multimedia

How can Remi use this system of equations to solve the riddle?

$$2x + y = 8$$
$$4x - y = 4$$

Two times a number x plus a number y equals eight. Four times the number x minus the number y equals four.

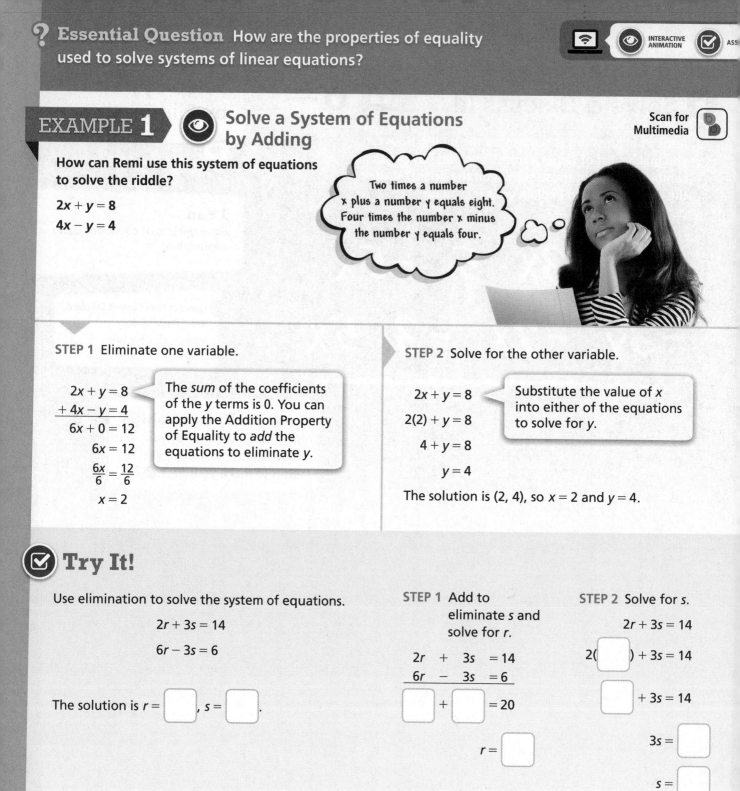

STEP 1 Eliminate one variable.

$$2x + y = 8$$
$$\underline{+\ 4x - y = 4}$$
$$6x + 0 = 12$$
$$6x = 12$$
$$\frac{6x}{6} = \frac{12}{6}$$
$$x = 2$$

The *sum* of the coefficients of the y terms is 0. You can apply the Addition Property of Equality to *add* the equations to eliminate y.

STEP 2 Solve for the other variable.

$$2x + y = 8$$
$$2(2) + y = 8$$
$$4 + y = 8$$
$$y = 4$$

Substitute the value of x into either of the equations to solve for y.

The solution is (2, 4), so x = 2 and y = 4.

✓ **Try It!**

Use elimination to solve the system of equations.

$$2r + 3s = 14$$
$$6r - 3s = 6$$

The solution is r = ☐ , s = ☐ .

STEP 1 Add to eliminate s and solve for r.

$$2r\ +\ 3s\ = 14$$
$$\underline{6r\ -\ 3s\ = 6}$$
$$☐\ +\ ☐\ = 20$$

$$r = ☐$$

STEP 2 Solve for s.

$$2r + 3s = 14$$
$$2(☐) + 3s = 14$$
$$☐ + 3s = 14$$
$$3s = ☐$$
$$s = ☐$$

Convince Me! What must be true about a system of equations for a term to be eliminated by adding or subtracting?

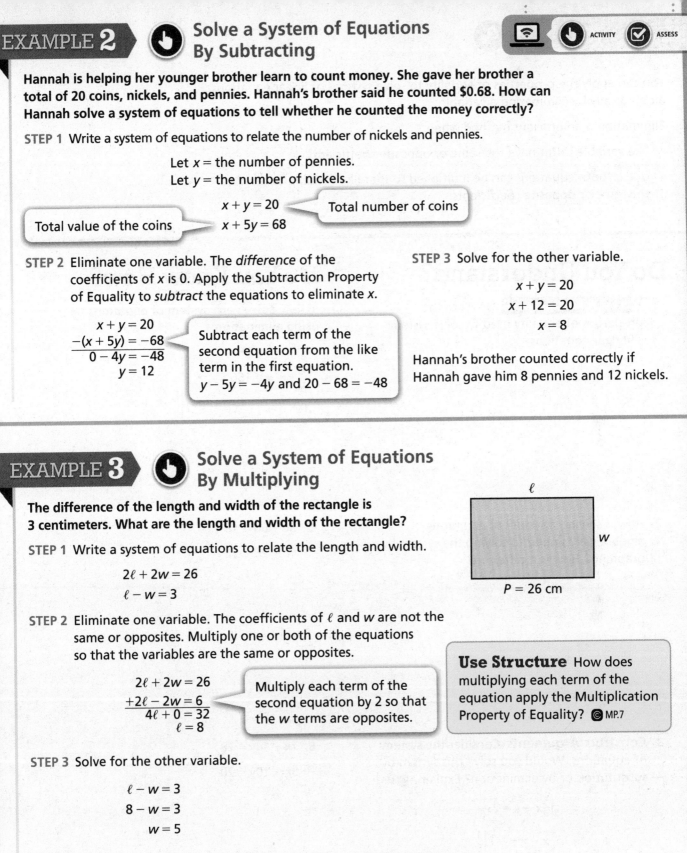

Hannah is helping her younger brother learn to count money. She gave her brother a total of 20 coins, nickels, and pennies. Hannah's brother said he counted $0.68. How can Hannah solve a system of equations to tell whether he counted the money correctly?

STEP 1 Write a system of equations to relate the number of nickels and pennies.

Let x = the number of pennies.
Let y = the number of nickels.

$$x + y = 20 \quad \text{— Total number of coins}$$

Total value of the coins → $x + 5y = 68$

STEP 2 Eliminate one variable. The *difference* of the coefficients of x is 0. Apply the Subtraction Property of Equality to *subtract* the equations to eliminate x.

$$\begin{array}{r} x + y = 20 \\ -(x + 5y) = -68 \\ \hline 0 - 4y = -48 \\ y = 12 \end{array}$$

Subtract each term of the second equation from the like term in the first equation.
$y - 5y = -4y$ and $20 - 68 = -48$

STEP 3 Solve for the other variable.

$$x + y = 20$$
$$x + 12 = 20$$
$$x = 8$$

Hannah's brother counted correctly if Hannah gave him 8 pennies and 12 nickels.

EXAMPLE **3** 🖐 Solve a System of Equations
By Multiplying

The difference of the length and width of the rectangle is 3 centimeters. What are the length and width of the rectangle?

STEP 1 Write a system of equations to relate the length and width.

$$2\ell + 2w = 26$$
$$\ell - w = 3$$

ℓ

w

$P = 26$ cm

STEP 2 Eliminate one variable. The coefficients of ℓ and w are not the same or opposites. Multiply one or both of the equations so that the variables are the same or opposites.

$$\begin{array}{r} 2\ell + 2w = 26 \\ +2\ell - 2w = 6 \\ \hline 4\ell + 0 = 32 \\ \ell = 8 \end{array}$$

Multiply each term of the second equation by 2 so that the w terms are opposites.

Use Structure How does multiplying each term of the equation apply the Multiplication Property of Equality? ⓒ MP.7

STEP 3 Solve for the other variable.

$$\ell - w = 3$$
$$8 - w = 3$$
$$w = 5$$

The length of the rectangle is 8 centimeters and the width is 5 centimeters.

☑ Try It!

Use elimination to solve the system of equations. $3x - 5y = -9$
$x + 2y = 8$

You can apply the properties of equality to solve systems of linear equations algebraically by eliminating a variable.

Elimination is an efficient method when:

- like variable terms have the same or opposite coefficients.

- one or both equations can be multiplied so that like variable terms have the same or opposite coefficients.

Do You Understand?

1. **Essential Question** How are the properties of equality used to solve systems of linear equations?

2. How is solving a system of equations algebraically similar to solving the system by graphing? How is it different?

3. **Construct Arguments** Consider the system of equations. Would you solve this system by substitution or by elimination? Explain. © MP.3

$$1\frac{3}{4}x + y = 2\frac{3}{16}$$

$$\frac{1}{4}x - y = -1\frac{11}{16}$$

Do You Know How?

In **4–6**, solve each system of equations by using elimination.

4. $y - x = 28$

   $y + x = 156$

5. $3c + 6d = 18$

   $6c - 2d = 22$

6. $7x + 14y = 28$

   $5x + 10y = 20$

Name: _____

Practice & Problem Solving

7. Leveled Practice Solve the system of equations using elimination.

$2x - 2y = -4$

$2x + y = 11$

Multiply the first equation by $\boxed{}$.

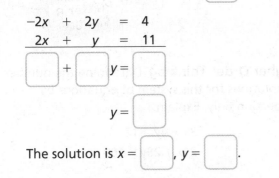

$$-2x \ + \ 2y \ = \ 4$$
$$\underline{2x \ + \quad y \ = \ 11}$$

$\boxed{} + \boxed{}\, y = \boxed{}$

$y = \boxed{}$

The solution is $x = \boxed{}$, $y = \boxed{}$.

$2x + y = 11$

$2x + \boxed{} = 11$

$2x = \boxed{}$

$x = \boxed{}$

---

8. Solve the system of equations using elimination.

$$2y - 5x = -2$$
$$3y + 2x = 35$$

9. If you add Natalie's age and Frankie's age, the result is 44. If you add Frankie's age to 3 times Natalie's age, the result is 70. Write and solve a system of equations using elimination to find their ages.

---

10. If possible, use elimination to solve the system of equations.

$$5x + 10y = 7$$
$$4x + 8y = 3$$

11. At a basketball game, a team made 56 successful shots. They were a combination of 1- and 2-point shots. The team scored 94 points in all. Use elimination to solve the system of equations to find the number of each type of shot.

$$x + y = 56$$
$$x + 2y = 94$$

---

12. Two trains, Train A and Train B, weigh a total of 312 tons. Train A is heavier than Train B. The difference in their weights is 170 tons. Use elimination to solve the system of equations to find the weight of each train.

$$a + b = 312$$
$$a - b = 170$$

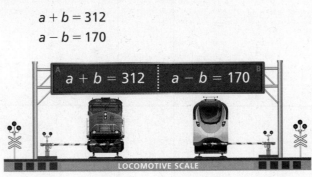

LOCOMOTIVE SCALE

13. A deli offers two platters of sandwiches. Platter A has 2 roast beef sandwiches and 3 turkey sandwiches. Platter B has 3 roast beef sandwiches and 2 turkey sandwiches.

    a. **Model with Math** Write a system of equations to represent the situation. © MP.4

    b. What is the cost of each sandwich?

Platter A
$31.00

Platter B
$29.00

14. Consider the system of equations.

$$x - 3.1y = 11.5$$
$$-x + 3.5y = -13.5$$

    a. Solve the system by elimination.

    b. If you solved this equation by substitution instead, what would the solution be? Explain.

15. **Higher Order Thinking** Determine the number of solutions for this system of equations by inspection only. Explain.

$$3x + 4y = 17$$
$$21x + 28y = 109$$

© **Assessment Practice**

16. Four times a number r plus half a number s equals twelve. Twice the number r plus a quarter of the number s equals eight. What are the two numbers?

17. Solve the system of equations.

$$3m + 3n = 36$$
$$8m - 5n = 31$$

3-ACT MATH ▶ ▶ ▶

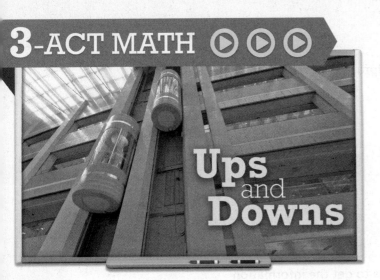

3-Act Mathematical Modeling:
Ups and Downs

📶 Go Online | PearsonRealize.com

© **Common Core Content Standards**
8.EE.C.8, 8.SP.A.3, 8.F.B.4
Mathematical Practices
MP.4, MP.5

ACT 1

1. After watching the video, what is the first question that comes to mind?

2. Write the Main Question you will answer.

3. Make a prediction to answer this Main Question.

The person who wins took the [   ].

4. Construct Arguments Explain how you arrived at your prediction. © MP.3

5. What information in this situation would be helpful to know? How would you use that information?

6. Use Appropriate Tools What tools can you use to get the information you need? Record the information as you find it. © MP.5

7. Model with Math Represent the situation using the mathematical content, concepts, and skills from this topic. Use your representation to answer the Main Question. © MP.4

8. What is your answer to the Main Question? Does it differ from your prediction? Explain.

Go Online | **PearsonRealize.com**

9. Write the answer you saw in the video.

10. Reasoning Does your answer match the answer in the video? If not, what are some reasons that would explain the difference? Ⓒ MP.2

11. Make Sense and Persevere Would you change your model now that you know the answer? Explain. Ⓒ MP.1

Reflect

12. Model with Math Explain how you used a mathematical model to represent the situation. How did the model help you answer the Main Question? Ⓒ MP.4

13. Reason Abstractly A classmate solved the problem using equations with independent variable *a* and dependent variable *b*. What do these variables represent in the situation? Ⓒ MP.2

SEQUEL

14. Generalize Write an equation or inequality to represent all numbers of flights for which the elevator is faster. Ⓒ MP.8

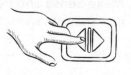

Go Online | PearsonRealize.com

What does it mean to solve a system of linear equations?

Vocabulary Review

Complete each definition and then provide an example of each vocabulary word.

Vocabulary
solution of a system of linear equations
system of linear equations

Definition	Example
Any ordered pair that makes all equations in the system true is a _____.	
A _____ is formed by two or more linear equations that use the same variables.	

Use Vocabulary in Writing

Describe how you can find the number of solutions of two or more equations by using the slope and the y-intercept. Use vocabulary terms in your description.

Concepts and Skills Review

Estimate Solutions by Inspection

Quick Review

The slopes and *y*-intercepts of the linear equations in a system determine the relationship between the lines and the number of solutions.

	Same Slope?	Same *y*-intercept?
No Solution	Yes	No
One Solution	No	n/a
Infinitely Many Solutions	Yes	Yes

Example

How many solutions does the system of equations have? Explain.

$y + 2x = 6$

$y - 8 = -2x$

Write each equation in slope-intercept form.

$y = -2x + 6$

$y = -2x + 8$

Identify the slope and *y*-intercept of each equation.

For the equation $y = -2x + 6$, the slope is -2 and the *y*-intercept is 6.

For the equation $y = -2x + 8$, the slope is -2 and the *y*-intercept is 8.

The equations have the same slope but different *y*-intercepts, so the system has no solution.

Practice

Determine whether the system of equations has one solution, no solution, or infinitely many solutions.

1. $y - 13 = 5x$

$y - 5x = 12$

2. $y = 2x + 10$

$3y - 6x = 30$

3. $-3x + \frac{1}{3}y = 12$

$2y = 18x + 72$

4. $y - \frac{1}{4}x = -1$

$y - 2 = 4x$

5. Michael and Ashley each buy *x* pounds of turkey and *y* pounds of ham. Turkey costs $3 per pound at Store A and $4.50 per pound at Store B. Ham costs $4 per pound at Store A and $6 per pound at Store B. Michael spends $18 at Store A, and Ashley spends $27 at Store B. Could Michael and Ashley have bought the same amount of turkey and ham? Explain.

Quick Review

Systems of equations can be solved by looking at their graphs. A system with one solution has one point of intersection. A system with infinitely many solutions has infinite points of intersection. A system with no solution has no points of intersection.

Example

Graph the system and determine its solution.

$y = x + 4$

$y = -2x + 1$

Graph each equation in the system on the same coordinate plane.

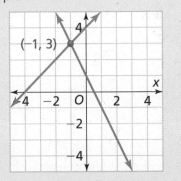

The point of intersection is $(-1, 3)$. This means the solution to the system is $(-1, 3)$.

Practice

Graph each system and find the solution(s).

1. $y = \frac{1}{2}x + 1$

$-2x + 4y = 4$

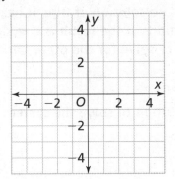

2. $y = -x - 3$

$y + x = 2$

3. $2y = 6x + 4$

$y = -2x + 2$

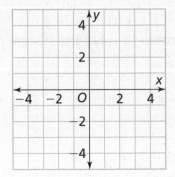

Quick Review

To solve a system by substitution, write one equation for a variable in terms of the other. Substitute the expression into the other equation and solve. If the result is false, the system has no solution. If true, it has infinitely many solutions. If the result is a value, substitute to solve for the other variable.

Example

Use substitution to solve the system.

$y = x + 1$
$y = 5x - 3$

Substitute $x + 1$ for y in the second equation.

$(x + 1) = 5x - 3$
$\quad\quad 4 = 4x$
$\quad\quad 1 = x$

Substitute 1 for x in the first equation.

$y = (1) + 1 = 2$

The solution is $x = 1$, $y = 2$.

Practice

Use substitution to solve each system.

1. $-3y = -2x - 1$
$\quad y = x - 1$

2. $y = 5x + 2$
$\quad 2y - 4 = 10x$

3. $2y - 8 = 6x$
$\quad y = 3x + 2$

4. $2y - 2 = 4x$
$\quad y = -x + 4$

Quick Review

To solve a system by elimination, multiply one or both equations to make opposite terms. Add (or subtract) the equations to eliminate one variable. Substitute to solve for the other variable.

Example

Use elimination to solve the system.

$2x - 9y = -5$
$4x - 6y = 2$

Multiply the first equation by -2. Then add.

$-4x + 18y = 10$
$\underline{\quad 4x - 6y = 2 \quad}$
$\quad\quad 12y = 12$
$\quad\quad\quad y = 1$

Substitute 1 for y in the first equation.

$2x - 9(1) = -5$
$2x - 9 = -5$
$\quad 2x = 4$
$\quad\quad x = 2$

The solution is $x = 2$, $y = 1$.

Practice

Use elimination to solve each system.

1. $-2x + 2y = 2$
$\quad 4x - 4y = 4$

2. $4x + 6y = 40$
$\quad -2x + y = 4$

3. A customer at a concession stand bought 2 boxes of popcorn and 3 drinks for $12. Another customer bought 3 boxes of popcorn and 5 drinks for $19. How much does a box of popcorn cost? How much does a drink cost?

Pathfinder

Shade a path from START to FINISH. Follow the solutions to the equations from least to greatest. You can only move up, down, right, or left.

I can...
solve multistep equations using the Distributive Property. © 8.EE.C.7b

START
↓

$2(d + 1)$ $= -38$	$3(2z + 3)$ $= -75$	$3(g + 4) = g$	$-2(t - 1) + 8$ $= 30$
$7x - 2(x - 11)$ $= -103$	$2(s + 6)$ $= 5(s + 12)$	$4(w - 7) = -48$	$6m + 3(4m + 18)$ $= -108$
$2w - 5(w + 4)$ $= -14$	$3c + 2(2c + 5)$ $= 3$	$2(q - 6) = -18$	$6 - 9(r - 3) = 69$
$-4(h - 2) = 8$	$2.5n + 1.1$ $= 4n - 1.9$	$-17 = \frac{1}{3}(9y + 12)$	$4a - 11 = a - 5$
$4(3 - 5k) = 92$	$-4(-2j + 7)$ $= -4$	$9b - 10$ $= 2(3b + 4)$	$12(7 - 2v) + 5v$ $= -68$

↓
FINISH

TOPIC 6

CONGRUENCE AND SIMILARITY

? Topic Essential Question

How can you show that two figures are either congruent or similar to one another?

Topic Overview

6-1 Analyze Translations

6-2 Analyze Reflections

6-3 Analyze Rotations

6-4 Compose Transformations

3-Act Mathematical Modeling: Tricks of the Trade

6-5 Understand Congruent Figures

6-6 Describe Dilations

6-7 Understand Similar Figures

6-8 Angles, Lines, and Transversals

6-9 Interior and Exterior Angles of Triangles

6-10 Angle-Angle Triangle Similarity

Topic Vocabulary

- alternate interior angles
- angle of rotation
- center of rotation
- congruent
- corresponding angles
- dilation
- enlargement
- exterior angle of a triangle
- image
- line of reflection
- reduction
- reflection
- remote interior angles
- rotation
- same-side interior angles
- scale factor
- similar
- transformation
- translation
- transversal

Lesson Digital Resources

 INTERACTIVE ANIMATION Interact with visual learning animations.

 ACTIVITY Use with *Solve & Discuss It, Expl* and *Explain It* activities, and to explore Exar

 VIDEOS Watch clips to support *3-Act Math Modeling Lessons* and *STEM Projects*.

 PRACTICE Practice what you've learned.

Go online | **PearsonRealize.com**

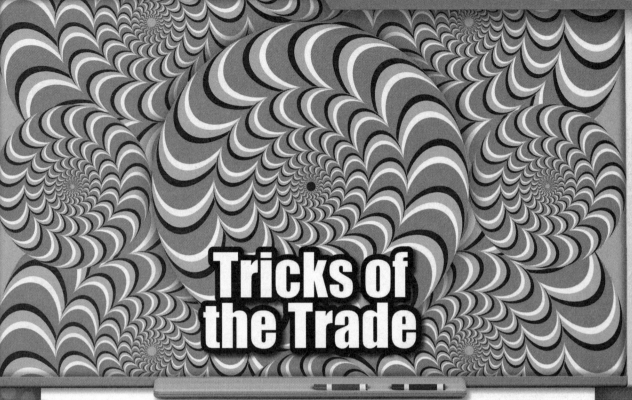

Tricks of the Trade

▶ ## Tricks of the Trade

All kinds of objects in nature have symmetry: beehives, pine cones, butterflies, and snowflakes, to name a few. If you look closely, you will start to see patterns left and right. Think about this during the 3-Act Mathematical Modeling lesson.

Additional Digital Resources

 TUTORIALS Get help from *Virtual Nerd*, right when you need it.

 KEY CONCEPT Review important lesson content.

 GLOSSARY Read and listen to English/Spanish definitions.

 ASSESSMENT Show what you've learned.

 MATH TOOLS Explore math with digital tools.

 GAMES Play Math Games to help you learn.

 ETEXT Interact with your Student's Edition online.

STEM Project

🛜 ▶ VIDEO

Did You Know?

Trees provide **wood for cooking** and **heating** for half of the world's population.

As trees grow, **carbon dioxide** is removed from the atmosphere for **photosynthesis**. Forests are called "carbon sinks" because one acre of forest absorbs six tons of carbon dioxide and puts out four tons of **oxygen**.

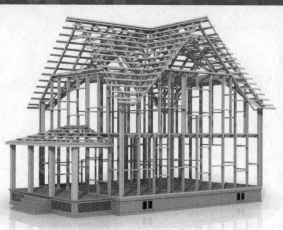

Carbon Dioxide   Oxygen

Sunlight

In addition to **providing oxygen** and **improving air quality**, trees conserve water and **soil** and preserve wildlife.

Trees provide **lumber for buildings**, tools, and furniture. Other products include rubber, sponges, cork, paper, **chocolate**, nuts, and fruit.

About **30%** of land is covered by forests.

Forests are now being **managed** to preserve wildlife and old growth forests, protect biodiversity, safeguard watersheds, and develop **recreation**, as well as extract timber.

Forests also need managed to prevent raging **wildfires**, **invasive species**, overgrazing, and disease.

Your Task: Forest Health

The proper management of forests is a growing science. You and your classmates will learn about forest health indicators and use what you know about similar triangles and ratios to gather and interpret data in order to assess the health of a forest.

Review What You Know!

Vocabulary

Choose the best term from the box to complete each definition.

adjacent angles

complementary angles

supplementary angles

vertical angles

1. _____ have a sum of 90°.

2. _____ share the same ray.

3. _____ are pairs of opposite angles made by intersecting lines.

4. _____ have a sum of 180°.

Multiplying Real Numbers

Simplify the expression.

5. $5 \times 2 = \boxed{}$

6. $6 \times \frac{1}{2} = \boxed{}$

7. $12 \times \frac{1}{3} = \boxed{}$

Identifying Points on a Coordinate Plane

Name the location of the point.

8. point W

9. point X

10. point Y

11. point Z

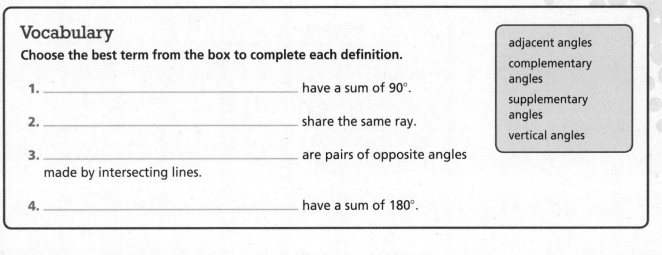

Supplementary Angles

The angles are supplementary. Find the missing angle measure.

12.

130°

13.

139°

Build Vocabulary

Use the graphic organizer to help you understand new vocabulary terms.

Reflection

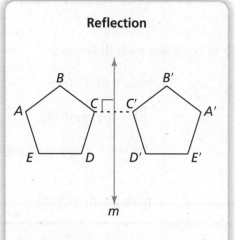

The *image* is congruent to the *preimage*.

Translation

The *image* is congruent to the *preimage*.

What transformation?
Congruent or similar?

Rotation (90°)

The *image* is congruent to the *preimage*.

Dilation

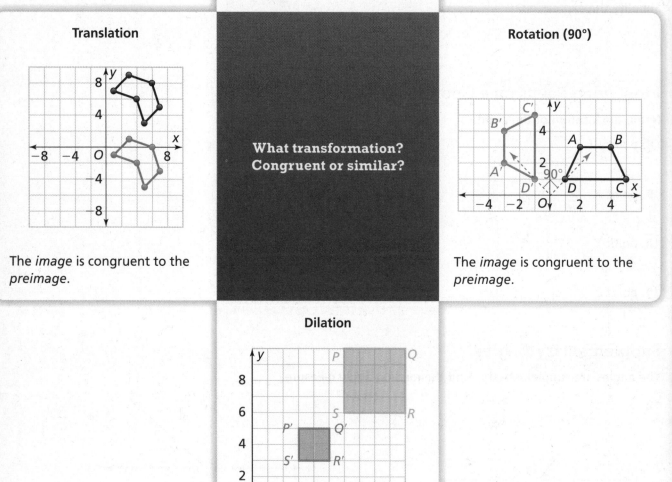

The *image* is similar to the *preimage*.

Solve & Discuss It!

ACTIVITY

Ashanti draws a trapezoid on the coordinate plane and labels it Figure 1. Then she draws Figure 2. How can she determine whether the figures have the same side lengths and the same angle measures?

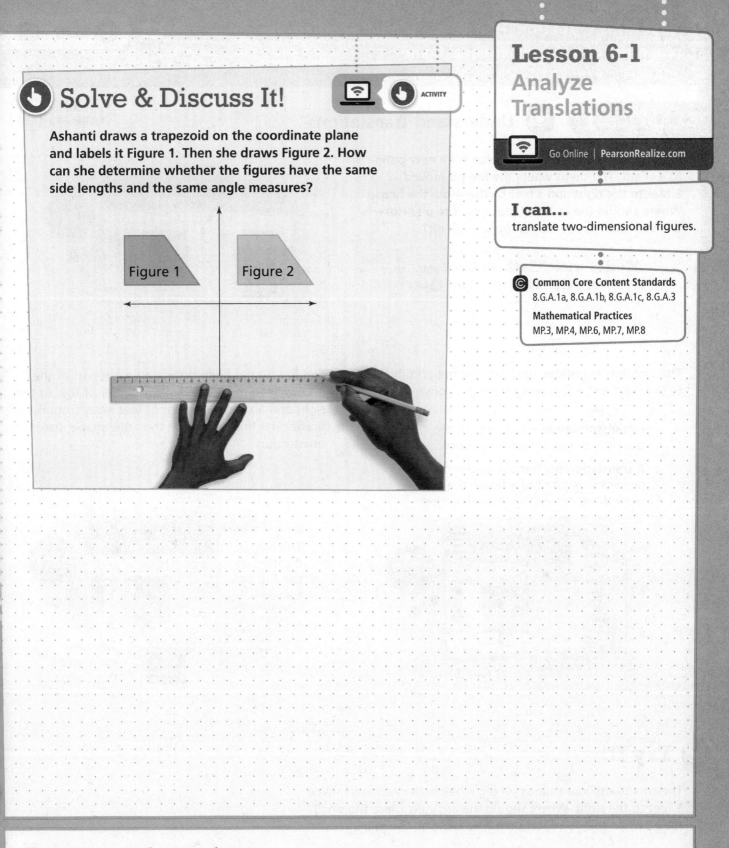

I can...
translate two-dimensional figures.

© **Common Core Content Standards**
8.G.A.1a, 8.G.A.1b, 8.G.A.1c, 8.G.A.3

Mathematical Practices
MP.3, MP.4, MP.6, MP.7, MP.8

Focus on math practices

Be Precise How do you know that the method you described shows whether the side lengths and angle measures are equal? Explain. © MP.6

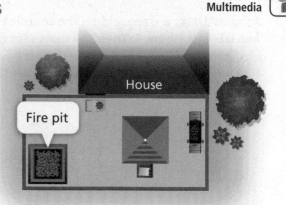

EXAMPLE 1 👁 Understand Translations

Scan for Multimedia

A landscape architect shows a plan for a new patio to a client. The client wants the fire pit moved 6 feet to the right and 3 feet farther from the house. Where should the architect place the fire pit? How will the client's request change the fire pit?

> **Model with Math** How can you represent the problem situation? © MP.4

The architect translates, or slides, the fire pit 6 feet to the right and 3 feet away from the house.

> A **transformation** is a change in the position, shape, or size of a figure.
>
> A **translation** is a transformation that moves every point of a figure the same distance and the same direction.

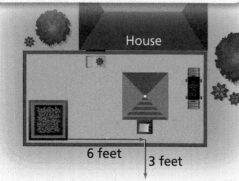

The fire pit has been translated. Each part of the pit has been moved an equal number of feet to the right and an equal number of feet away from the house. The fire pit still has the same shape, size, and orientation.

☑ Try It!

The clients also want the small table below the window moved 5 feet to the right. Where should the architect place the small table? Draw the new location of the table on the plan.

Convince Me! An equilateral triangle with side lengths 5 inches is translated 3 units down and 2 units right. Describe the shape and dimensions of the translated figure.

EXAMPLE **2**

Translate a Figure on a Coordinate Plane

Polygon *ABCD* has vertices
A(−1, 6), *B*(4, 5), *C*(2, 2), and
D(−2, 0). Graph and label the
vertices of *ABCD* and *A′B′C′D′*,
its image after a translation of
8 units down and 3 units left.

In a transformation, the
original figure is the preimage.
The resulting figure is the
image. The image of point A is
point *A′*, read "A prime."

STEP 1 Graph polygon *ABCD*.

STEP 2 Translate each vertex
8 units down and
3 units left.

STEP 3 Draw and label the
vertices of polygon
A′B′C′D′.

The corresponding
side lengths are
equal.

$AB = A'B'$

$BC = B'C'$

$CD = C'D'$

$AD = A'D'$

A translation maps
angles to angles with
the same measure.

$m\angle A = m\angle A'$

$m\angle B = m\angle B'$

$m\angle C = m\angle C'$

$m\angle D = m\angle D'$

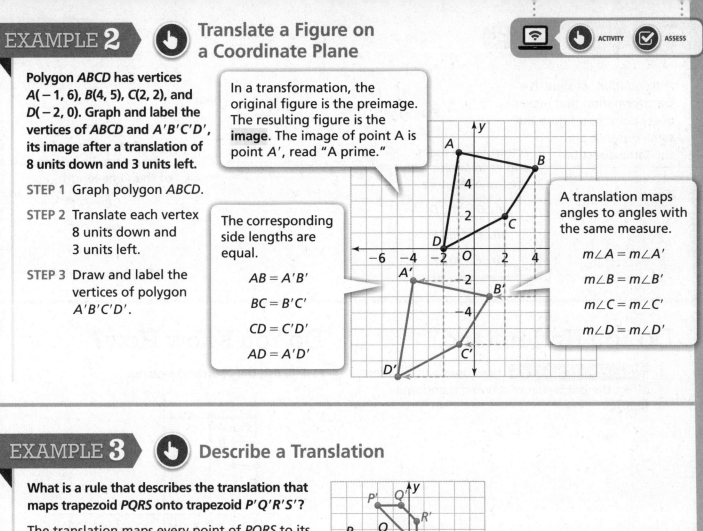

EXAMPLE **3**   **Describe a Translation**

**What is a rule that describes the translation that
maps trapezoid *PQRS* onto trapezoid *P′Q′R′S′*?**

The translation maps every point of *PQRS* to its
corresponding point of *P′Q′R′S′*.

Use Structure How do you know
which vertex of the trapezoid to use
to determine the rule? © MP.7

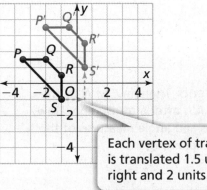

Each vertex of trapezoid *PQRS*
is translated 1.5 units to the
right and 2 units up.

☑ Try It!

Triangle *ABC* is translated 5 units right and 1 unit down.
Graph and label the image *A′B′C′*. If $m\angle A = 30°$, what
is $m\angle A'$?

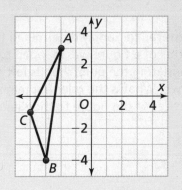

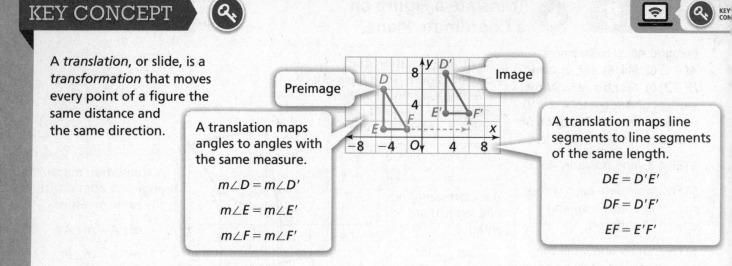

A *translation*, or slide, is a *transformation* that moves every point of a figure the same distance and the same direction.

Preimage

Image

A translation maps angles to angles with the same measure.

$m\angle D = m\angle D'$

$m\angle E = m\angle E'$

$m\angle F = m\angle F'$

A translation maps line segments to line segments of the same length.

$DE = D'E'$

$DF = D'F'$

$EF = E'F'$

Do You Understand?

1. **Essential Question** How does a translation affect the properties of a two-dimensional figure?

2. **Construct Arguments** Triangle *L'M'N'* is the image of triangle *LMN* after a translation. How are the side lengths and angle measures of the triangles related? Explain. © MP.3

3. **Generalize** Sanjay determined that one vertex of a figure was mapped to its image by translating the point 2 units left and 7 units down. What is the rule that maps the other vertices of the figure to their images? © MP.8

Do You Know How?

In 4–6, use the coordinate plane.

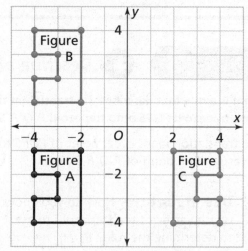

4. Which figure is a translation of Figure A? Explain.

5. Graph the translation of Figure A 3 units right and 4 units up.

6. Describe the translation needed to move Figure B to the same position as the image from Item 5.

Practice & Problem Solving

7. Graph *G′R′A′M′*, the image of *GRAM* after a translation 11 units right and 2 units up.

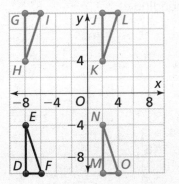

8. △*A′B′C′* is a translation of △*ABC*. Describe the translation.

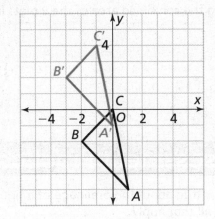

9. Which triangle is the image of △*DEF* after a translation? Describe the translation.

10. The vertices of figure *QRST* are translated 3 units left and 11 units down to form figure *Q′R′S′T′*. Explain the similarities and differences between the two figures.

11. Graph the image of the given triangle after a translation 3 units right and 2 units up.

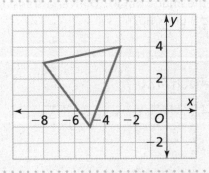

12. Quadrilateral *P′Q′R′S′* is the image of quadrilateral *PQRS* after a translation.

  a. If the length of side *PQ* is about 2.8 units, what is the length of side *P′Q′*?

  b. If *m∠R* = 75°, what is *m∠R′*?

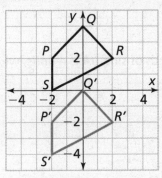

13. **Higher Order Thinking** A farmer has a plot of land shaped like the figure in the graph. There is another identical plot of land 120 yards east and 100 yards north of the original plot.

    a. Draw the image after the given translation.

    b. Find the combined area of the 2 plots in square yards.

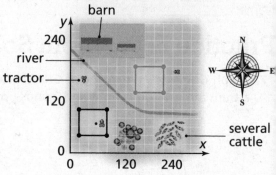

Assessment Practice

14. What is true about the preimage of a figure and its image created by a translation? Select all that apply.

    ☐ Each point in the image moves the same distance and direction from the preimage.

    ☐ Each point in the image has the same *x*-coordinate as the corresponding point in the preimage.

    ☐ The preimage and the image are the same size.

    ☐ The preimage and the image are the same shape.

15. The vertices of parallelogram *QUAD* are $Q(-7, -7)$, $U(-6, -4)$, $A(-2, -4)$, and $D(-3, -7)$.

    PART A

    Graph and label the image of QUAD after a translation 11 units right and 9 units up.

    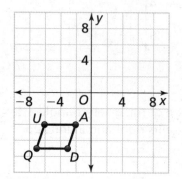

    PART B

    If $m\angle U = 110°$, what is $m\angle U'$?

    PART C

    If the length of side *UA* is 4 units, what is the length of side *U'A'*?

Go Online | PearsonRealize.com

Solve & Discuss It! ACTIVITY

Dale draws a triangle on grid paper and labels it Figure 1. Then using his pencil as a guide, he draws another triangle directly on the opposite side of the pencil so that the vertical side is now one square to the right of the pencil instead of one square to the left of the pencil. He labels this triangle Figure 2. How are the figures the same? How are they different?

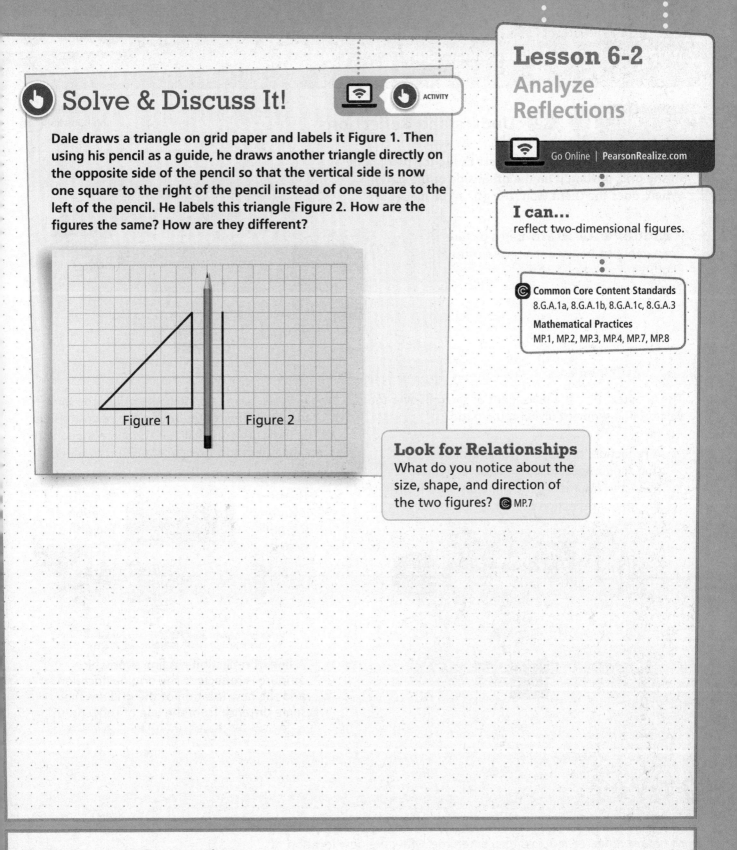

Figure 1   Figure 2

I can...
reflect two-dimensional figures.

Common Core Content Standards
8.G.A.1a, 8.G.A.1b, 8.G.A.1c, 8.G.A.3

Mathematical Practices
MP.1, MP.2, MP.3, MP.4, MP.7, MP.8

Look for Relationships
What do you notice about the size, shape, and direction of the two figures? MP.7

Focus on math practices

Reasoning Dale draws a line in place of his pencil and folds the grid paper along the line. How do the triangles align when the grid paper is folded? Explain. MP.2

INTERACTIVE ANIMATION   ASS

EXAMPLE 1 👁 **Understand Reflections**

Scan for Multimedia

The client also wants the architect to flip the placement of the grill, putting it on the other side of the patio. Where does the client want the grill to be placed?

Model with Math Can a picture or an object be used to represent the problem situation? © MP.4

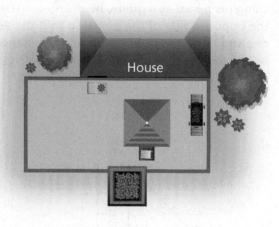

The architect flips the placement of the grill over the vertical line segment dividing the patio.

A **reflection**, or flip, is a transformation that flips a figure over a *line of reflection*. Reflected figures are the same distance from the line of reflection but on opposite sides.

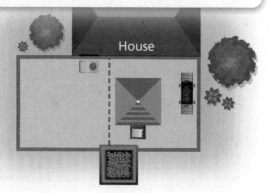

The grill has been reflected. The grill is the same distance from the center but on the opposite side of the patio. The grill still has the same shape and size. The orientation, or direction, has changed.

The new location of the grill.

The original location of the grill.

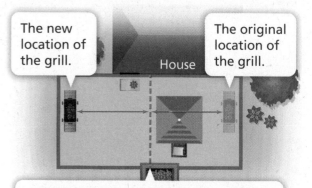

A **line of reflection** is a line over which a figure is reflected. The original location and the new location of the grill are the same distance from the line of reflection.

☑ Try It!

While updating the design, the architect accidentally clicked on the chair and reflected it across the center line. Draw the new location of the chair on the plan.

Convince Me! How do the preimage and image compare after a reflection?

Polygon *ABCDE* has vertices *A*(−5, 2), *B*(−5, 4), *C*(−4, 5), *D*(−3, 5) and *E*(−3, 2). Graph and label the vertices of *ABCDE* and its image, *A'B'C'D'E'*, after a reflection across the *x*-axis.

STEP 1   Graph polygon *ABCDE*.

STEP 2   Show how each vertex of *ABCDE* maps to its image after a reflection across the *x*-axis.

STEP 3   Draw and label the vertices of polygon *A'B'C'D'E'*.

Since point *A* is 2 units above the *x*-axis, point *A'* will be 2 units below the *x*-axis.

The corresponding side lengths and angle measures remain the same but their positions and orientations are different.

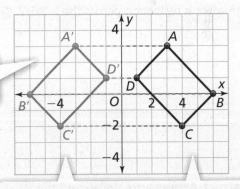

Try It!

Quadrilateral *KLMN* has vertices at *K*(2, 6), *L*(3, 8), *M*(5, 4), and *N*(3, 2). It is reflected across the *y*-axis, resulting in quadrilateral *K'L'M'N'*. What are the coordinates of point *N'*?

EXAMPLE **3** 👆 Describe a Reflection

What is a rule that describes the reflection that maps parallelogram *ABCD* onto parallelogram *A'B'C'D'*?

A reflection maps every point of *ABCD* to the corresponding point of *A'B'C'D'*.

Parallelogram *A'B'C'D'* is the image of parallelogram *ABCD* after a reflection across the *y*-axis.

Generalize When reflecting across the *y*-axis, the *y*-coordinate of the vertex of the image remains the same and the *x*-coordinate is the opposite. $(x, y) \rightarrow (−x, y)$ ©MP.8

Each point of preimage *ABCD* is the same distance from the line of reflection as the corresponding point of image *A'B'C'D'*.

Try It!

Polygon *ABCDE* is reflected across the line *x* = −2. Graph and label the image *A'B'C'D'E'*. Is *m∠A* = *m∠A'*? Explain.

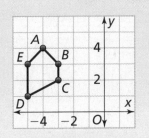

A **reflection**, or flip, is a transformation that flips a figure across a line of reflection. The preimage and image are the same distance from the line of reflection but on opposite sides. They have the same size and shape but different orientations.

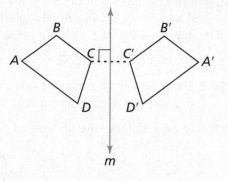

Do You Understand?

1. **Essential Question** How does a reflection affect the properties of a two-dimensional figure?

2. **Generalize** What do you notice about the corresponding coordinates of the preimage and image after a reflection across the *x*-axis? © MP.8

3. **Construct Arguments** Jorge said the *y*-values would stay the same when you reflect a preimage across the line $y = 5$ since the *y*-values stay the same when you reflect a preimage across the *y*-axis. Is Jorge correct? Explain. © MP.3

Do You Know How?

4. Is △*X'Y'Z'* a reflection of △*XYZ* across line *g*?

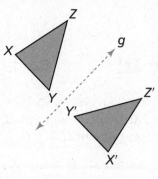

Use the coordinate grid below for 5 and 6.

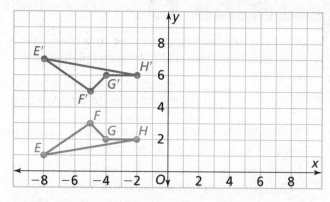

5. Describe the reflection of figure *EFGH*.

6. Draw the image that would result from a reflection of figure *EFGH* across the line $x = -1$.

Name: _____

Practice & Problem Solving

7. Leveled Practice Trapezoid *ABCD* is shown.
Draw the reflection of trapezoid *ABCD* across the *y*-axis.

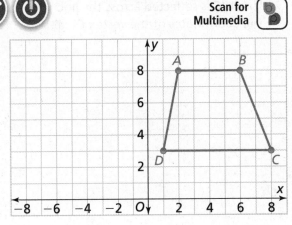

Identify the points of the preimage.

A ☐

B ☐

C ☐

D ☐

Identify the points of the image.

A′ ☐

B′ ☐

C′ ☐

D′ ☐

Plot the points and draw trapezoid *A′B′C′D′*.

8. Reasoning Is triangle *A′B′C′* a reflection of triangle *ABC* across the line? Explain. © MP.2

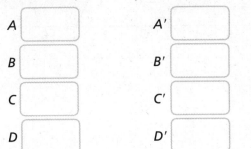

9. Your friend gives you the graph of quadrilateral *ABCD* and its image, quadrilateral *A′B′C′D′*. What reflection produces this image?

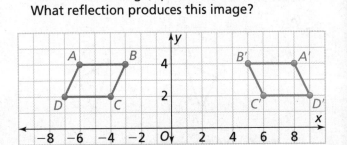

10. Construct Arguments Your friend incorrectly says that the reflection of △*EFG* to its image △*E′F′G′* is a reflection across the *x*-axis. © MP.3

a. What is your friend's mistake?

b. What is the correct description of the reflection?

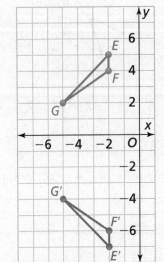

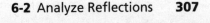

11. Make Sense and Persevere The vertices of △ABC are A(−5, 5), B(−2, 5), and C(−2, 3). If △ABC is reflected across the line y = −1, find the coordinates of the vertex C'. Ⓒ MP.1

12. Higher Order Thinking What reflection of the parallelogram ABCD results in image A'B'C'D'?

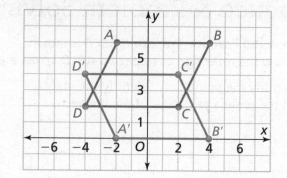

13. △JAR has vertices J(4, 5), A(6, 4), and R(5, 2). What graph shows △JAR and its image after a reflection across the line x = 1?

PART A

Ⓐ
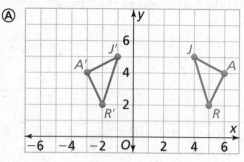

Ⓒ
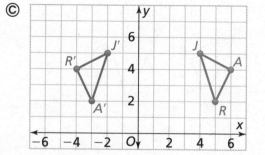

Ⓑ
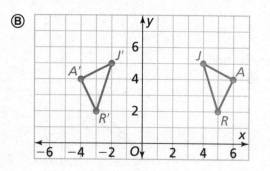

Ⓓ
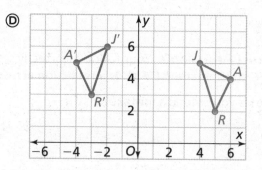

PART B

The measure of ∠A = 90°. What is m∠A'?

Go Online | PearsonRealize.com

Explain It!

Maria boards a car at the bottom of the Ferris wheel. She rides to the top, where the car stops. Maria tells her friend that she completed $\frac{1}{4}$ turn before the car stopped.

ACTIVITY

Lesson 6-3
Analyze Rotations

Go Online | PearsonRealize.com

I can...
rotate a two-dimensional figure.

© **Common Core Content Standards**
8.G.A.1a, 8.G.A.1b, 8.G.A.1c, 8.G.A.3
Mathematical Practices
MP.2, MP.3, MP.4

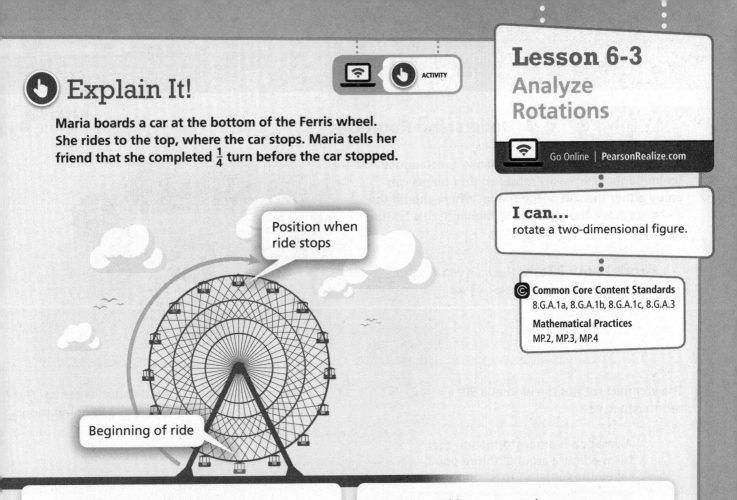

Position when ride stops

Beginning of ride

A. Do you agree with Maria? Explain.

B. How could you use angle measures to describe the change in position of the car?

Focus on math practices

Construct Arguments How can you describe Maria's change in position when her car returns to the position at which she began the ride? © MP.3

309

INTERACTIVE ANIMATION

EXAMPLE **1** 👁 **Understand Rotations**

Scan for Multimedia

One feature of the new patio plan is a rectangular umbrella that can easily rotate so that clients can enjoy either the sun or the shade. Where should the architect move the umbrella to highlight this feature for his clients?

> **Model with Math** How can you describe the rotation of the umbrella? Ⓒ MP.4

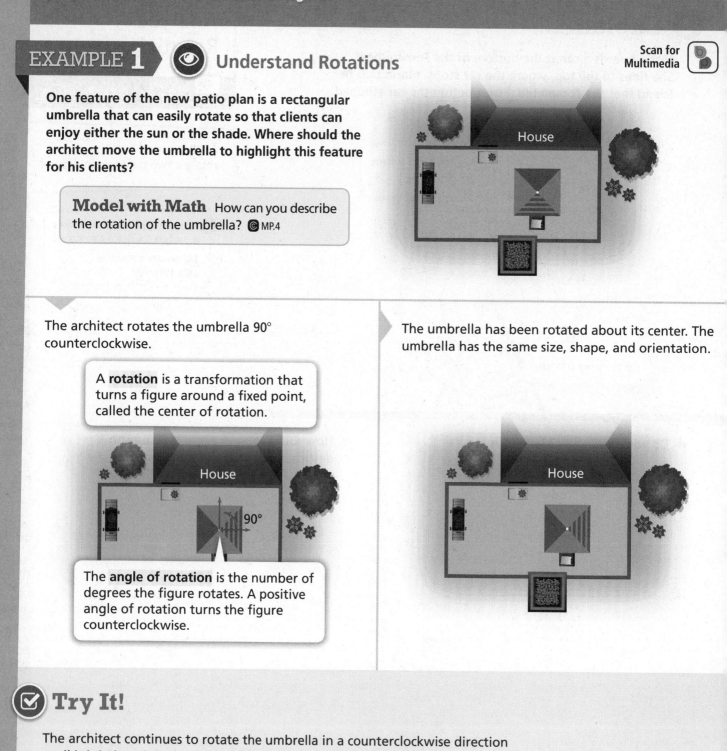

House

The architect rotates the umbrella 90° counterclockwise.

> A **rotation** is a transformation that turns a figure around a fixed point, called the center of rotation.

House

90°

> The **angle of rotation** is the number of degrees the figure rotates. A positive angle of rotation turns the figure counterclockwise.

The umbrella has been rotated about its center. The umbrella has the same size, shape, and orientation.

House

☑ **Try It!**

The architect continues to rotate the umbrella in a counterclockwise direction until it is in its original position. What is the angle of this rotation?

Convince Me! How does an image compare to its preimage after a −45° rotation?

 Go Online | PearsonRealize.com

EXAMPLE 2 👆 Complete a Rotation

What are the coordinates of the image of trapezoid *ABCD* after a 90° rotation about the origin?

STEP 1 Draw a ray from the origin to point *D*. Then use a protractor to draw a 90° angle in the counterclockwise direction.

STEP 2 Plot point *D′* the same distance from the origin as point *D*.

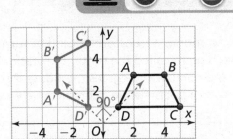

STEP 3 Use the same method to map each vertex of trapezoid *ABCD* to its image. Draw trapezoid *A′B′C′D′*.

$A(2, 3) \rightarrow A'(-3, 2)$

$B(4, 3) \rightarrow B'(-3, 4)$

$C(5, 1) \rightarrow C'(-1, 5)$

$D(1, 1) \rightarrow D'(-1, 1)$

Generalize The *x*- and *y*-coordinates of a point change as shown in the table below when rotated in a counterclockwise direction about the origin. © MP.8

Angle of Rotation	Rule
90°	$(x, y) \rightarrow (-y, x)$
180°	$(x, y) \rightarrow (-x, -y)$
270°	$(x, y) \rightarrow (y, -x)$

✅ Try It!

The coordinates of the vertices of quadrilateral *HIJK* are *H*(1, 4), *I*(3, 2), *J*(−1, −4), and *K*(−3, −2). If quadrilateral *HIJK* is rotated 270° about the origin, what are the vertices of the resulting image, quadrilateral *H′I′J′K′*?

EXAMPLE 3 👆 Describe a Rotation

Describe the rotation that maps parallelogram *ABCD* to parallelogram *A′B′C′D′*.

STEP 1 Draw rays from the origin through point *A* and point *A′*.

STEP 2 Measure the angle formed by the rays.

A 270° rotation about the origin maps parallelogram *ABCD* to parallelogram *A′B′C′D′*.

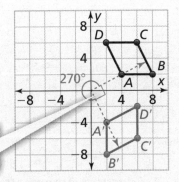

> This rotation could also be described as a −90°, or 90° clockwise, rotation.

✅ Try It!

Describe the rotation that maps △*FGH* to △*F′G′H′*.

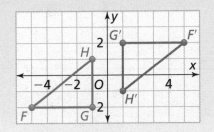

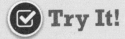

A rotation is a transformation that turns a figure about a fixed point called the center of rotation. The angle of rotation is the number of degrees the figure is rotated. The x- and y-coordinates change in predictable ways when rotated.

Counterclockwise Rotations about the Origin

Angle of Rotation	Transformation
90°	$(x, y) \rightarrow (-y, x)$
180°	$(x, y) \rightarrow (-x, -y)$
270°	$(x, y) \rightarrow (y, -x)$

Do You Understand?

1. **?** **Essential Question** How does a rotation affect the properties of a two-dimensional figure?

2. **Reasoning** If a preimage is rotated 360 degrees about the origin how can you describe its image? **©** MP.2

3. **Construct Arguments** In Example 3, side *AB* is parallel to side *DC*. How are side *A'B'* and side *D'C'* related? Explain. **©** MP.3

Do You Know How?

4. The coordinates of the vertices of rectangle *ABCD* are *A*(3, −2), *B*(3, 2), *C*(−3, 2), and *D*(−3, −2).

   a. Rectangle *ABCD* is rotated 90° about the origin. What are the coordinates of the vertices of rectangle *A'B'C'D'*?

   b. What are the measures of the angles of *A'B'C'D'*?

5. Describe the counterclockwise rotation that maps △*QRS* to △*Q'R'S'*.

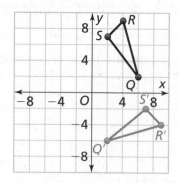

Practice & Problem Solving

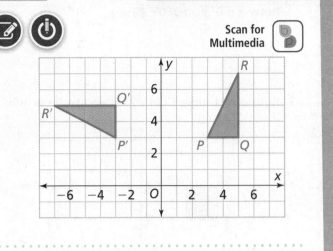

6. What is the angle of rotation about the origin that maps △PQR to △P'Q'R'?

7. Is △X'Y'Z' a rotation of △XYZ? Explain.

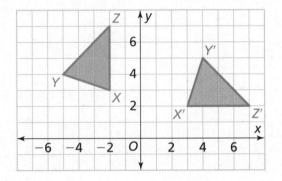

8. △PQR is rotated 270° about the origin. Graph and label the coordinates of P', Q', and R'.

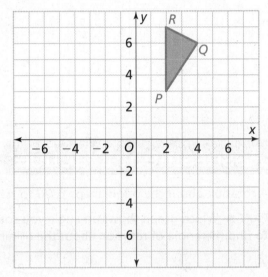

9. Is △P'Q'R' a 270° rotation of △PQR about the origin? Explain.

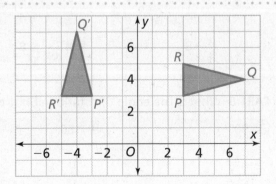

10. Reasoning Explain why any rotation can be described by an angle between 0° and 360°. © MP.2

11. Rotate rectangle *KLMN* 270° about the origin.

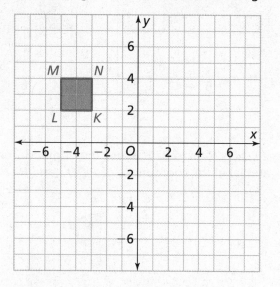

12. Higher Order Thinking An architect is designing a new windmill with four sails. In her sketch, the sails' center of rotation is the origin, (0, 0), and the tip of one of the sails, point *Q*, has coordinates (2, −3). She wants to make another sketch that shows the windmill after the sails have rotated 270° about their center of rotation. What would be the coordinates of *Q*′?

© Assessment Practice

13. A rotation about the origin maps △*TRI* to △*T′R′I′*.

PART A Which graph shows an angle you could measure to find the angle of rotation about the origin?

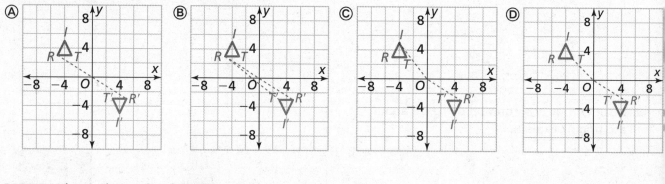

PART B What is the angle of rotation about the origin?

Ⓐ 90°   Ⓑ 180°   Ⓒ 270°   Ⓓ 360°

Solve & Discuss It!

ACTIVITY

How can you map Figure A onto Figure B?

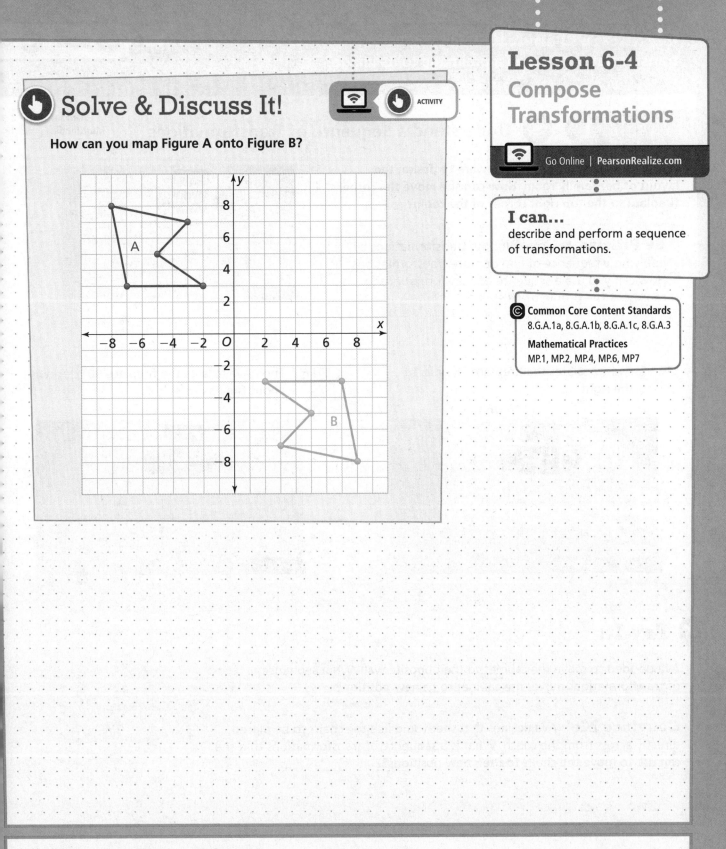

I can...
describe and perform a sequence of transformations.

© **Common Core Content Standards**
8.G.A.1a, 8.G.A.1b, 8.G.A.1c, 8.G.A.3

Mathematical Practices
MP.1, MP.2, MP.4, MP.6, MP7

Focus on math practices

Look for Relationships Is there another transformation or sequence of transformations that will map Figure A to Figure B? © MP.7

EXAMPLE 1   👁 Understand a Sequence of Transformations

Scan for Multimedia

Ava is using interior design software to design the layout of her family room. How can she move the corner fireplace to the top right corner of the room?

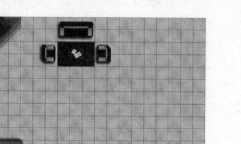

Be Precise You can compose transformations by applying a sequence of two or more transformations. How can you use a sequence of transformations to represent the problem? © MP.6

STEP 1 Ava translates the fireplace 15 units to the right.

15 Units

STEP 2 Then Ava rotates the fireplace 90° clockwise about the its center.

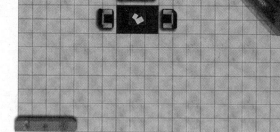

☑ Try It!

Ava decided to move the cabinet to the opposite wall. What sequence of transformations moves the cabinet to its new position?

Convince Me! Ava decides that she would like the chairs to be placed directly across from the couch. What is a sequence of transformations that she can use to move the chairs to their new positions?

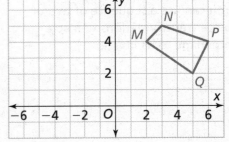

EXAMPLE 2 — Complete a Sequence of Transformations on a Coordinate Plane

Translate quadrilateral *MNPQ* 7 units left, and then reflect it across the line $x = -3$.

This is called a *glide reflection*, because it is a sequence of a translation and a reflection.

Be Precise The image of point N' is N'' (read "N double prime"). © MP.6

STEP 1 Translate quadrilateral *MNPQ* 7 units left.

Each point moves 7 units left.

STEP 2 Reflect quadrilateral $M'N'P'Q'$ across the line $x = -3$.

Reflect each point across the line of reflection.

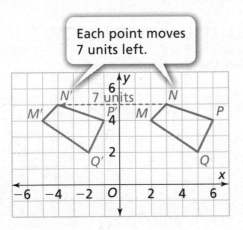

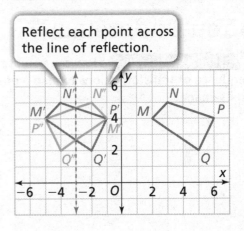

EXAMPLE 3 — Describe a Sequence of Transformations

What is a sequence of transformations that maps △*ABC* onto △*A"B"C"*?

STEP 1 Translate △*ABC* 8 units right and 6 units down to map it onto △*A'B'C'*.

STEP 2 Reflect △*A'B'C'* across the *y*-axis to map it onto △*A"B"C"*.

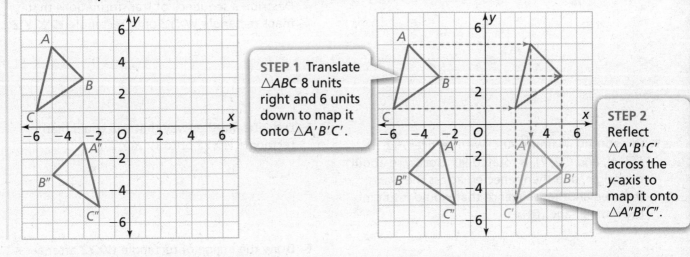

Try It!

What is another sequence of transformations that maps △*ABC* onto △*A"B"C"*?

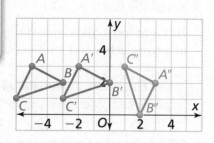
You can use a sequence of two or more transformations to map a preimage to its image.

You can map △ABC onto △A″B″C″ by a translation 3 units right followed by a 90° clockwise rotation about the origin.

Do You Understand?

1. **Essential Question** How can you use a sequence of transformations to map a preimage to its image?

2. **Make Sense and Persevere** A preimage is rotated 180° about the origin and then rotated 180° about the origin again. Compare the preimage and image. ⓒ MP.1

3. **Reasoning** A figure *ABC*, with vertices *A*(2, 1), *B*(7, 4), and *C*(2, 7), is rotated 90° clockwise about the origin, and then reflected across the *y*-axis. Describe another sequence that would result in the same image. ⓒ MP.2

Do You Know How?

In **4–6**, use the diagram below.

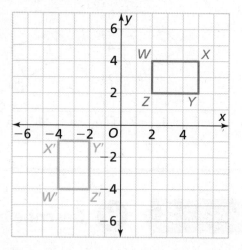

4. Describe a sequence of transformations that maps rectangle *WXYZ* onto rectangle *W′X′Y′Z′*.

5. Describe another way that you could map rectangle *WXYZ* onto *W′X′Y′Z′*.

6. Draw the image of rectangle *WXYZ* after a reflection across the line *y* = 1 and a translation 1 unit right. Label the image *W″X″Y″Z″*.

Name: _____

Practice & Problem Solving

7. Leveled Practice Describe a sequence of transformations that maps △QRS onto △TUV.

A translation ⬜ units left and ⬜ units down,

followed by a ⬜ across the ⬜ .

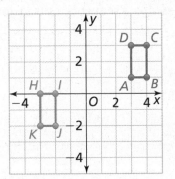

8. Model with Math A family moves a table, shown as rectangle EFGH, by translating it 3 units left and 3 units down followed by a 90° rotation about the origin. Graph E′F′G′H′ to show the new location of the table. © MP.4

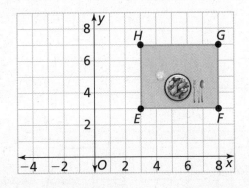

9. Describe a sequence of transformations that maps quadrilateral ABCD to quadrilateral HIJK.

10. Map △QRS to △Q′R′S′ with a reflection across the y-axis followed by a translation 6 units down.

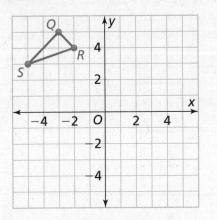

11. Higher Order Thinking A student says that he was rearranging furniture at home and he used a glide reflection to move a table with legs from one side of the room to the other. Will a glide reflection result in a functioning table? Explain.

12. PART A Which sequence of transformations maps rectangle *ABCD* onto rectangle *A'B'C'D'*?

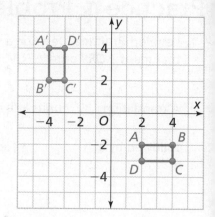

Ⓐ translation 6 units down, rotation 90° about the origin, translation 6 units down, reflection across the *x*-axis

Ⓑ reflection across the *x*-axis, translation 6 units down, reflection across the *y*-axis, translation 6 units right

Ⓒ rotation 90° about the origin, reflection across the *x*-axis, translation 6 units left, translation 6 units up

Ⓓ translation 6 units left, reflection across the *y*-axis, translation 6 units down, rotation 180° about the origin

PART B Describe a sequence of transformations that maps *A'B'C'D'* onto *ABCD*.

13. PART A Which figure is the image of Figure A after a reflection across the *x*-axis and a translation 4 units right?

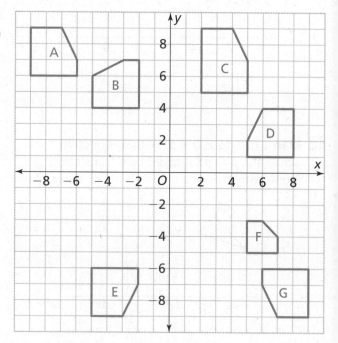

Ⓐ Figure B

Ⓑ Figure C

Ⓒ Figure D

Ⓓ Figure E

PART B Which figure can be transformed into Figure G after a rotation 90° about the origin, then a translation 13 units right and 4 units down?

Ⓐ Figure B

Ⓑ Figure D

Ⓒ Figure E

Ⓓ Figure F

3-ACT MATH ▷ ▷ ▷

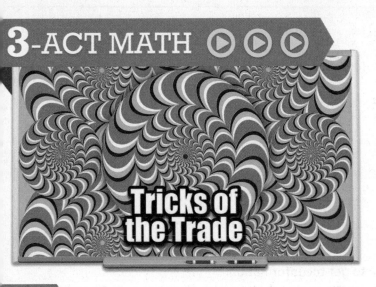

Tricks of the Trade

3-Act Mathematical Modeling:
Tricks of the Trade

📶 Go Online | PearsonRealize.com

© **Common Core Content Standards**
8.G.A.1, 8.G.A.2
Mathematical Practices
MP.4

ACT 1

1. After watching the video, what is the first question that comes to mind?

2. Write the Main Question you will answer.

3. Make a prediction to answer this Main Question.

4. **Construct Arguments** Explain how you arrived at your prediction. © MP.3

5. What information in this situation would be helpful to know? How would you use that information?

6. Use Appropriate Tools What tools can you use to get the information you need? Record the information as you find it. Ⓒ MP.5

7. Model with Math Represent the situation using the mathematical content, concepts, and skills from this topic. Use your representation to answer the Main Question. Ⓒ MP.4

8. What is your answer to the Main Question? Does it differ from your prediction? Explain.

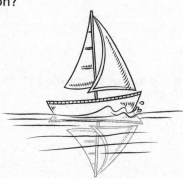

 Go Online | PearsonRealize.com

9. Write the answer you saw in the video.

10. Reasoning Does your answer match the answer in the video? If not, what are some reasons that would explain the difference? © MP.2

11. Make Sense and Persevere Would you change your model now that you know the answer? Explain. © MP.1

Reflect

12. Model with Math Explain how you used a mathematical model to represent the situation. How did the model help you answer the Main Question? Ⓒ MP.4

13. Make Sense and Persevere When did you struggle most while solving the problem? How did you overcome that obstacle? Ⓒ MP.1

14. Be Precise Find another optical illusion online involving shapes that look different but are the same. Explain how you know the shapes are the same. Ⓒ MP.6

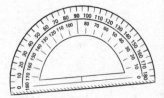

Go Online | PearsonRealize.com

👆 Solve & Discuss It!

Simone plays a video game in which she moves shapes into empty spaces. After several rounds, her next move must fit the blue piece into the dashed space. How can Simone move the blue piece to fit in the space?

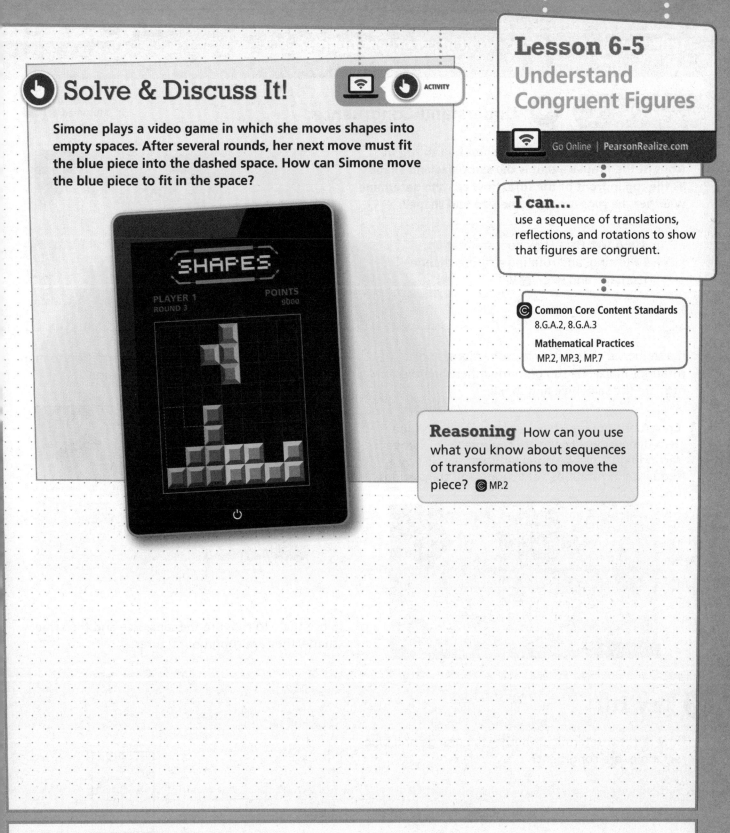

I can...
use a sequence of translations, reflections, and rotations to show that figures are congruent.

© **Common Core Content Standards**
8.G.A.2, 8.G.A.3

Mathematical Practices
MP.2, MP.3, MP.7

Reasoning How can you use what you know about sequences of transformations to move the piece? © MP.2

Focus on math practices

Construct Arguments How do you know that the piece that fits into the space is the same as the original blue shape? Explain. © MP.3

EXAMPLE 1 ⊙ Understand Congruence

Scan for
Multimedia

Ava wants to place a flame-resistant hearth rug in front of the fireplace that is the same size and shape as the rug in front of the sofa. How can she determine whether the rugs are the same size and shape?

> **Reasoning** How does translating, reflecting, and rotating a figure change its shape and size? ⓒ MP.2

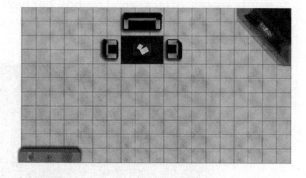

If a sequence of translations, reflections, and rotations maps one rug onto the other then the rugs are the same size and shape.

> *Congruent figures* have the same size and shape. Two-dimensional figure are **congruent** (≅) if the second figure can be obtained from the first by a sequence of rotations, reflections, and translations.

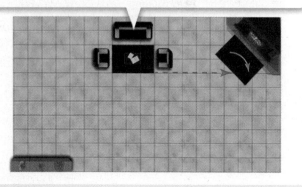

Ava uses a translation followed by a rotation to map the living room rug onto the hearth rug.

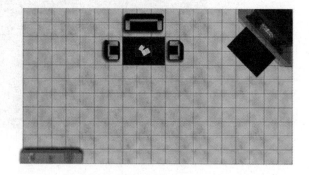

Since the two rugs are the same size and the same shape, they are congruent figures.

☑ Try It!

How can you determine whether the orange and blue rectangles are congruent?

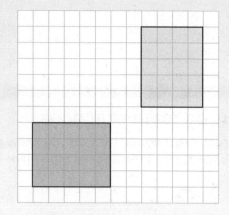

Convince Me! Quadrilateral *PQRS* is congruent to quadrilateral *P'Q'R'S'*. What do you know about how these figures relate?

 Go Online | PearsonRealize.com

A. Is quadrilateral ABCD congruent to quadrilateral QRST?

> **Look for Relationships** Is there a sequence of transformations that will map one of the figures onto the other? © MP.7

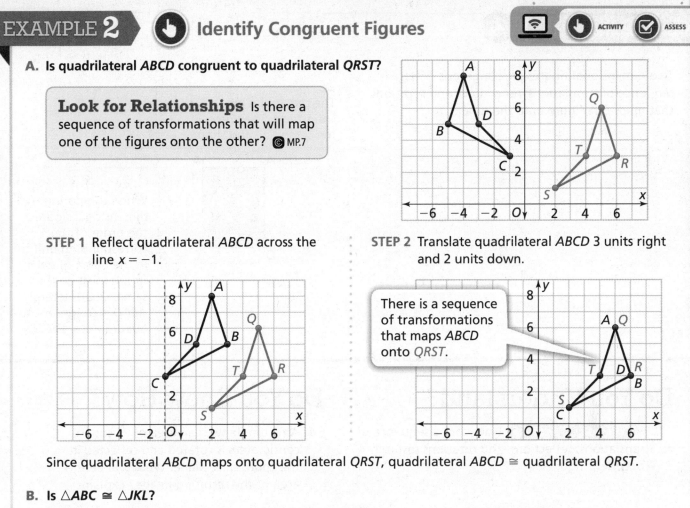

STEP 1 Reflect quadrilateral ABCD across the line x = −1.

STEP 2 Translate quadrilateral ABCD 3 units right and 2 units down.

> There is a sequence of transformations that maps ABCD onto QRST.

Since quadrilateral ABCD maps onto quadrilateral QRST, quadrilateral ABCD ≅ quadrilateral QRST.

B. Is △ABC ≅ △JKL?

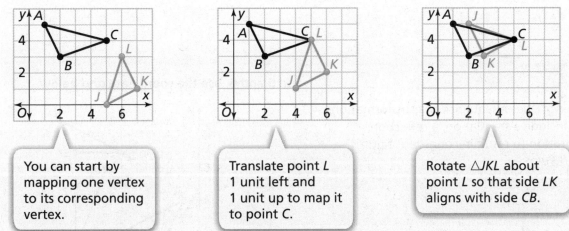

> You can start by mapping one vertex to its corresponding vertex.

> Translate point L 1 unit left and 1 unit up to map it to point C.

> Rotate △JKL about point L so that side LK aligns with side CB.

There is no sequence of transformations that maps △JKL directly onto △ABC, so △ABC is NOT congruent to △JKL.

Try It!

Are the figures congruent? Explain.

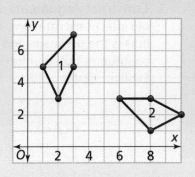

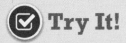

Two-dimensional figures are congruent if there is a sequence of translations, reflections, and rotations that maps one figure onto the other.

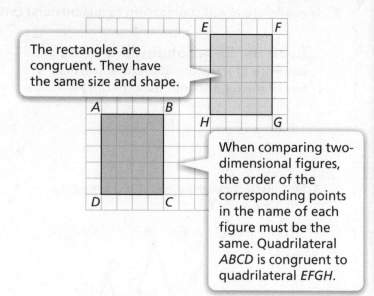

The rectangles are congruent. They have the same size and shape.

When comparing two-dimensional figures, the order of the corresponding points in the name of each figure must be the same. Quadrilateral *ABCD* is congruent to quadrilateral *EFGH*.

Do You Understand?

1. **Essential Question** How does a sequence of translations, reflections, and rotations result in congruent figures?

2. **Reasoning** Does a sequence of transformations have to include a translation, a reflection, and a rotation to result in congruent figures? Explain. © MP.2

3. **Construct Arguments** Is there a sequence of reflections, rotations, and translations that makes the preimage and image not only congruent, but identical in orientation? Explain. © MP.3

Do You Know How?

4. A rectangle with an area of 25 square centimeters is rotated and reflected in the coordinate plane. What will be the area of the resulting image? Explain.

In 5 and 6, use the coordinate grid below.

5. Is △*ABC* ≅ △*DEF*? Explain.

6. Is △*ABC* ≅ △*GHI*? Explain.

 Go Online | PearsonRealize.com

Practice & Problem Solving

Scan for
Multimedia

7. △Q′R′S′ is the image of △QRS after a reflection across the
y-axis and a translation 6 units down. Is the image the same
size and shape as the preimage?

△QRS and △Q′R′S′ 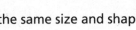 the same size and shape.

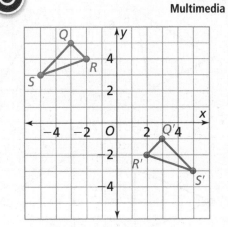

8. Is △DEF ≅ △D′E′F′? Explain.

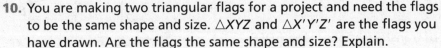

9. Construct Arguments Describe a way to
show that quadrilateral *ABCD* is congruent to
quadrilateral *A′B′C′D′*. Ⓒ MP.3

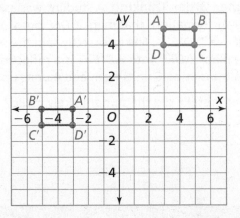

10. You are making two triangular flags for a project and need the flags
to be the same shape and size. △XYZ and △X′Y′Z′ are the flags you
have drawn. Are the flags the same shape and size? Explain.

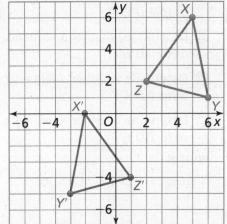

11. Which two triangles are congruent? Describe the sequence of transformations that maps one figure onto the other.

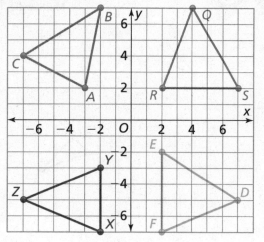

12. Is △*LMN* ≅ △*XYZ*? Explain.

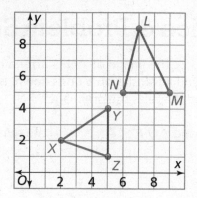

13. Higher Order Thinking A student was asked to describe a sequence of transformations that maps △*DEF* onto △*D'E'F'*, given that △*DEF* ≅ △*D'E'F'*. She incorrectly said the sequence of transformations that maps △*DEF* onto △*D'E'F'* is a reflection across the *x*-axis, followed by a translation 6 units right and 4 units up.

What mistake did the student likely make?

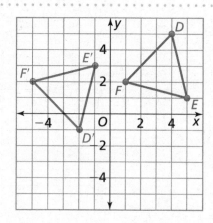

14. PART A

How can you determine whether △*DEF* ≅ △*D'E'F'*?

Ⓐ Determine whether a sequence of rotations maps △*DEF* onto △*D'E'F'*.

Ⓑ Determine whether a sequence of transformations maps △*DEF* onto △*D'E'F'*.

Ⓒ Determine whether a sequence of translations maps △*DEF* onto △*D'E'F'*.

Ⓓ Determine whether a sequence of reflections maps △*DEF* onto △*D'E'F'*.

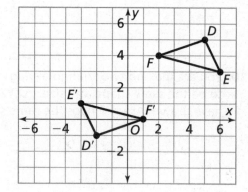

PART B

Is △*DEF* ≅ △*D'E'F'*? Explain.

Name: _____

1. **Vocabulary** Describe three transformations where the image and preimage have the same size and shape. *Lesson 6-1, Lesson 6-2, and Lesson 6-3*

For 2–6, use the figures below.

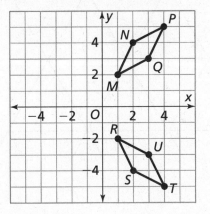

2. What are the coordinates of each point after quadrilateral *RSTU* is rotated 90° about the origin? *Lesson 6-3*

3. What are the coordinates of each point after quadrilateral *MNPQ* is translated 2 units right and 5 units down? *Lesson 6-1*

4. What are the coordinates of each point after quadrilateral *MNPQ* is reflected across the *x*-axis? *Lesson 6-2*

5. Which series of transformations maps quadrilateral *MNPQ* onto quadrilateral *RSTU*? *Lesson 6-4*

   Ⓐ reflection across the *x*-axis, translation 4 units down

   Ⓑ reflection across the *y*-axis, translation 4 units down

   Ⓒ rotation 180° about the origin, and then reflection across the *x*-axis

   Ⓓ rotation 180° about the origin, and then reflection across the *y*-axis

6. Is quadrilateral *MNPQ* congruent to quadrilateral *RSTU*? Explain. *Lesson 6-5*

How well did you do on the mid-topic checkpoint? Fill in the stars. ☆☆☆

MID-TOPIC
PERFORMANCE TASK

A tessellation is a design in a plane that uses one or more congruent figures, with no overlaps and no gaps, to cover the entire plane. A tessellation of an equilateral triangle is shown.

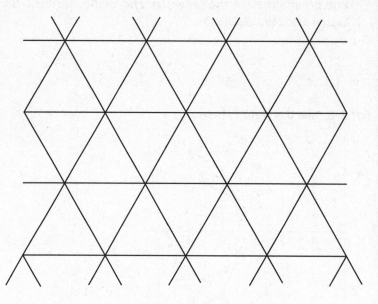

PART A

Explain how the tessellation of an equilateral triangle is formed using reflections.

PART B

Explain how the tessellation of an equilateral triangle is formed using rotations.

PART C

Which of the regular polygon(s) below can be tessellated using a series of transformations?

square   pentagon   hexagon

Go Online | **Pearson**Realize.com

👆 Solve & Discuss It!

📶 👆 ACTIVITY

A landscape architect designs a small splash pad represented by △ABC. Then she decides to make the splash pad larger as shown by △ADE. How are the splash pad designs alike? How are they different?

Look for Relationships
How can you use what you know about scale drawings to compare and contrast the designs? © MP.7

I can...
dilate two-dimensional figures

© **Common Core Content Standards**
8.G.A.3, 8.G.A.4

Mathematical Practices
MP.2, MP.3, MP.7, MP.8

Focus on math practices

Reasoning Paul wants to make two square picnic tables. One table will have side lengths that are $\frac{1}{2}$ the lengths of the second table. How do the tables compare? Explain. © MP.2

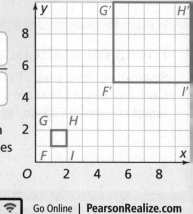

EXAMPLE 1 👁 **Understand Dilations**

Scan for Multimedia

The landscape architect designs two open green spaces for another area of the park. She designs the larger space so that the length of each side is three times the length of its corresponding side in the smaller green space. Where should the architect draw the larger green space?

Look for Relationships How can you use what you know about scale drawings to determine the space? ⓒ MP.7

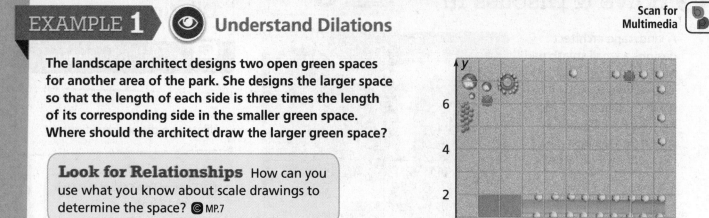

The architect dilates the smaller space by a scale factor of 3. A **dilation** is a transformation that moves each point along the ray through the point, starting from a fixed center, and multiplies distances from the center by a common scale factor.

The **scale factor**, *r*, is the ratio of a length in the image to the corresponding length in the preimage.

The fixed center of this dilation is the origin *O*. A dilation with fixed center *O* and scale factor *r* maps any point *P* to *P'* such that $OP' = rOP$.
$$OA' = rOA$$
$$OB' = rOB$$
$$OC' = rOC$$
$$OD' = rOD$$

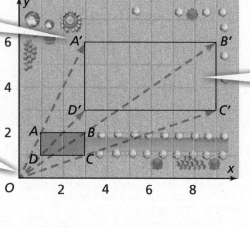

The image of a dilation has the same shape, angle measures, and orientation, but different side lengths.

☑ **Try It!**

$F'G'H'I'$ is the image of *FGHI* after a dilation with center at the origin. What is the scale factor?

The ratio of a side length in $F'G'H'I'$ to a corresponding side length in *FGHI* is: ⬜/⬜

The scale factor is ⬜.

Convince Me! Quadrilateral *WXYZ* is the image of quadrilateral *FGHI* after a dilation with center at the origin and a scale factor of 3.5. What are the coordinates of the vertices of quadrilateral *WXYZ*?

Go Online | PearsonRealize.com

EXAMPLE **2** 👆 **Dilate to Enlarge a Figure on a Coordinate Plane**

🔲📶 👆 ACTIVITY ✅ ASSESS

What are the coordinates of the image of *ABCD* after a dilation with center (0, 0) and a scale factor of 2?

STEP 1 Identify the coordinates of each vertex of the preimage.

$A(2, -2), B(2, 1), C(4, 0), D(4, -1)$

STEP 2 Dilate to find the coordinates of the vertices of $A'B'C'D'$.

You can find the image points of a dilation in the coordinate plane with center at the origin by multiplying the coordinates of the preimage by the scale factor.

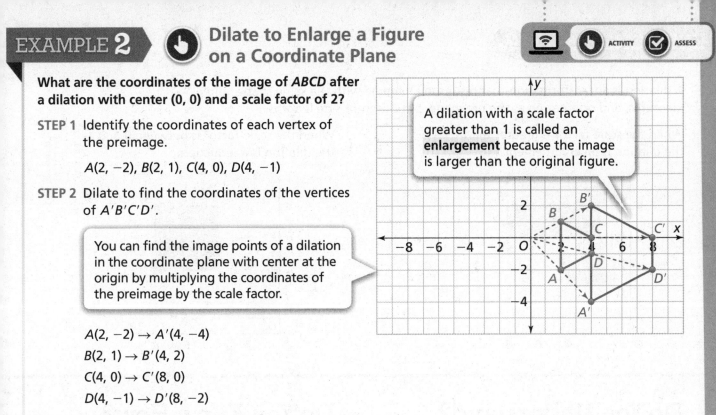

A dilation with a scale factor greater than 1 is called an **enlargement** because the image is larger than the original figure.

$A(2, -2) \rightarrow A'(4, -4)$
$B(2, 1) \rightarrow B'(4, 2)$
$C(4, 0) \rightarrow C'(8, 0)$
$D(4, -1) \rightarrow D'(8, -2)$

STEP 3 Graph $A'B'C'D'$.

EXAMPLE **3** 👆 **Dilate to Reduce a Figure**

What are the coordinates of the image of *PQRS* after a dilation with center (0, 0) and a scale factor of $\frac{1}{2}$?

STEP 1 Identify the coordinates of each vertex of the preimage.

$P(6, 10), Q(10, 10), R(10, 6), S(6, 6)$

STEP 2 Dilate to find the coordinates of the vertices of $P'Q'R'S'$.

$P(6, 10) \rightarrow P'(3, 5)$
$Q(10, 10) \rightarrow Q'(5, 5)$
$R(10, 6) \rightarrow R'(5, 3)$
$S(6, 6) \rightarrow S'(3, 3)$

Multiply the coordinates by the scale factor $\frac{1}{2}$.

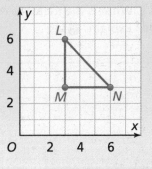

A dilation with a scale factor between 0 and 1 is called a **reduction** because the image is smaller than the original figure.

STEP 3 Graph $P'Q'R'S'$.

✅ **Try It!**

A dilation maps point $L(3, 6)$ to its image $L'(2, 4)$. Complete the dilation of figure *LMN* and label the image $L'M'N'$. What is the scale factor? What is the length of side $M'N'$?

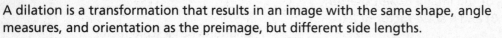
A dilation is a transformation that results in an image with the same shape, angle measures, and orientation as the preimage, but different side lengths.

When the scale factor is greater than 1, the dilation is an enlargement.

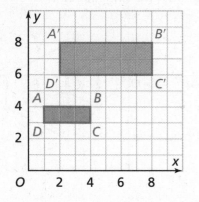

When the scale factor is between 0 and 1, the dilation is a reduction.

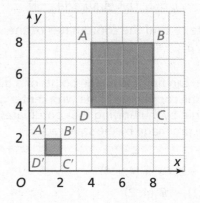

Do You Understand?

1. **Essential Question** What is the relationship between a preimage and its image after a dilation?

2. **Generalize** When will a dilation be a reduction? When will it be an enlargement? © MP.8

3. **Reasoning** Flora draws a rectangle with points at (12, 12), (15, 12), (15, 9) and (12, 9). She dilates the figure with center at the origin and a scale factor of $\frac{3}{4}$. What is the measure of each angle in the image? Explain. © MP.2

Do You Know How?

In 4–6, use the coordinate grid below.

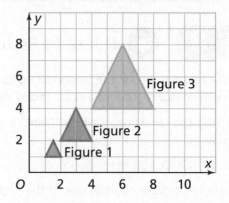

4. Figure 3 is the image of Figure 1 after a dilation with center at the origin. What is the scale factor? Explain.

5. What are the coordinates of the image of Figure 2 after a dilation with center at the origin and a scale factor of 3?

6. Which figures represent a dilation with a scale factor of $\frac{1}{2}$?

Practice & Problem Solving

7. Leveled Practice Draw the image of △*DEF* after a dilation with center (0, 0) and scale factor of 2.

Find the coordinates of each point in the original figure.

D([ ] , ([ ])   *E*([ ] , ([ ])   *F*([ ] , ([ ])

Multiply each coordinate by [ ] .

Find the coordinates of each point in the image:

D'([ ] , ([ ])   *E'*([ ] , ([ ])   *F'*([ ] , ([ ])

Graph the image.

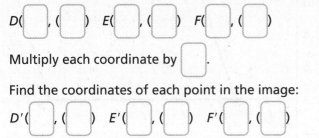

8. Find the scale factor for the dilation shown.

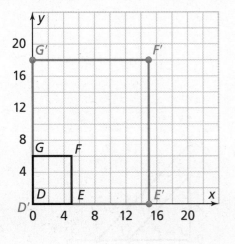

9. Critique Reasoning For the dilation with center (0, 0) shown on the graph, your friend says the scale factor is $\frac{5}{2}$. What is the correct scale factor? What mistake did your friend likely make? © MP.3

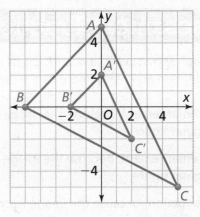

10. The smaller figure is the image of a dilation of the larger figure. The origin is the center of dilation. Tell whether the dilation is an enlargement or a reduction. Then find the scale factor of the dilation.

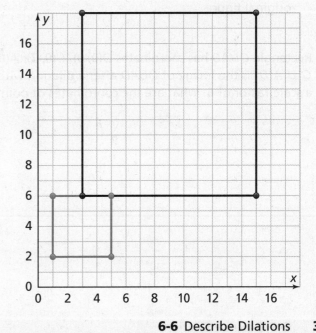

11. **Higher Order Thinking** $Q'R'S'T'$ is the image of QRST after a dilation with center at the origin.

   a. Find the scale factor.

   b. Find the area of each parallelogram. What is the relationship between the areas?

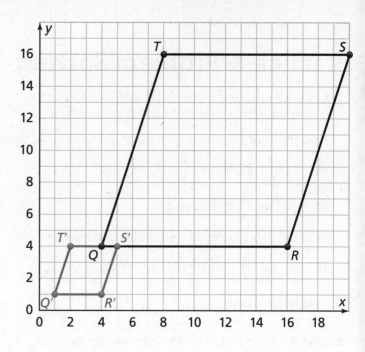

Assessment Practice

12. The graph shows $\triangle JKL$ and $\triangle J'K'L'$, its image after a dilation. Is the dilation an enlargement or a reduction? Explain.

   Ⓐ An enlargement, because the image is larger than the original figure

   Ⓑ An enlargement, because the image is smaller than the original figure

   Ⓒ A reduction, because the image is smaller than the original figure

   Ⓓ A reduction, because the image is larger than the original figure

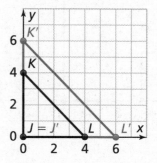

13. Rectangle QUAD has coordinates Q(0, 0), U(0, 3), A(6, 3), and D(6, 0). Q'U'A'D' is the image of QUAD after a dilation with center (0, 0) and a scale factor of 6. What are the coordinates of point D'? Explain.

👆 Solve & Discuss It!

Andrew draws the two figures shown on a coordinate plane. How are the two figures alike? How are they different? How do you know?

📶 👆 ACTIVITY

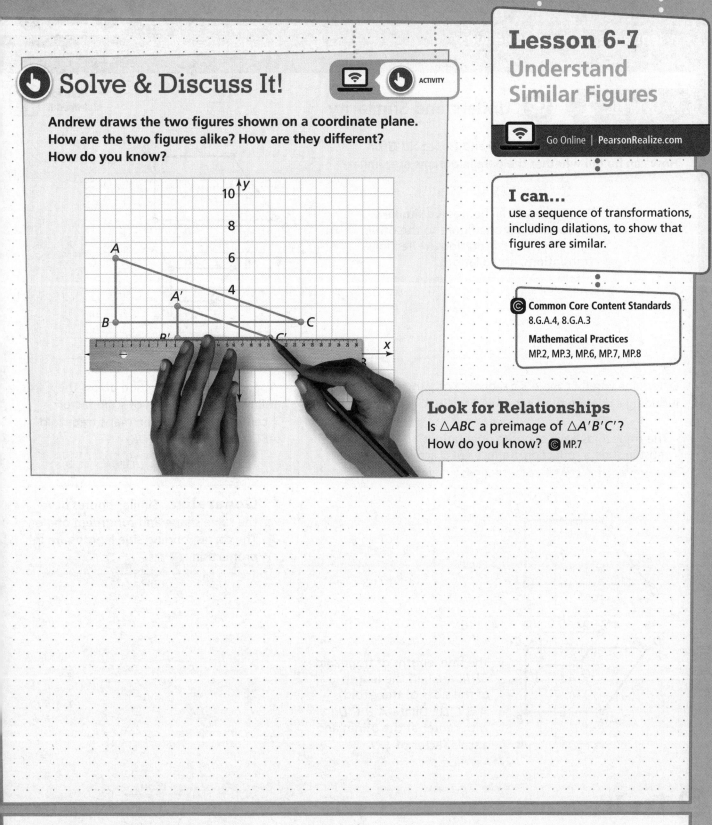

I can...
use a sequence of transformations, including dilations, to show that figures are similar.

ⓒ **Common Core Content Standards**
8.G.A.4, 8.G.A.3

Mathematical Practices
MP.2, MP.3, MP.6, MP.7, MP.8

Look for Relationships
Is △ABC a preimage of △A'B'C'? How do you know? ⓒ MP.7

Focus on math practices

Reasoning How can you use the coordinates of the vertices of the triangles to identify the transformation that maps △ABC to △A'B'C'? Explain. ⓒ MP.2

? Essential Question How are similar figures related by a sequence of transformations?

EXAMPLE 1 **Understand Similarity**

Scan for Multimedia

Albert graphed trapezoid *ABCD* and trapezoid *GHJK*. How can he tell whether the parallelograms are similar?

> Two-dimensional figures are **similar** (~) if you can map one figure to the other by a sequence of rotations, reflections, translations, and dilations.

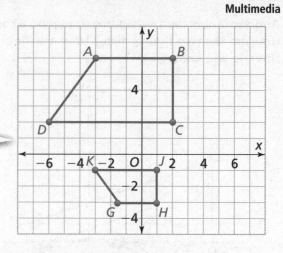

Determine whether there is a sequence of transformations, including a dilation that maps *ABCD* to *GHJK*.

> The trapezoids have opposite orientations, so the sequence must include a reflection. Reflect *ABCD* across the *x*-axis.

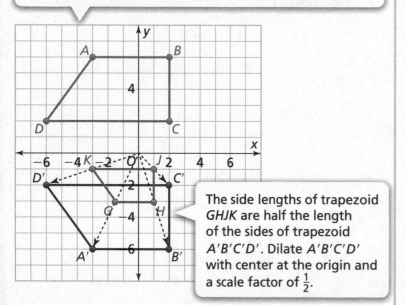

> The side lengths of trapezoid *GHJK* are half the length of the sides of trapezoid *A'B'C'D'*. Dilate *A'B'C'D'* with center at the origin and a scale factor of $\frac{1}{2}$.

A sequence of a reflection across the *x*-axis followed by a dilation of scale factor $\frac{1}{2}$ centered at the origin maps trapezoid *ABCD* to trapezoid *GHJK*.

$$ABCD \sim GHJK$$

> **Generalize** Similar figures have the same shape and congruent angles. The corresponding side lengths are in proportion. © MP.8

☑ Try It!

Is △*ABC* similar to △*A'B'C'*?

The triangles ☐ similar.

Convince Me! What sequence of transformations shows that △*ABC* is similar to △*A'B'C'*?

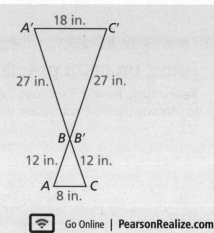

340 6-7 Understand Similar Figures

Go Online | PearsonRealize.com

EXAMPLE **2** Complete a Similarity Transformation

ACTIVITY   ASSESS

Quadrilateral *JKLM* has coordinates *J*(2, −1), *K*(1, −2), *L*(1, −3), and *M*(3, −2). Graph *J″K″L″M″*, the image of *JKLM* by a dilation with center (0, 0) and scale factor 3 and a reflection across the *y*-axis.

STEP 1 Graph the dilation.

Find the coordinates of the dilated image, *J′K′L′M′*.

$J(2, -1) \rightarrow J'(6, -3)$

$K(1, -2) \rightarrow K'(3, -6)$

$L(1, -3) \rightarrow L'(3, -9)$

$M(3, -2) \rightarrow M'(9, -6)$

Multiply each coordinate by the scale factor, 3.

STEP 2 Graph the reflection.

Find the coordinates of the reflected image, *J″K″L″M″*.

$J'(6, -3) \rightarrow J''(-6, -3)$

$K'(3, -6) \rightarrow K''(-3, -6)$

$L'(3, -9) \rightarrow L''(-3, -9)$

$M'(9, -6) \rightarrow M''(-9, -6)$

To reflect across the *y*-axis, (*x*, *y*) becomes (−*x*, *y*).

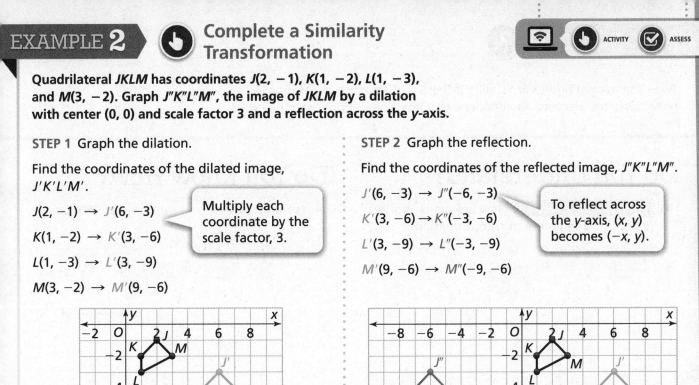

EXAMPLE **3** Identify Similar Figures

Is *ABCD* similar to *EFGH*? Explain.

Compare corresponding coordinates.

$A(4, 4) \rightarrow E(-2, -2)$

$B(8, 4) \rightarrow F(-4, -2)$

$C(10, -2) \rightarrow G(-5, 1)$

$D(2, -2) \rightarrow H(-1, 1)$

$(x, y) \rightarrow (-0.5x, -0.5y)$

Yes, *ABCD* ~ *EFGH* because a rotation of 180° about the origin and a dilation with a scale factor of 0.5 about the origin maps *ABCD* to *EFGH*.

a. Graph the image of *JKL* after a reflection across the line *x* = 1 followed by a dilation with a scale factor of $\frac{1}{2}$ and center of dilation point *J′*.

b. Is △*JKL* similar to △*PQR*?

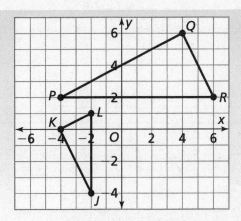

Two-dimensional figures are similar if there is a sequence of rotations, reflections, translations, and dilations that maps one figure onto the other.

Do You Understand?

1. **Essential Question** How are similar figures related by a sequence of transformations?

2. **Be Precise** How do the angle measures and side lengths compare in similar figures? © MP.6

3. **Generalize** Does a given translation, reflection, or rotation, followed by a given dilation, always map a figure to the same image as that same dilation followed by that same translation, reflection, or rotation? Explain. © MP.8

Do You Know How?

4. Is trapezoid *ABCD* ~ trapezoid *EFGH*? Explain.

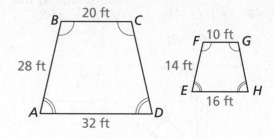

Use the graph for 5 and 6.

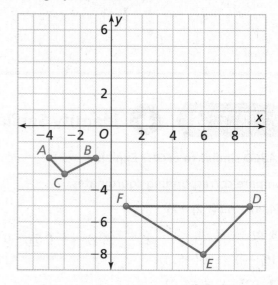

5. △*ABC* is dilated by a factor of 2 with a center of dilation at point *C*, reflected across the *x*-axis, and translated 3 units up. Graph the resulting similar figure.

6. Is △*ABC* similar to △*DEF*? Explain.

Practice & Problem Solving ✏️ ⏻

7. Leveled Practice *RSTU* and *VXYZ* are quadrilaterals.
Given *RSTU ~ VXYZ*, describe a sequence of
transformations that maps *RSTU* to *VXYZ*.

* reflection across the ☐

* translation ☐ unit(s) left and ☐ unit(s) down

* dilation with center (0,0) and a scale factor of ☐

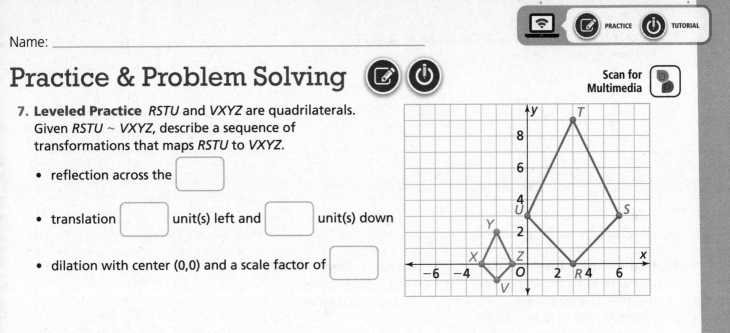

8. Reasoning Is △*MNO* similar to △*PQO*?
Explain. © MP.2

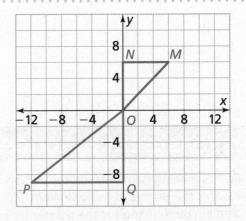

9. △*PQR* is dilated by a scale factor of 2 with
center of dilation (0, 0) and rotated 180° about
the origin. Graph the resulting similar △*XYZ*.

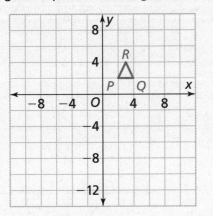

10. Describe a sequence of transformations that
shows that quadrilateral *RSTU* is similar to
quadrilateral *VXYZ*.

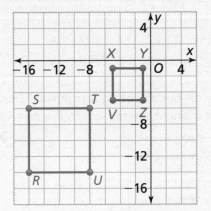

11. Construct Arguments Is △PQR similar to △XYZ? Explain. © MP.3

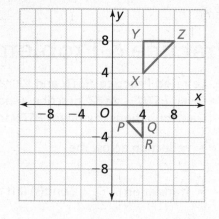

12. Higher Order Thinking Given △JKL ~ △XYZ, find two possible coordinates for missing point Y. For each coordinate chosen, describe a sequence of transformations, including a dilation, that will map △JKL to △XYZ.

© Assessment Practice

13. Rajesh is making pennants in preparation for a school soccer game. He wants the pennants to be similar triangles. Which of these triangles could he use for the pennants?

Ⓐ △QRS and △TVW

Ⓑ △QRS and △XYZ

Ⓒ △TVW and △JKL

Ⓓ △TVW and △XYZ

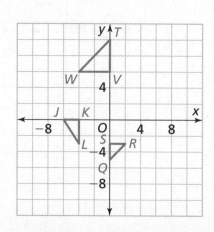

14. Are the given pairs of figures similar? Draw a line to match the pairs of triangles on the left to the correct description on the right.

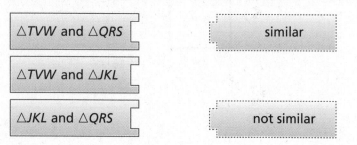

△TVW and △QRS	similar
△TVW and △JKL	
△JKL and △QRS	not similar

Solve & Discuss It!

ACTIVITY

Draw two parallel lines.

Then draw a line that intersects both lines. Which angles have equal measures?

Go Online | PearsonRealize.com

I can...
identify and find the measures of angles formed by parallel lines and a transversal.

Common Core Content Standards
8.G.A.5

Mathematical Practices
MP.2, MP.5, MP.7

Use Appropriate Tools What tools can you use to determine which angles have equal measures? © MP.5

Focus on math practices

Reasoning What properties or definitions can you use to describe which angles have equal measures? © MP.2

INTERACTIVE ANIMATION   ASS

EXAMPLE 1 ▸ 👁 Identify Angles Created by Parallel Lines Cut by a Transversal

Scan for Multimedia

Sarah is building a handrail for a ramp. According to the design plan, the posts must be parallel. How can Sarah determine how the angles formed by the posts and the ramp are related?

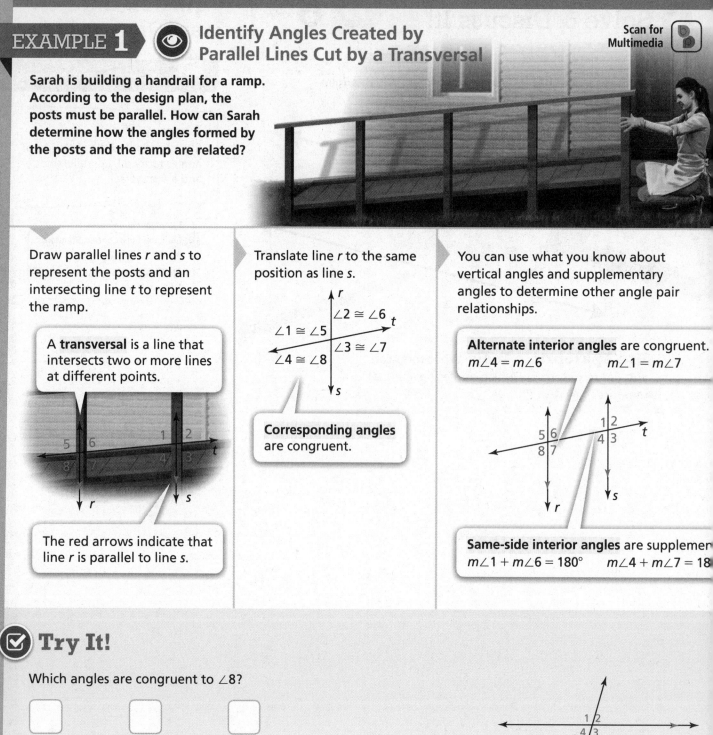

Draw parallel lines *r* and *s* to represent the posts and an intersecting line *t* to represent the ramp.

A **transversal** is a line that intersects two or more lines at different points.

The red arrows indicate that line *r* is parallel to line *s*.

Translate line *r* to the same position as line *s*.

$\angle 2 \cong \angle 6$
$\angle 1 \cong \angle 5$
$\angle 3 \cong \angle 7$
$\angle 4 \cong \angle 8$

Corresponding angles are congruent.

You can use what you know about vertical angles and supplementary angles to determine other angle pair relationships.

Alternate interior angles are congruent.
$m\angle 4 = m\angle 6$ $m\angle 1 = m\angle 7$

Same-side interior angles are supplemen
$m\angle 1 + m\angle 6 = 180°$ $m\angle 4 + m\angle 7 = 18$

☑ Try It!

Which angles are congruent to ∠8?

☐ ☐ ☐

Which angles are supplementary to ∠8?

☐ ☐ ☐ ☐

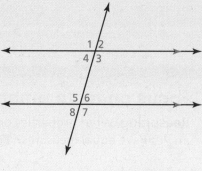

Convince Me! Use what you know about other angle relationships to explain why ∠4 and ∠5 are supplementary angles.

Go Online | PearsonRealize.com

EXAMPLE 2 👆 **Find Unknown Angle Measures** 📶 👆 ACTIVITY ☑ ASSESS

In the figure, $a \parallel b$. What are the measures of $\angle 4$ and $\angle 5$? Explain.

Use what you know about the angles created when parallel lines are cut by a transversal.

$m\angle 4 = 99°$ ⟵ The 99° angle and $\angle 4$ are corresponding angles.

$m\angle 4 + m\angle 5 = 180°$ ⟵ $\angle 4$ and $\angle 5$ are supplementary angles.

$\qquad m\angle 5 = 180° - 99°$

$\qquad m\angle 5 = 81°$

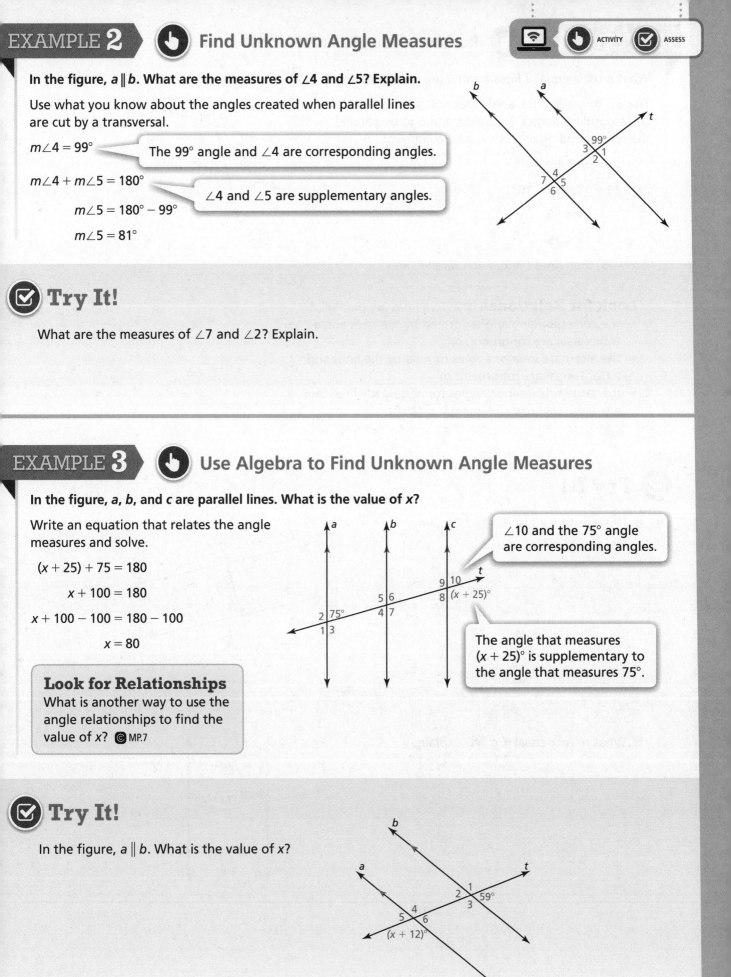

☑ Try It!

What are the measures of $\angle 7$ and $\angle 2$? Explain.

EXAMPLE 3 👆 **Use Algebra to Find Unknown Angle Measures**

In the figure, a, b, and c are parallel lines. What is the value of x?

Write an equation that relates the angle measures and solve.

$(x + 25) + 75 = 180$

$\qquad x + 100 = 180$

$x + 100 - 100 = 180 - 100$

$\qquad\qquad x = 80$

$\angle 10$ and the 75° angle are corresponding angles.

The angle that measures $(x + 25)°$ is supplementary to the angle that measures 75°.

Look for Relationships
What is another way to use the angle relationships to find the value of x? Ⓒ MP.7

☑ Try It!

In the figure, $a \parallel b$. What is the value of x?

EXAMPLE **4** 👆 **Reason about Parallel Lines**

What must *x* equal if lines *c* and *d* are parallel? Explain.

The 60° angle and the angle that measures 2*x* + 10 are corresponding angles. For lines *c* and *d* to be parallel, the corresponding angles must be congruent.

$$2x + 10 = 60$$

$$2x + 10 - 10 = 60 - 10$$

$$2x = 50$$

$$x = 25$$

If *x* = 25, then lines *c* and *d* are parallel lines.

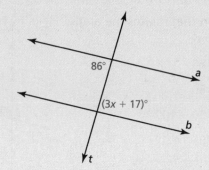

> **Look for Relationships** Two lines are parallel if
> - the corresponding angles formed by the lines and a transversal are congruent, or
> - the alternate interior angles formed by the lines and a transversal are congruent, or
> - the same-side interior angles formed by the lines and a transversal are supplementary. ©MP.7

☑ Try It!

a. What must *x* equal if *a* ∥ *b*? Explain.

b. What must *x* equal if *g* ∥ *h*? Explain.

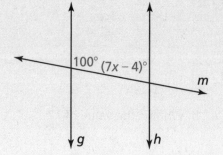

 Go Online | PearsonRealize.com

EY CONCEPT

If parallel lines are intersected by a transversal, then

- Corresponding angles are congruent.
- Alternate interior angles are congruent.
- Same-side interior angles are supplementary.

∠1 and ∠5 are corresponding angles.

∠4 and ∠5 are same-side interior angles.

∠6 and ∠4 are alternate interior angles.

Do You Understand?

1. **Essential Question** What are the relationships among angles that are created when a line intersects two parallel lines?

2. When parallel lines are cut by a transversal, how can you use a translation to describe how angles are related?

3. How many angles are created when two parallel lines are cut by a transversal? How many different angle measures are there?

4. **Use Structure** How can you use angle measures to tell whether two lines are parallel? © MP.7

Do You Know How?

In 5–7, use the figure below.

5. Which angles are congruent to ∠8?

6. If $m\angle 4 = 70°$, what is $m\angle 6$? Explain.

7. If $m\angle 1 = 95°$, write an equation that could be used to find the measure of ∠8. Find $m\angle 8$.

8. What must x equal if line a is parallel to line b?

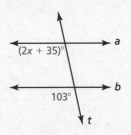

$(2x + 35)°$

$103°$

Practice & Problem Solving

9. If $p \parallel q$, what is the value of u?

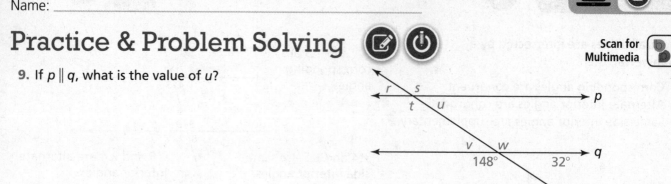

10. Are $\angle K$ and $\angle B$ corresponding angles? Explain.

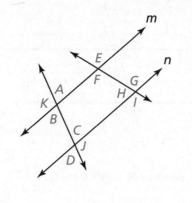

11. Streets A and B run parallel to each other. The measure of $\angle 6$ is 155°. What is the measure of $\angle 4$?

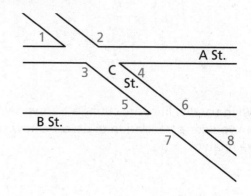

12. Reasoning The figure shows the design of a rectangular windowpane. The four horizontal lines are parallel. The measure of $\angle 6$ is 53°. What is the measure of $\angle 12$? Write and solve an equation to find the answer. ⓒ MP.2

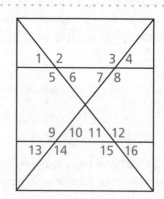

13. In the figure, $m \parallel n$. If $m\angle 8$ is $(4x + 7)°$ and $m\angle 2$ is $107°$, what is the value of x? Explain.

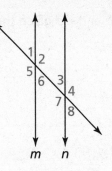

14. For the given figure, can you conclude $m \parallel n$? Explain.

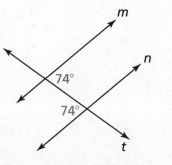

15. Line m is parallel to line n. Find the value of x and each missing angle measure.

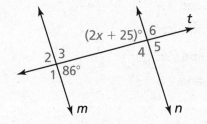

16. Higher Order Thinking

a. Find the value of x given that $r \parallel s$.

$m\angle 1 = (63 - x)°$

$m\angle 2 = (72 - 2x)°$

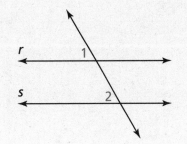

b. Find $m\angle 1$ and $m\angle 2$.

17. Find the measures of ∠b and ∠d given that $m \parallel n$.

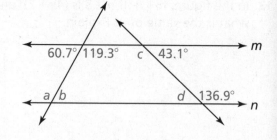

18. In the figure, $g \parallel p$. Which angles are alternate interior angles? Select all that apply.

☐ ∠q and ∠r

☐ ∠q and ∠t

☐ ∠q and ∠k

☐ ∠r and ∠t

☐ ∠r and ∠k

☐ ∠u and ∠q

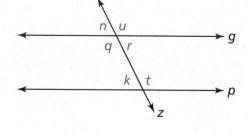

19. In the figure, $p \parallel q$. On a recent math test, Jacob incorrectly listed the value of w as 101.

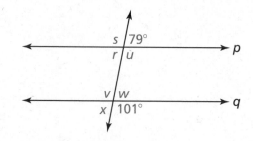

PART A

Find the value of w.

PART B

What mistake did Jacob likely make?

👆 Solve & Discuss It!

📶   👆 ACTIVITY

Nell cuts tile to make a decorative strip
for a kitchen backsplash. She must
cut the tiles precisely to be congruent
triangles. She plans to place the tiles
between two pieces of molding,
as shown. What is $m\angle 1$? Explain.

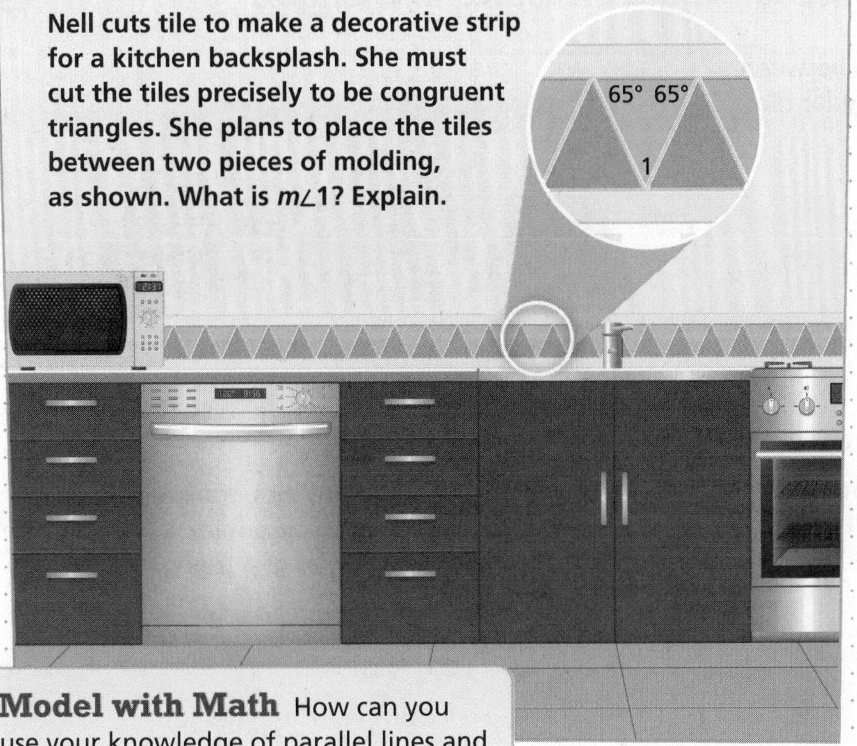

65° 65°

1

Model with Math How can you
use your knowledge of parallel lines and
transversals to solve the problem? © MP.4

© **Common Core Content Standards**
8.G.A.5

Mathematical Practices
MP.2, MP.4, MP.7, MP.8

Focus on math practices

Reasoning What assumption(s) did you need to make to find
$m\angle 1$? Explain why your assumption(s) is reasonable. © MP.2

EXAMPLE 1 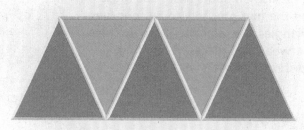 **Relate Interior Angle Measures in Triangles**

Scan for Multimedia

How can you describe the relationship between the three interior angles of each triangular tile in the backsplash?

You can rotate and place the congruent tiles side-by-side to form the alternating pattern.

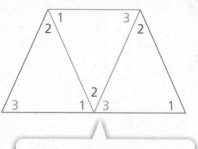

∠1, ∠2, and ∠3 appear to fit together to form a line.

Use what you know about lines, transversals, and angle pair relationships to determine a relationship between the interior angles of a triangle.

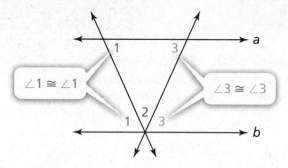

∠1 ≅ ∠1   ∠3 ≅ ∠3

Alternate interior angles are congruent, so a ∥ b. Since ∠1, ∠2, and ∠3 form line b, a straight angle, $m\angle1 + m\angle2 + m\angle3 = 180°$.

Generalize The sum of the measures of the interior angles of a triangle is 180°. © MP.8

✓ Try It!

Find the unknown angle measure in the triangle at the right.

Convince Me! Could a triangle have interior angle measures of 23°, 71°, and 96°? Explain.

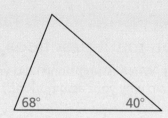

68°   40°

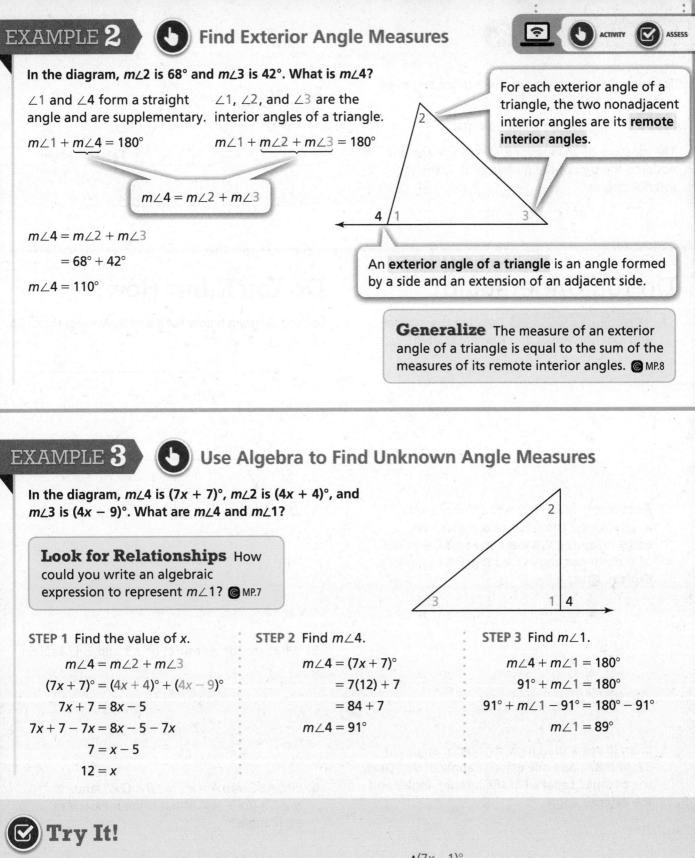

EXAMPLE 2 ⟩ 👆 Find Exterior Angle Measures

🔲 ⏱ ACTIVITY   ☑ ASSESS

In the diagram, $m\angle2$ is 68° and $m\angle3$ is 42°. What is $m\angle4$?

$\angle1$ and $\angle4$ form a straight angle and are supplementary.

$\angle1$, $\angle2$, and $\angle3$ are the interior angles of a triangle.

$m\angle1 + m\angle4 = 180°$

$m\angle1 + m\angle2 + m\angle3 = 180°$

$m\angle4 = m\angle2 + m\angle3$

$m\angle4 = m\angle2 + m\angle3$

$= 68° + 42°$

$m\angle4 = 110°$

For each exterior angle of a triangle, the two nonadjacent interior angles are its **remote interior angles**.

An **exterior angle of a triangle** is an angle formed by a side and an extension of an adjacent side.

Generalize The measure of an exterior angle of a triangle is equal to the sum of the measures of its remote interior angles. © MP.8

EXAMPLE 3 ⟩ 👆 Use Algebra to Find Unknown Angle Measures

In the diagram, $m\angle4$ is $(7x + 7)°$, $m\angle2$ is $(4x + 4)°$, and $m\angle3$ is $(4x − 9)°$. What are $m\angle4$ and $m\angle1$?

Look for Relationships How could you write an algebraic expression to represent $m\angle1$? © MP.7

STEP 1 Find the value of x.

$m\angle4 = m\angle2 + m\angle3$

$(7x + 7)° = (4x + 4)° + (4x − 9)°$

$7x + 7 = 8x − 5$

$7x + 7 − 7x = 8x − 5 − 7x$

$7 = x − 5$

$12 = x$

STEP 2 Find $m\angle4$.

$m\angle4 = (7x + 7)°$

$= 7(12) + 7$

$= 84 + 7$

$m\angle4 = 91°$

STEP 3 Find $m\angle1$.

$m\angle4 + m\angle1 = 180°$

$91° + m\angle1 = 180°$

$91° + m\angle1 − 91° = 180° − 91°$

$m\angle1 = 89°$

☑ Try It!

What is the measure of the exterior angle shown?

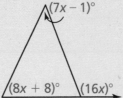

$(7x − 1)°$

$(8x + 8)°$ $(16x)°$

The sum of the measures of the interior angles of a triangle is 180°.

$$m\angle 1 + m\angle 2 + m\angle 3 = 180°$$

The measure of an exterior angle of a triangle is equal to the sum of the measures of its remote interior angles.

$$m\angle 2 + m\angle 3 = m\angle 4$$

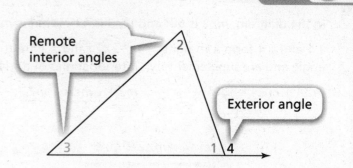

Remote interior angles

Exterior angle

Do You Understand?

1. **Essential Question** How are the interior and exterior angles of a triangle related?

2. **Reasoning** Maggie draws a triangle with a right angle. The other two angles have equal measures. What are the possible values of the exterior angles for Maggie's triangle? Explain. © MP.2

3. Brian draws a triangle with interior angles of 32° and 87°, and one exterior angle of 93°. Draw the triangle. Label all of the interior angles and the exterior angle.

Do You Know How?

Use the diagram below for 4 and 5. Assume that a ∥ b.

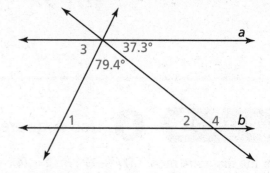

4. What are the measures of ∠1 and ∠2? Explain.

5. What are the measures of ∠3 and ∠4? Explain.

6. In △ABC, $m\angle A = x°$, $m\angle B = (2x)°$, and $m\angle C = (6x + 18)°$. What is the measure of each angle?

Practice & Problem Solving

7. Leveled Practice For the figure shown, find $m\angle 1$.

Angle 1 is an [   ] angle of the triangle.

$m\angle 1$ is equal to the sum of its [   ].

$m\angle 1 = $ [   ]$^\circ$ $+$ [   ]$^\circ$

$m\angle 1 = $ [   ]$^\circ$

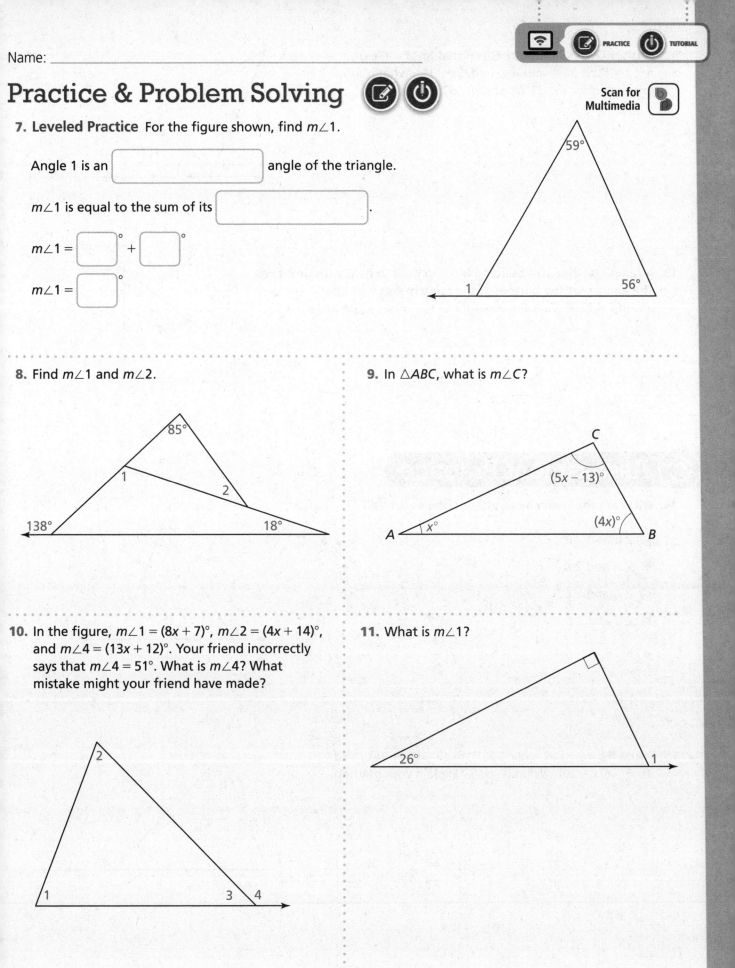

8. Find $m\angle 1$ and $m\angle 2$.

9. In $\triangle ABC$, what is $m\angle C$?

10. In the figure, $m\angle 1 = (8x + 7)^\circ$, $m\angle 2 = (4x + 14)^\circ$, and $m\angle 4 = (13x + 12)^\circ$. Your friend incorrectly says that $m\angle 4 = 51^\circ$. What is $m\angle 4$? What mistake might your friend have made?

11. What is $m\angle 1$?

12. Higher Order Thinking Given that $m\angle 1 = (16x)°$, $m\angle 2 = (8x + 21)°$, and $m\angle 4 = (25x + 19)$, what is an expression for $m\angle 3$? What is $m\angle 3$?

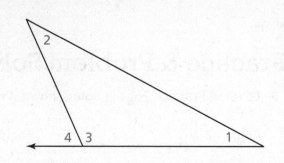

13. A ramp attached to a building is being built to help with deliveries. The angle that the bottom of the ramp makes with the ground is 37.2°. Find the measure of the other acute angle.

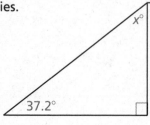

14. What are the two remote interior angles for $\angle F$?

Ⓐ $\angle C$ and $\angle B$

Ⓑ $\angle A$ and $\angle B$

Ⓒ $\angle A$ and $\angle C$

Ⓓ $\angle E$ and $\angle D$

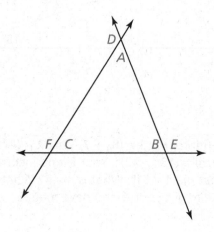

15. In the figure, $m\angle 1 = (3x + 12)°$, $m\angle 2 = (3x + 18)°$, and $m\angle 3 = (7x + 10)°$. What is $m\angle 3$? Explain your method.

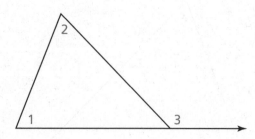

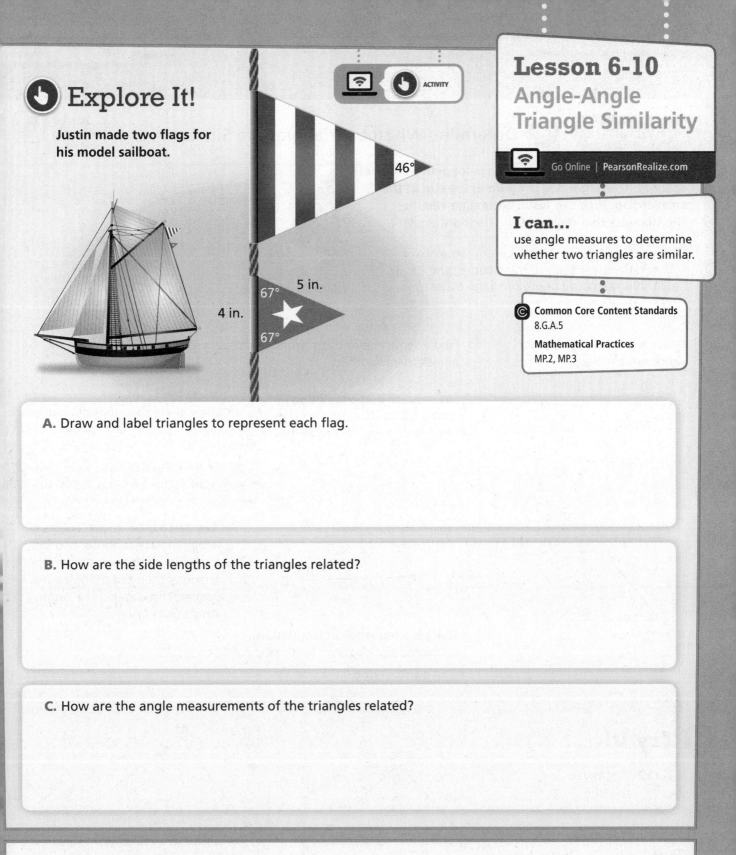

Explore It!

Justin made two flags for his model sailboat.

ACTIVITY

46°

67° 5 in.

4 in.

67°

I can...
use angle measures to determine whether two triangles are similar.

Common Core Content Standards
8.G.A.5

Mathematical Practices
MP.2, MP.3

A. Draw and label triangles to represent each flag.

B. How are the side lengths of the triangles related?

C. How are the angle measurements of the triangles related?

Focus on math practices

Reasoning Justin makes a third flag that has sides that are shorter than the sides of the small flag. Two of the angles for each flag measure the same. Are the third angles for each flag the same measure? Explain. © MP.2

EXAMPLE 1  **Determine Whether Triangles are Similar**

Scan for Multimedia

Justin designs another pair of flags for another model sailboat. The larger flag is 1.5 times the size of the smaller flag. How can Justin determine whether the triangles that represent the flags are similar?

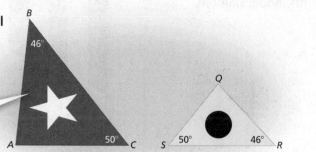

Remember, figures are similar if a sequence of rotations, reflections, translations, and dilations maps one figure onto the other.

Draw and label triangles to represent the flags.

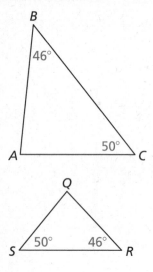

Find a sequence of transformations that maps one pair of congruent angles to each other.

A rotation and translation map ∠S to ∠C.

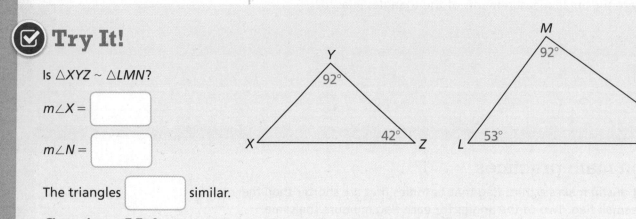

∠R and ∠B are corresponding angles. Because ∠R ≅ ∠B, $\overline{AB}$ is parallel to $\overline{QR}$.

BC = 1.5 · RS so a dilation from center C with scale factor 1.5 maps △ABC to △QRS

Generalize If two angles of a triangle are congruent to the corresponding angles of another triangle, then the triangles are similar. This is called the Angle-Angle (AA) Criterion.

There is a sequence of translations, rotations, and dilations that maps △ABC to △QRS.

So △ABC ~ △QRS.

☑ **Try It!**

Is △XYZ ~ △LMN?

m∠X = ☐

m∠N = ☐

The triangles ☐ similar.

Convince Me! Use what you know about transformations and parallel lines to explain why the Angle-Angle Criterion is true for all triangles.

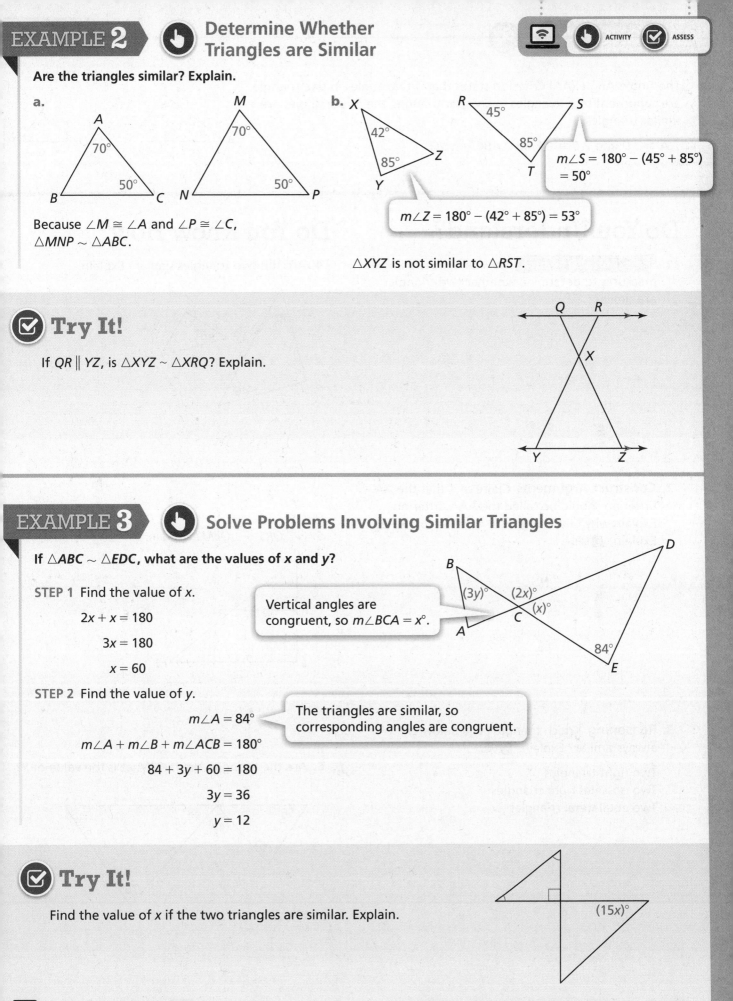

EXAMPLE 2 · Determine Whether Triangles are Similar

ACTIVITY   ASSESS

Are the triangles similar? Explain.

a.

A 70°
B 50° C

M 70°
N 50° P

Because ∠M ≅ ∠A and ∠P ≅ ∠C, △MNP ~ △ABC.

b.

X 42°
Y 85° Z

R 45° S
85°
T

$m\angle S = 180° - (45° + 85°) = 50°$

$m\angle Z = 180° - (42° + 85°) = 53°$

△XYZ is not similar to △RST.

✓ Try It!

If $QR \parallel YZ$, is $\triangle XYZ \sim \triangle XRQ$? Explain.

EXAMPLE 3 · Solve Problems Involving Similar Triangles

If △ABC ~ △EDC, what are the values of x and y?

STEP 1 Find the value of x.

$2x + x = 180$

$3x = 180$

$x = 60$

Vertical angles are congruent, so $m\angle BCA = x°$.

B (3y)° (2x)°
A (x)°
C
D
84°
E

STEP 2 Find the value of y.

$m\angle A = 84°$

The triangles are similar, so corresponding angles are congruent.

$m\angle A + m\angle B + m\angle ACB = 180°$

$84 + 3y + 60 = 180$

$3y = 36$

$y = 12$

✓ Try It!

Find the value of x if the two triangles are similar. Explain.

(15x)°

Go Online | PearsonRealize.com   **6-10** Angle-Angle Triangle Similarity   **361**

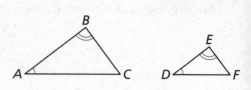

The Angle-Angle (AA) Criterion states that if two angles in one triangle are congruent to two angles in another triangle, the two triangles are similar triangles.

$\angle A \cong \angle D$ and $\angle B \cong \angle E$, so $\triangle ABC \sim \triangle DEF$.

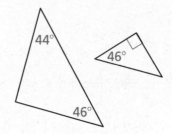

Do You Understand?

1. **Essential Question** How can you use angle measures to determine whether two triangles are similar?

2. **Construct Arguments** Claire says that the AA Criterion should be called the AAA Criterion. Explain why Claire might say this. Do you agree? Explain. © MP.3

3. **Reasoning** Which triangle pairs below are always similar? Explain. © MP.2

   Two right triangles
   Two isosceles right triangles
   Two equilateral triangles

Do You Know How?

4. Are the two triangles similar? Explain.

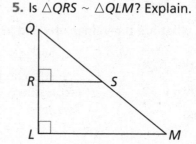

5. Is $\triangle QRS \sim \triangle QLM$? Explain.

6. Are the triangles similar? What is the value of x?

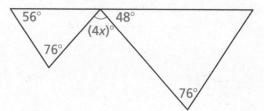

 Go Online | PearsonRealize.com

Practice & Problem Solving ✏️ ⏻

7. Is △XYZ ~△XTU?

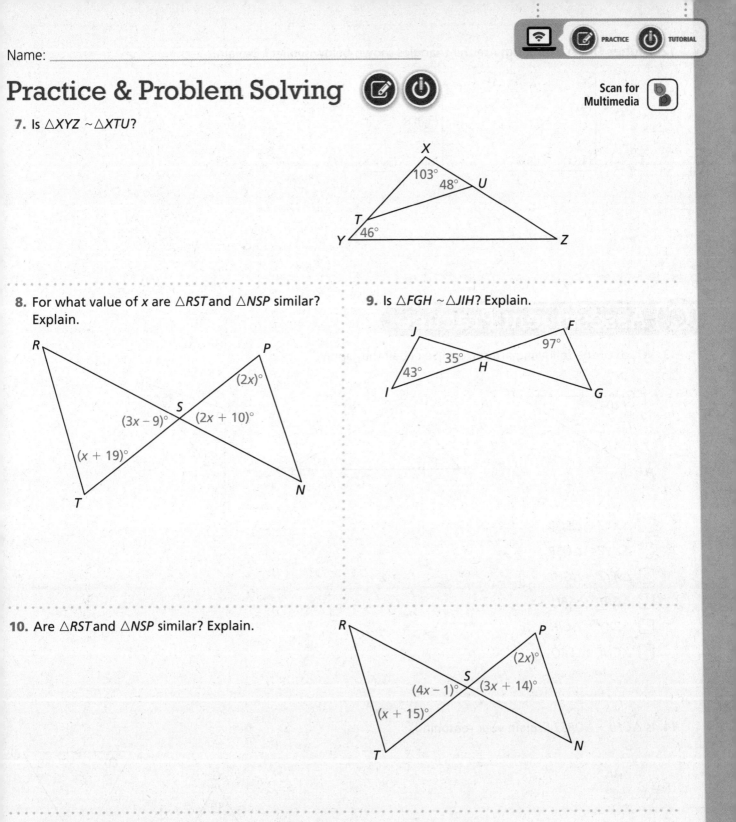

8. For what value of x are △RST and △NSP similar? Explain.

9. Is △FGH ~△JIH? Explain.

10. Are △RST and △NSP similar? Explain.

11. Contruct Arguments Describe how to use angle relationships to decide whether any two triangles are similar. Ⓒ MP.3

12. Higher Order Thinking Are the triangles shown below similar? Explain.

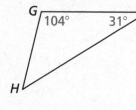

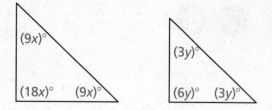

Assessment Practice

13. Which of the following are correct? Select all that apply.

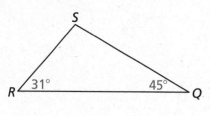

☐ △XYZ ~△SQR

☐ △XYZ ~△QSR

☐ △XYZ ~△GHI

☐ △GIH ~△SRQ

☐ △ZXY ~△GIH

☐ △GHI ~△SRQ

14. Is △GHI ~△QRS? Explain your reasoning.

Go Online | PearsonRealize.com

? Topic Essential Question

How can you show that two figures are either congruent or similar to one another?

Vocabulary Review

Complete each sentence by matching each vocabulary word to its definition. Assume pairs of lines are parallel.

Vocabulary Term	Definition
1. Alternate interior angles	lie on the same side of the transversal and in corresponding positions.
2. Same-side interior angles	lie within a pair of lines and on opposite sides of a transversal.
3. Corresponding angles	are two adjacent interior angles corresponding to each exterior angle of a triangle.
4. An exterior angle of a triangle	is formed by a side and an extension of an adjacent side of a triangle.
5. Remote interior angles of a triangle	lie within a pair of lines and on the same side of a transversal.

Use Vocabulary in Writing

Describe a way to show that $\triangle ABC$ is congruent to $\triangle DEF$. Use vocabulary terms from this Topic in your description.

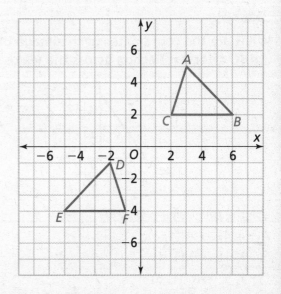

Concepts and Skills Review

Analyze Translations

Quick Review

A translation is a transformation that maps each point of the preimage the same distance and in the same direction.

Example

Translate △*XYZ* 5 units right and 3 units up.

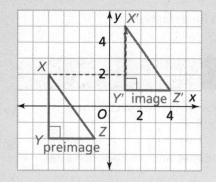

Practice

1. Draw the image after a translation 3 units left and 2 units up.

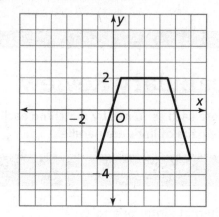

Analyze Reflections

Quick Review

Reflected figures are the same distance from the line of reflection but on opposite sides.

Example

What are the coordinates of the image of △*ABC* after a reflection across the *y*-axis?

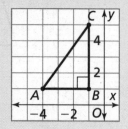

Use the rule $(x, y) \rightarrow (-x, y)$.

$A(-4, 1) \rightarrow A'(4, 1)$

$B(-1, 1) \rightarrow B'(1, 1)$

$C(-1, 5) \rightarrow C'(1, 5)$

Practice

Use the figure.

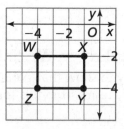

1. What are the coordinates of the image of rectangle *WXYZ* after a reflection across the *x*-axis?

2. What are the coordinates of the image of *WXYZ* after a reflection across the *y*-axis?

Quick Review

A rotation turns a figure about a fixed point, called the *center of rotation*. The angle of rotation is the number of degrees the figure is rotated.

Example

What are the coordinates of the image of △*ABC* after a 90° rotation about the origin?

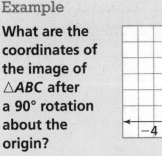

Use the rule $(x, y) \rightarrow (-y, x)$.

$A(1, 4) \rightarrow A'(-4, 1)$

$B(4, 4) \rightarrow B'(-4, 4)$

$C(4, 1) \rightarrow C'(-1, 4)$

Practice

Use the figure.

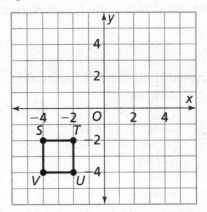

1. What are the coordinates of the image of quadrilateral *STUV* after a 180° rotation about the origin?

2. What are the coordinates of the image of quadrilateral *STUV* after a 270° rotation about the origin?

Quick Review

To compose a sequence of transformations, perform one transformation, and then use the resulting image to perform the next transformation.

Example

How can you use a sequence of transformations to map Figure A onto Figure B?

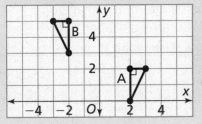

Translate Figure A 3 units up, and then reflect Figure A across the *y*-axis.

Practice

1. Translate rectangle *ABCD* 5 units down, and then reflect it across the *y*-axis.

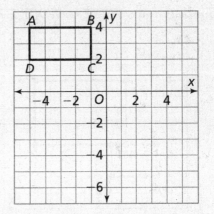

LESSON 6-5 | Understand Congruent Figures

Quick Review

Two figures are congruent if a sequence of transformations maps one figure onto the other.

Example

How can you determine if Figure A is congruent to Figure B?

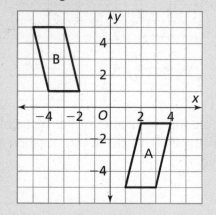

Reflect Figure A across the y-axis, and then translate Figure A 6 units up and 1 unit left.

Practice

1. Is quadrilateral A congruent to quadrilateral B? Explain.

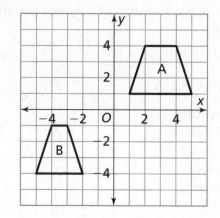

LESSON 6-6 | Describe Dilations

Quick Review

A dilation results in an image that is the same shape but not the same size as the preimage.

Example

What dilation maps WXYZ to W'X'Y'Z'?

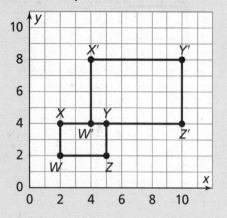

A dilation with center at the origin and a scale factor of 2 maps WXYZ to W'X'Y'Z'.

Practice

Use the figure.

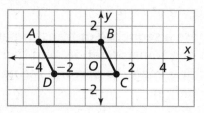

1. What are the coordinates of the image of parallelogram ABCD after a dilation with center (0, 0) and a scale factor of 3?

2. What are the coordinates of the image of parallelogram ABCD after a dilation with center (0, 0) and a scale factor of $\frac{1}{2}$?

Quick Review

Two-dimensional figures are similar if there is a sequence of translations, reflections, rotations, and dilations that maps one figure onto the other figure. Similar figures have the same shape, congruent angles, and proportional side lengths.

Example

Is rectangle $ABCD \sim$ rectangle $A'B'C'D'$?

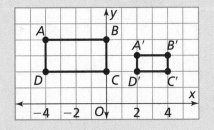

All the angles are right angles.

$$\frac{AB}{A'B'} = \frac{BC}{B'C'} = \frac{CD}{C'D'} = \frac{AD}{A'D'} = \frac{2}{1} = 2$$

The figures have congruent angle measures and proportional side lengths, so they are similar.

Practice

Use the figure.

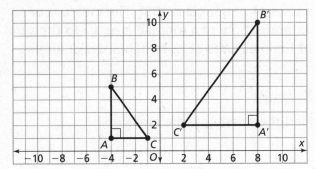

1. Is $\triangle ABC$ similar to $\triangle A'B'C'$? Explain.

2. What sequence of transformations shows that $\triangle ABC$ is similar to $\triangle A'B'C'$?

Quick Review

When parallel lines are intersected by a transversal, corresponding angles are congruent, alternate interior angles are congruent, and same-side interior angles are supplementary.

Example

If $m \parallel n$, what is the value of x?

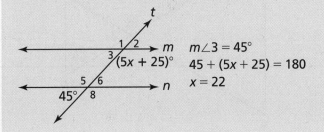

$m\angle 3 = 45°$

$45 + (5x + 25) = 180$

$x = 22$

Practice

In the figure, $a \parallel b$. What is the value of x?

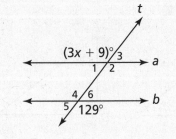

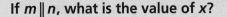

Quick Review

The sum of the measures of the interior angles of a triangle is 180°. The measure of an exterior angle of a triangle is equal to the sum of the measures of its remote interior angles.

Example

Find the missing angle measure.

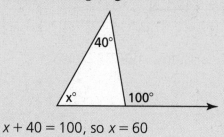

$x + 40 = 100$, so $x = 60$

Practice

1. Find the missing angle measure.

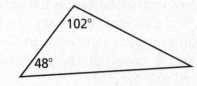

2. Find the value of x.

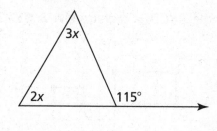

Quick Review

By the AA Criterion, if two angles in one triangle are congruent to two angles in another triangle, then the triangles are similar.

Example

Is △ABC ~ △DEF? Explain.

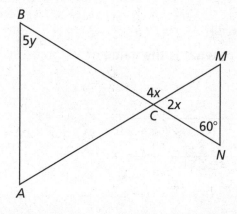

$m\angle B = 180° - 90° - 37° = 53°$

$m\angle A = m\angle D = 90°$ and $m\angle B = m\angle E = 53°$

Because two angles of the triangles are congruent, the triangles are similar by the AA Criterion.

Practice

1. $AB \parallel XY$. Is △ABC ~ △XYC? Explain.

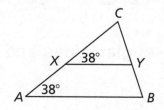

2. Find the values of x and y given that △ABC is similar to △MNC.

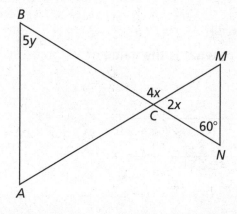

Crisscrossed

Solve each equation. Write your answers in the cross-number puzzle below. Each digit, negative sign, and decimal point of your answer goes in its own box.

I can... solve multistep equations. © 8.EE.C.7b

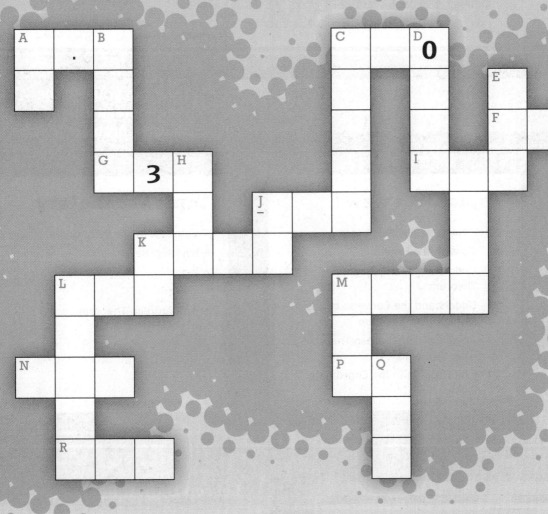

ACROSS

A $9n + 13 = 3n + 62.2$

C $\frac{1}{5}x + 13 = x - 107$

F $\frac{3}{4}k + 7 = \frac{1}{8}k + 27$

G $\frac{1}{3}t = t - 154$

I $g + 43 = 3g - 975$

J $\frac{1}{2}c + 13 = 3c + 48$

K $0.2m = -13(m + 330)$

L $-12 - r = -17.2$

M $4,500 - b = -3b + 4,098$

N $\frac{1}{4}w = 2(w - 87.5)$

P $\frac{1}{8}y + 17 = 2y - 118$

R $4p = 2(p + 7.1)$

DOWN

A $5q + 1 = 6q - 79$

B $5(z - 0.52) = 8$

C $2(a - 5) = a + 2.54$

D $8(n + 2) = 22$

E $5(t + 40) = -t - 34$

H $4h + 18 = 2(h + 10.3)$

K $4y - 1 = 3(-5 - y)$

L $d - 15.6 = 2d - 556.3$

M $3.5q - 145.5 = 5q$

Q $4(x + 2) = 5(x - 38.4)$

TOPIC 7

UNDERSTAND AND APPLY THE PYTHAGOREAN THEOREM

? Topic Essential Question

How can you use the Pythagorean Theorem to solve problems?

Topic Overview

3-Act Mathematical Modeling:
Go with the Flow

7-1 Understand the Pythagorean Theorem

7-2 Understand the Converse of the Pythagorean Theorem

7-3 Apply the Pythagorean Theorem to Solve Problems

7-4 Find Distance in the Coordinate Plane

Topic Vocabulary

- Converse of the Pythagorean Theorem
- hypotenuse
- leg
- proof
- Pythagorean Theorem

Lesson Digital Resources

 INTERACTIVE ANIMATION Interact with visual learning animations.

 ACTIVITY Use with *Solve & Discuss It, Explo* and *Explain It* activities, and to explore Exam

 VIDEOS Watch clips to support *3-Act Mathe Modeling Lessons* and *STEM Projects*.

 PRACTICE Practice what you've learned.

Go online | **PearsonRealize.com**

Go with the Flow

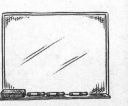

▶ Go with the Flow

You may have noticed that when you double the base and the height of a triangle, the area is more than doubled. The same is true for doubling the sides of a square or the radius of a circle. So what is the relationship? Think about this during the 3-Act Mathematical Modeling lesson.

 VIDEO

Did You Know?

Over **two billion** people will face **water shortages** by 2050 according to a 2015 United Nations Environment Program report.

Using **water wisely** saves money on water and energy bills and extends the life of supply and wastewater facilities.

Rainwater can be **collected** and stored for use in irrigation, industrial uses, flushing toilets, washing clothes and cars, or it can be purified for use as everyday drinking water.

This **alternative water source** reduces the use of fresh water from reservoirs and wells.

Roofs of buildings or large tarps are used to collect rainwater.

A rainwater **collection system** for a building roof that measures 28 feet by 40 feet can provide 700 gallons of water—enough water to support two people for a year—from a rainfall of 1.0 inch.

Even a **5 foot by 7 foot tarp** can collect **2 gallons** of water from a rainfall total of only 0.1 in.

The **rainwater harvesting** market is expected to **grow 5%** from 2016 to 2020.

Your Task: Rainy Days

Rainwater collection is an inexpensive way to save water in areas where it is scarce. One inch of rain falling on a square roof with an area of 100 ft² collects 62 gallons of water that weighs over 500 pounds. You and your classmates will research the necessary components of a rainwater collection system. Then you will use what you know about right triangles to design a slanted roof system that will be used to collect rainwater.

Review What You Know!

Vocabulary

Choose the best term from the box to complete each definition.

1. The _____ of a number is a factor that when multiplied by itself gives the number.

2. A _____ is a line segment that connects two vertices of a polygon and is not a side.

3. The _____ of a figure is the distance around it.

4. A _____ is a triangle with one right angle.

Simplify Expressions with Exponents

Simplify the expression.

5. $3^2 + 4^2$

6. $2^2 + 5^2$

7. $10^2 - 8^2$

Square Roots

Determine the square root.

8. $\sqrt{81}$

9. $\sqrt{144}$

10. $\sqrt{225}$

Distance on a Coordinate Plane

Determine the distance between the two points.

11.

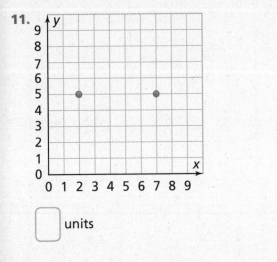

☐ units

12.

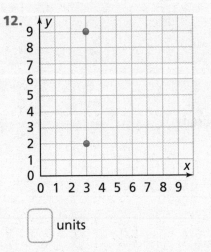

☐ units

Build Vocabulary

Use the graphic organizer to help you understand new vocabulary terms.

Term	Definition	Example
conjecture		
converse of the Pythagorean Theorem		
hypotenuse		
leg		
proof		
Pythagorean Theorem		
theorem		

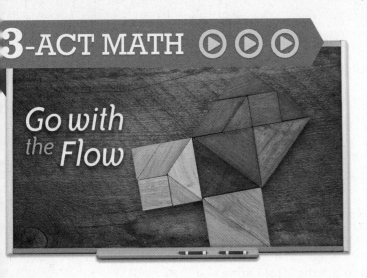

Go with the Flow

3-Act Mathematical Modeling:
Go With the Flow

📶 Go Online | PearsonRealize.com

© **Common Core Content Standards**
8.G.B.6
Mathematical Practices
MP.4

ACT 1

1. After watching the video, what is the first question that comes to mind?

2. Write the Main Question you will answer.

3. Make a prediction to answer this Main Question.

[   ] % will fit in the third square.

4. Construct Arguments Explain how you arrived at your prediction. © MP.3

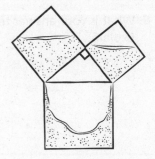

5. What information in this situation would be helpful to know? How would you use that information?

6. Use Appropriate Tools What tools can you use to get the information you need? Record the information as you find it. © MP.5

7. Model With Math Represent the situation using the mathematical content, concepts, and skills from this topic. Use your representation to answer the Main Question. © MP.4

8. What is your answer to the Main Question? Does it differ from your prediction? Explain.

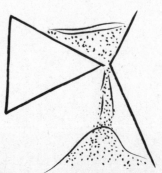

    Go Online | PearsonRealize.com

9. Write the answer you saw in the video.

10. **Reasoning** Does your answer match the answer in the video? If not, what are some reasons that would explain the difference? © MP.2

11. **Make Sense and Persevere** Would you change your model now that you know the answer? Explain. © MP.1

Reflect

12. Model with Math Explain how you used a mathematical model to represent the situation. How did the model help you answer the Main Question? ⓒ MP.4

13. Reason Abstractly How did you represent the situation using symbols? How did you use those symbols to solve the problem? ⓒ MP.2

14. Construct Arguments Explain why you can use an area formula when the problem involves comparing volumes. ⓒ MP.3

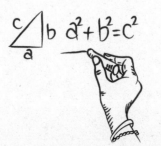

Go Online | PearsonRealize.com

Explain It!

ACTIVITY

Lesson 7-1
Understand the Pythagorean Theorem

Go Online | PearsonRealize.com

I can...
use the Pythagorean Theorem to find unknown sides of triangles.

© **Common Core Content Standards**
8.G.B.6, 8.G.B.7

Mathematical Practices
MP.3, MP.7, MP.8

Kelly drew a right triangle on graph paper. Kelly says that the sum of the areas of squares with side lengths a and b is the same as the area of a square with side length c.

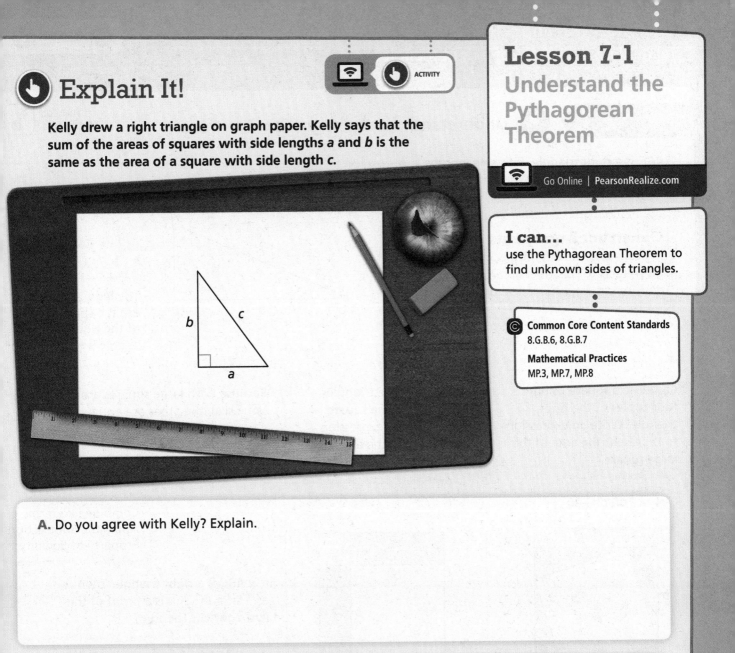

A. Do you agree with Kelly? Explain.

B. Sam drew a different right triangle with side lengths $a = 5$, $b = 12$, and $c = 13$. Is the relationship Kelly described true for Sam's right triangle? Explain.

Focus on math practices

Generalize Kelly draws another right triangle. What would you expect to be the relationship between the areas of the squares drawn on each side of the triangle? Explain. © MP.8

381

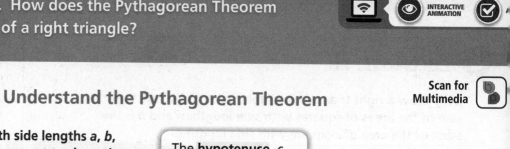

? Essential Question How does the Pythagorean Theorem relate the side lengths of a right triangle?

EXAMPLE 1 👁 **Understand the Pythagorean Theorem**

Scan for Multimedia

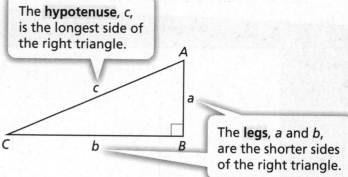

△*ABC* is a right triangle with side lengths *a*, *b*, and *c*. Construct a logical argument to show that $a^2 + b^2 = c^2$.

The **hypotenuse**, *c*, is the longest side of the right triangle.

Construct Arguments When you think logically and use definitions, properties, and given facts to construct an argument, you are developing a mathematical proof. ©MP.3

The **legs**, *a* and *b*, are the shorter sides of the right triangle.

Compose a square using four copies of the right triangle. Write an expression to represent the area of the large square.

$A = \frac{1}{2}bh$ or $\frac{1}{2}ab$

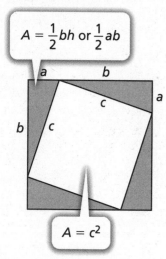

$A = c^2$

The total area of the large square is $A = 4(\frac{1}{2}ab) + c^2$.

Rearrange the triangles inside the same square and write an expression to represent the area of the large square.

$A = ab$ $A = a^2$

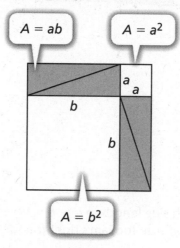

$A = b^2$

The total area of the large square is
$A = ab + ab + a^2 + b^2$

Because both large squares are exactly the same size, the areas are equal.

$4(\frac{1}{2}ab) + c^2 = ab + ab + a^2 + b^2$

$2ab + c^2 = 2ab + a^2 + b^2$

$c^2 = a^2 + b^2$

Combine like terms. Apply the Subtraction Property of Equality.

If △*ABC* is a right triangle, then $a^2 + b^2 = c^2$. This is a proof of the **Pythagorean Theorem**.

A logical mathematical argument in which every statement of fact is supported by a reason is called a **proof**.

✅ **Try It!**

A right triangle has side lengths 15 centimeters, 25 centimeters, and 20 centimeters. How can you use the Pythagorean Theorem to write an equation that describes how the side lengths are related?

Convince Me! How do you know that the geometric proof of the Pythagorean Theorem shown above can be applied to all right triangles?

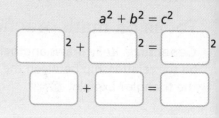

$a^2 + b^2 = c^2$

☐² + ☐² = ☐²

☐ + ☐ = ☐

EXAMPLE 2

Use the Pythagorean Theorem to Find the Length of the Hypotenuse

ACTIVITY   ASSESS

What is the length of the hypotenuse of the right triangle?

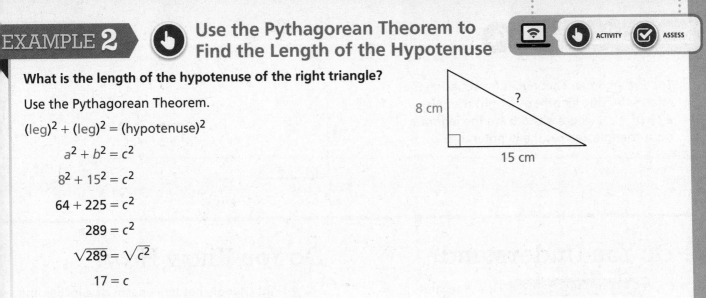

Use the Pythagorean Theorem.

$(\text{leg})^2 + (\text{leg})^2 = (\text{hypotenuse})^2$

$$a^2 + b^2 = c^2$$

$$8^2 + 15^2 = c^2$$

$$64 + 225 = c^2$$

$$289 = c^2$$

$$\sqrt{289} = \sqrt{c^2}$$

$$17 = c$$

The length of the hypotenuse is 17 centimeters.

EXAMPLE 3

Use the Pythagorean Theorem to Find the Length of a Leg

Mara is repairing the trim on one side of a display case sketched at the right. She has a piece of trim that is 20 inches long. Does Mara have enough trim to repair the display case?

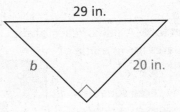

The display case is in the shape of a right triangle. Use the Pythagorean Theorem to find the missing side length.

$$a^2 + b^2 = c^2$$

$$20^2 + b^2 = 29^2 \quad \text{Substitute the given information.}$$

$$400 + b^2 = 841$$

$$400 + b^2 - 400 = 841 - 400$$

$$b^2 = 441$$

$$\sqrt{b^2} = \sqrt{441}$$

$$b = 21$$

Mara needs a 21-inch piece of trim, so she does not have enough trim to repair the display case.

✅ Try It!

A right triangle has a hypotenuse length of 32 meters. It has one leg with a length of 18 meters. What is the length of the other leg? Express your answer as a square root.

The Pythagorean Theorem is an equation that relates the side lengths of a right triangle, $a^2 + b^2 = c^2$, where a and b are the legs of a right triangle and c is the hypotenuse.

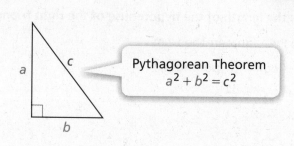

Pythagorean Theorem
$a^2 + b^2 = c^2$

Do You Understand?

1. **Essential Question** How does the Pythagorean Theorem relate the side lengths of a right triangle?

2. **Use Structure** A side of each of the three squares forms a side of a right triangle.

   Would any three squares form the sides of a right triangle? Explain. © MP.7

   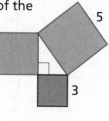

3. **Construct Arguments** Xavier said the missing length is about 18.5 units. Without calculating, how can you tell that Xavier solved incorrectly? © MP.3

   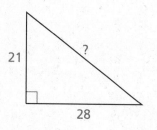

Do You Know How?

4. A right triangle has leg lengths of 4 inches and 5 inches. What is the length of the hypotenuse? Write the answer as a square root and round to the nearest tenth of an inch.

5. Find the missing side length to the nearest tenth of a foot.

   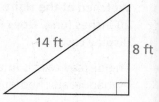

6. Find the missing side length to the nearest tenth of a millimeter.

   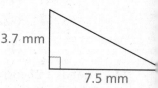

Go Online | PearsonRealize.com

Name: _____

Practice & Problem Solving

Leveled Practice In **7** and **8**, find the missing side length of each triangle.

7.

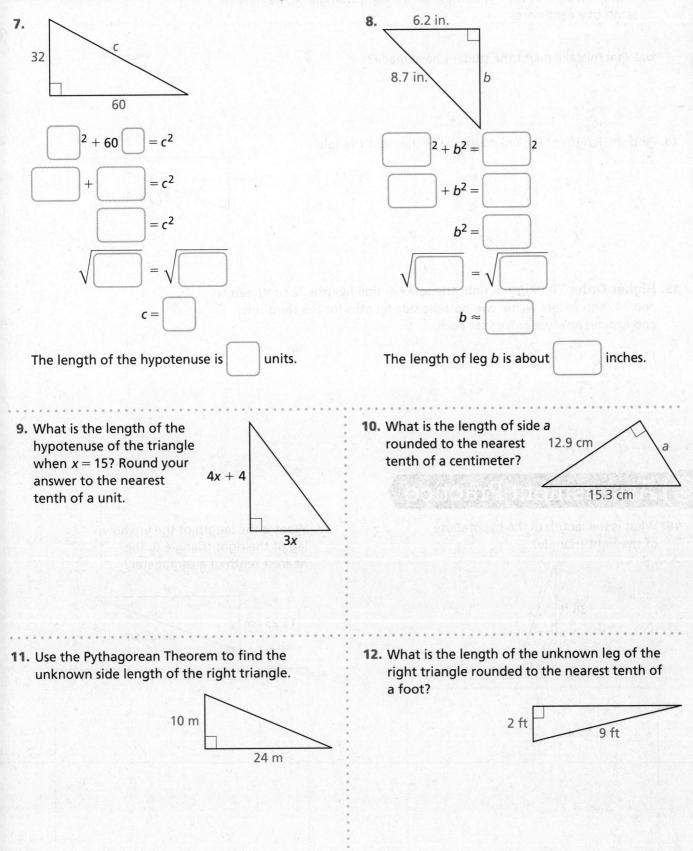

32

c

60

$\boxed{}^2 + 60\boxed{} = c^2$

$\boxed{} + \boxed{} = c^2$

$\boxed{} = c^2$

$\sqrt{\boxed{}} = \sqrt{\boxed{}}$

$c = \boxed{}$

The length of the hypotenuse is $\boxed{}$ units.

8. 6.2 in.

8.7 in.   b

$\boxed{}^2 + b^2 = \boxed{}^2$

$\boxed{} + b^2 = \boxed{}$

$b^2 = \boxed{}$

$\sqrt{\boxed{}} = \sqrt{\boxed{}}$

$b \approx \boxed{}$

The length of leg b is about $\boxed{}$ inches.

---

9. What is the length of the hypotenuse of the triangle when $x = 15$? Round your answer to the nearest tenth of a unit.

$4x + 4$

$3x$

10. What is the length of side a rounded to the nearest tenth of a centimeter?

12.9 cm   a

15.3 cm

---

11. Use the Pythagorean Theorem to find the unknown side length of the right triangle.

10 m

24 m

12. What is the length of the unknown leg of the right triangle rounded to the nearest tenth of a foot?

2 ft

9 ft

13. A student is asked to find the length of the hypotenuse of a right triangle. The length of one leg is 32 centimeters, and the length of the other leg is 26 centimeters. The student incorrectly says that the length of the hypotenuse is 7.6 centimeters.

    a. Find the length of the hypotenuse of the right triangle to the nearest tenth of a centimeter.

    b. What mistake might the student have made?

---

14. Find the length of the unknown leg of the right triangle.

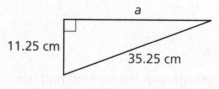

---

15. Higher Order Thinking A right triangle has side lengths 12 centimeters and 14 centimeters. Name two possible side lengths for the third side, and explain how you solved for each.

©️ Assessment Practice

16. What is the length of the hypotenuse of the right triangle?

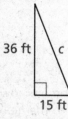

17. What is the length of the unknown leg of the right triangle to the nearest tenth of a centimeter?

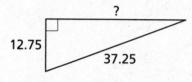

Solve & Discuss It!

ACTIVITY

Kayla has some straws that she will use for an art project. She wants to glue three of the straws onto a sheet of paper, without overlapping, to make the outline of a right triangle.

Which three straws could Kayla use to make a right triangle? Explain.

6 cm

5 cm

7 cm

12 cm

13 cm

3 cm

4 cm

I can...
use the Converse of the Pythagorean Theorem to identify right triangles.

© **Common Core Content Standards**
8.G.B.6, 8.G.B.7

Mathematical Practices
MP.3, MP.4, MP.7, MP.8

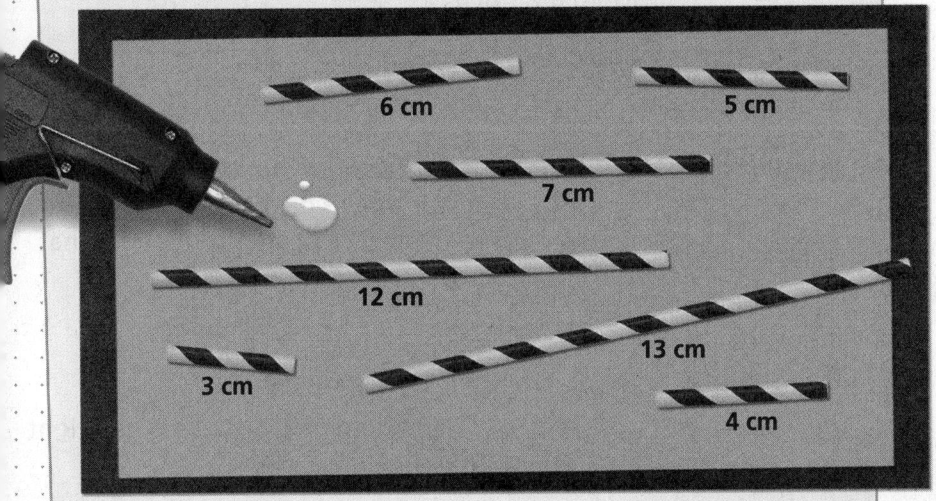

Look for Relationships How could you use the Pythagorean Theorem to determine whether the lengths form a right triangle? © MP.7

Focus on math practices

Use Structure Could Kayla use the straws that form a right triangle to make a triangle that is not a right triangle? Explain. © MP.7

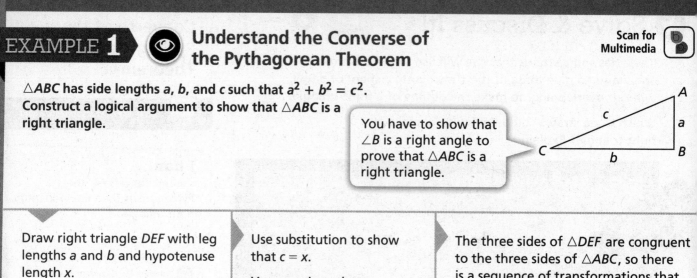

EXAMPLE 1 👁 **Understand the Converse of the Pythagorean Theorem**

Scan for Multimedia

$\triangle ABC$ has side lengths a, b, and c such that $a^2 + b^2 = c^2$. Construct a logical argument to show that $\triangle ABC$ is a right triangle.

> You have to show that $\angle B$ is a right angle to prove that $\triangle ABC$ is a right triangle.

Draw right triangle *DEF* with leg lengths a and b and hypotenuse length x.

> By the Pythagorean Theorem, $a^2 + b^2 = x^2$.

Use substitution to show that $c = x$.

You are given that $a^2 + b^2 = c^2$.

You know that $a^2 + b^2 = x^2$.

By substitution, $x^2 = c^2$.

$$x^2 = c^2$$
$$\sqrt{x^2} = \sqrt{c^2}$$
$$x = c$$

The three sides of $\triangle DEF$ are congruent to the three sides of $\triangle ABC$, so there is a sequence of transformations that maps $\triangle DEF$ to $\triangle ABC$.

$$\triangle ABC \cong \triangle DEF$$
$$\angle B \cong \angle E$$

$\angle B$ is a right angle, so $\triangle ABC$ is a right triangle.

This is a proof of the **Converse of the Pythagorean Theorem**.

> **Generalize** If $a^2 + b^2 = c^2$, then $\triangle ABC$ is a right triangle. Ⓒ MP.8

✓ Try It!

A triangle has side lengths 4 inches, 5 inches, and 7 inches. Is the triangle a right triangle?

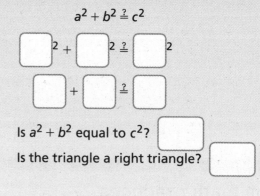

$$a^2 + b^2 \overset{?}{=} c^2$$

$$\boxed{}^2 + \boxed{}^2 \overset{?}{=} \boxed{}^2$$

$$\boxed{} + \boxed{} \overset{?}{=} \boxed{}$$

Is $a^2 + b^2$ equal to c^2? $\boxed{}$

Is the triangle a right triangle? $\boxed{}$

Convince Me! Explain the proof of the Converse of the Pythagorean Theorem in your own words.

EXAMPLE 2 Apply the Converse of the Pythagorean Theorem to Identify Right Triangles

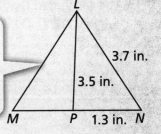
A. Is △*XYZ* a right triangle?

X

7 in.

25 in.

Y   24 in.   Z

Apply the Converse of the Pythagorean Theorem.

$$a^2 + b^2 \stackrel{?}{=} c^2$$

$$7^2 + 24^2 \stackrel{?}{=} 25^2$$

$$49 + 576 \stackrel{?}{=} 625$$

$$625 = 625$$

△*XYZ* is a right triangle.

B. The side lengths of a triangle are 6 inches, 4.5 inches, and 3.75 inches. Is this triangle a right triangle?

Apply the Converse of the Pythagorean Theorem.

$$a^2 + b^2 \stackrel{?}{=} c^2$$

$$4.5^2 + 3.75^2 \stackrel{?}{=} 6^2$$

$$20.25 + 14.0625 \stackrel{?}{=} 36$$

$$34.3125 \neq 36$$

> How do you know which side lengths are *a*, *b*, and *c*?

This triangle is not a right triangle.

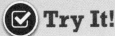 **Try It!**

A triangle has side lengths 10 feet, $\sqrt{205}$ feet, and $\sqrt{105}$ feet. Is this a right triangle? Explain.

EXAMPLE 3 Use the Converse of the Pythagorean Theorem to Analyze Shapes

Rey drew the isosceles triangle *LMN* and the segment *LP*. How can Rey tell whether the segment drawn is the height of the triangle?

Use the Converse of the Pythagorean Theorem to determine whether △*LPN* is a right triangle.

$$a^2 + b^2 \stackrel{?}{=} c^2$$

$$1.3^2 + 3.5^2 \stackrel{?}{=} 3.7^2$$

$$1.69 + 12.25 \stackrel{?}{=} 13.69$$

$$13.94 \neq 13.69$$

Segment *LP* is not the height of △*LMN*.

> Remember, the corresponding base and height of a triangle are perpendicular. If segment *LP* is the height of △*LMN*, then △*LPN* is a right triangle.

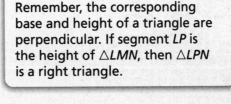

L

3.7 in.

3.5 in.

M   P   1.3 in. N

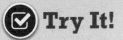 **Try It!**

A triangle is inside a trapezoid. Is the triangle a right triangle? Explain.

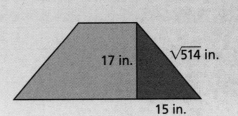

17 in. $\sqrt{514}$ in.

15 in.

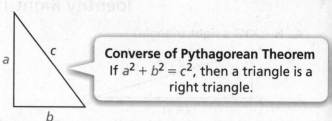

The Converse of the Pythagorean Theorem states that if the sum of the squares of the lengths of two sides of a triangle is equal to the square of the length of the third side, the triangle is a right triangle.

Converse of Pythagorean Theorem
If $a^2 + b^2 = c^2$, then a triangle is a right triangle.

Do You Understand?

1. **Essential Question** How can you determine whether a triangle is a right triangle?

2. **Construct Arguments** A triangle has side lengths of 3 centimeters, 5 centimeters, and 4 centimeters. Abe used the Converse of the Pythagorean Theorem to determine whether it is a right triangle.

$$3^2 + 5^2 \overset{?}{=} 4^2$$

$$9 + 25 \overset{?}{=} 16$$

$$34 \neq 16$$

Abe concluded that it is not a right triangle. Is Abe correct? Explain. © MP.3

3. **Use Structure** When you are given three side lengths for a triangle, how do you know which length to substitute for a, b, or c in the Pythagorean Theorem? © MP.7

Do You Know How?

4. Is the triangle a right triangle? Explain.

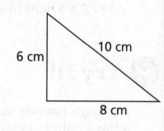

5. Is the triangle a right triangle? Explain.

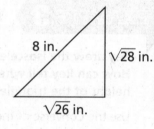

6. Is the purple triangle a right triangle? Explain.

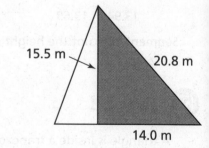

Name: _____

Practice & Problem Solving

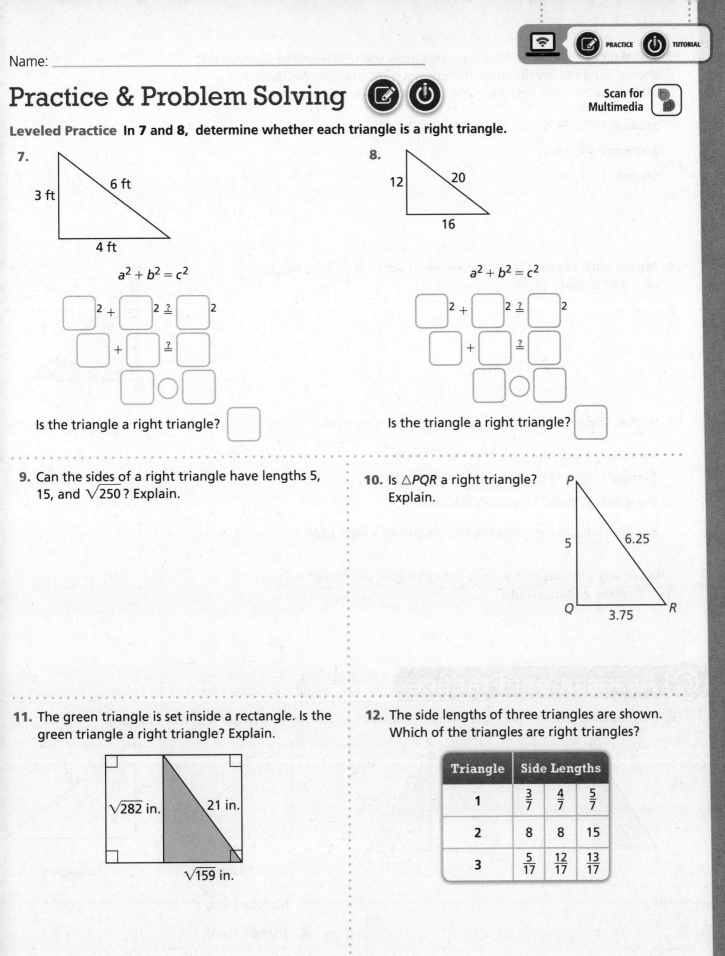

Scan for Multimedia

Leveled Practice In **7** and **8**, determine whether each triangle is a right triangle.

7.

3 ft, 6 ft, 4 ft

$a^2 + b^2 = c^2$

$\boxed{}^2 + \boxed{}^2 \overset{?}{=} \boxed{}^2$

$\boxed{} + \boxed{} \overset{?}{=} \boxed{}$

$\boxed{} \; \bigcirc \; \boxed{}$

Is the triangle a right triangle? $\boxed{}$

8.

12, 20, 16

$a^2 + b^2 = c^2$

$\boxed{}^2 + \boxed{}^2 \overset{?}{=} \boxed{}^2$

$\boxed{} + \boxed{} \overset{?}{=} \boxed{}$

$\boxed{} \; \bigcirc \; \boxed{}$

Is the triangle a right triangle? $\boxed{}$

9. Can the sides of a right triangle have lengths 5, 15, and $\sqrt{250}$? Explain.

10. Is △*PQR* a right triangle? Explain.

Triangle PQR: P, 5, 6.25, Q, 3.75, R

11. The green triangle is set inside a rectangle. Is the green triangle a right triangle? Explain.

$\sqrt{282}$ in., 21 in., $\sqrt{159}$ in.

12. The side lengths of three triangles are shown. Which of the triangles are right triangles?

Triangle	Side Lengths		
1	$\frac{3}{7}$	$\frac{4}{7}$	$\frac{5}{7}$
2	8	8	15
3	$\frac{5}{17}$	$\frac{12}{17}$	$\frac{13}{17}$

13. **Construct Arguments** Three students draw triangles with the side lengths shown. All three say that their triangle is a right triangle. Which students are incorrect? What mistake might they have made? Ⓒ MP.3

    Student 1: 22, 33, 55

    Student 2: 44, 33, 77

    Student 3: 33, 44, 55

14. **Model with Math** △*JKL* is an isosceles triangle. Is $\overline{KM}$ the height of △*JKL*? Explain. Ⓒ MP.4

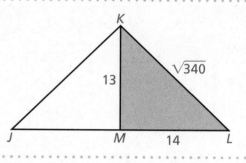

15. **Higher Order Thinking** The side lengths of three triangles are given.

    Triangle 1: $\sqrt{229}$ units, $\sqrt{225}$ units, 22 units

    Triangle 2: $\sqrt{11\frac{1}{3}}$ units, $\sqrt{13\frac{2}{3}}$ units, 5 units

    Triangle 3: 16 units, 17 units, $\sqrt{545}$ units

    a. Which lengths represent the side lengths of a right triangle?

    b. For any triangles that are not right triangles, use two of the sides to make a right triangle.

Ⓒ Assessment Practice

16. Which shaded triangle is a right triangle? Explain.

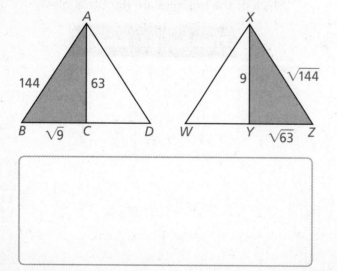

17. Which triangle is a right triangle?

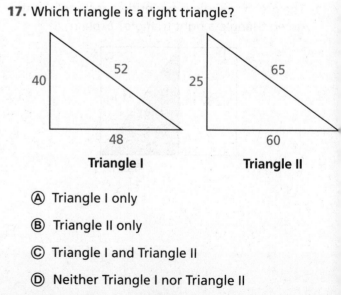

Triangle I   Triangle II

   Ⓐ Triangle I only

   Ⓑ Triangle II only

   Ⓒ Triangle I and Triangle II

   Ⓓ Neither Triangle I nor Triangle II

Name: _____

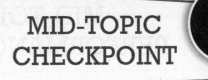
1. Vocabulary How are the hypotenuse and the legs of a right triangle related? *Lesson 7-1*

2. Given that △*PQR* has side lengths of 12.5 centimeters, 30 centimeters, and 32.5 centimeters, prove △*PQR* is a right triangle. *Lesson 7-2*

3. Ella said that if she knows the lengths of just two sides of any triangle, then she can find the length of the third side by using the Pythagorean Theorem. Is Ella correct? Explain. *Lesson 7-1*

4. Find the unknown side length. Round to the nearest tenth. *Lesson 7-1*

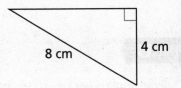

8 cm

4 cm

5. The lengths of the legs of a right triangle are 4.5 inches and 6 inches. What is the length of the hypotenuse? *Lesson 7-1*

6. Which lengths represent the sides of a right triangle? Select all that apply. *Lesson 7-2*

- ☐ 5 cm, 10 cm, 15 cm
- ☐ 7 in., 14 in., 25 in.
- ☐ 13 m, 84 m, 85 m
- ☐ 5 ft, 11 ft, 12 ft
- ☐ 6 ft, 9 ft, $\sqrt{117}$ ft

How well did you do on the mid-topic checkpoint? Fill in the stars.

☆ ☆ ☆

MID-TOPIC PERFORMANCE TASK

Javier is standing near a tree. He holds an electronic tape measure near his eyes and finds the three distances shown.

PART A

Javier says that he can now use the Pythagorean Theorem to find the height of the tree. Explain. Use vocabulary terms in your explanation.

25 ft

?

PART B

7 ft

9 ft

Find the height of the tree. Round to the nearest tenth. Show your work.

PART C

Javier moves backward so that his horizontal distance from the tree is 3 feet greater. Will the distance from his eyes to the top of the tree also be 3 feet greater? Explain.

PART D

Could Javier change his horizontal distance from the tree so that the distance from his eyes to the top of the tree is only 20 feet? Explain.

Lesson 7-3
Apply the
Pythagorean
Theorem to
Solve Problems

📶 Go Online | PearsonRealize.com

👆 Solve & Discuss It!

📶 👆 ACTIVITY

Carlos is giving his friend in another state a new umbrella as a gift. He wants to ship the umbrella in a box he already has. Which box can Carlos use to ship the umbrella? Explain.

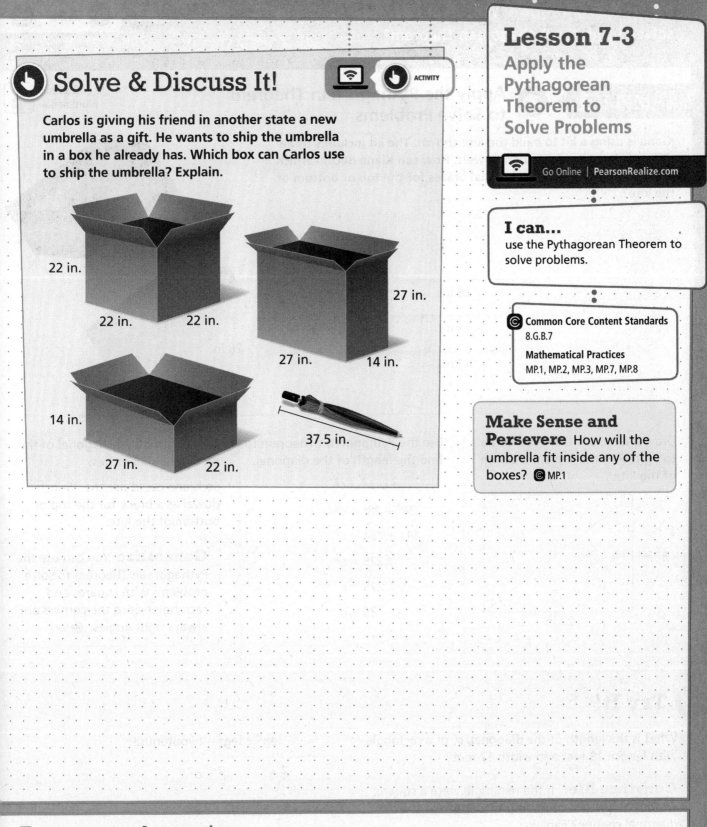

22 in.

22 in.   22 in.

27 in.

27 in.   14 in.

14 in.

27 in.   22 in.

37.5 in.

I can...
use the Pythagorean Theorem to solve problems.

© **Common Core Content Standards**
8.G.B.7

Mathematical Practices
MP.1, MP.2, MP.3, MP.7, MP.8

Make Sense and Persevere How will the umbrella fit inside any of the boxes? © MP.1

Focus on math practices

Construct Arguments Tim says that the diagonal of any of the boxes will always be longer than the sides. Is Tim correct? Explain. © MP.3

? **Essential Question** What types of problems can be solved using the Pythagorean Theorem?

INTERACTIVE ANIMATION   A

EXAMPLE 1 ◉ **Apply the Pythagorean Theorem to Solve Problems**

Scan for Multimedia

Kiana is using a kit to build the kite shown. The kit includes three different lengths of wooden dowels. How can Kiana decide which pieces of wood to use as diagonal braces for the top or bottom of the kite?

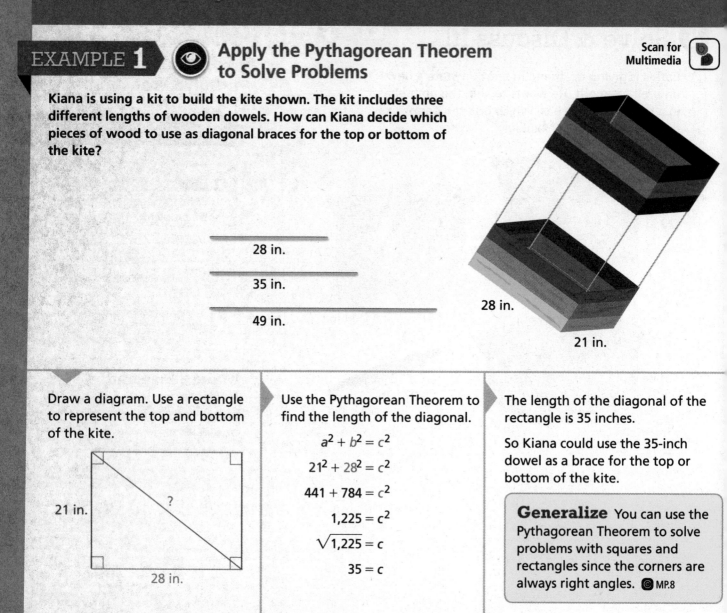

28 in.

35 in.

49 in.

28 in.

21 in.

Draw a diagram. Use a rectangle to represent the top and bottom of the kite.

21 in.
?
28 in.

Use the Pythagorean Theorem to find the length of the diagonal.

$$a^2 + b^2 = c^2$$

$$21^2 + 28^2 = c^2$$

$$441 + 784 = c^2$$

$$1{,}225 = c^2$$

$$\sqrt{1{,}225} = c$$

$$35 = c$$

The length of the diagonal of the rectangle is 35 inches.

So Kiana could use the 35-inch dowel as a brace for the top or bottom of the kite.

Generalize You can use the Pythagorean Theorem to solve problems with squares and rectangles since the corners are always right angles. © MP.8

☑ **Try It!**

What is the length of the diagonal, d, of a rectangle with length 19 feet and width 17 feet?

Convince Me! If the rectangle were a square, would the process of finding the length of the diagonal change? Explain.

$\text{leg}^2 + \text{leg}^2 = \text{hypotenuse}^2$

$$\boxed{}^2 + \boxed{}^2 = d^2$$

$$\boxed{} + \boxed{} = d^2$$

$$\boxed{} = d^2$$

$$\boxed{} \approx d$$

| EXAMPLE 2 | Apply the Pythagorean Theorem to Triangles in Three Dimensions | | ACTIVITY | ASSESS |

Alex has a column aquarium with a rectangular base that has a height of 66 inches, a length of 10 inches, and a width of 14.5 inches. What is the longest piece of choya wood that Alex can buy to fit in his tank?

STEP 1 Draw and label a diagram to represent the aquarium.

Length of choya wood, c

66 in.

d

10 in.

14.5 in.

STEP 2 Find the length of the diagonal, d, of the bottom of the tank.

$$10^2 + 14.5^2 = d^2$$
$$100 + 210.25 = d^2$$
$$310.25 = d^2$$
$$17.6 \approx d$$

STEP 3 Use the Pythagorean Theorem to find the length of the choya wood.

$$66^2 + 17.6^2 = c^2$$
$$4,356 + 310.25 = c^2$$
$$4,666.25 = c^2$$
$$68.3 \approx c$$

A piece of choya wood that is about 68.3 inches long is the longest piece of choya wood Alex can buy.

| EXAMPLE 3 | Apply the Converse of the Pythagorean Theorem to Solve Problems |

Sandra bought a triangular shelf to hang in the corner of her room. Will this shelf fit in the 90° corner? Explain.

Use the Converse of the Pythagorean Theorem to determine if the triangle is a right triangle.

$$a^2 + b^2 \overset{?}{=} c^2$$
$$18^2 + 24^2 \overset{?}{=} 30^2$$
$$324 + 576 \overset{?}{=} 900$$
$$900 = 900$$

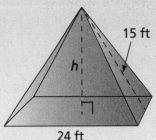

24 in.

18 in.

30 in.

The shelf is in the shape of a right triangle. It will fit in the corner.

✓ Try It!

A company wants to rent a tent that has a height of at least 10 feet for an outdoor show. Should they rent the tent shown at the right? Explain.

15 ft

h

24 ft

You can use the Pythagorean Theorem and its converse to solve problems involving right triangles.

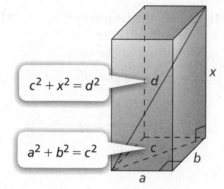

$c^2 + x^2 = d^2$

$a^2 + b^2 = c^2$

Do You Understand?

1. **Essential Question** What types of problems can be solved using the Pythagorean Theorem?

2. **Look for Structure** How is using the Pythagorean Theorem in a rectangular prism similar to using it in a rectangle? © MP.7

3. **Construct Arguments** Glen found the length of the hypotenuse of a right triangle using $\sqrt{a^2 + b^2}$. Gigi used $\sqrt{(a + b)^2}$. Who is correct? Explain. © MP.3

Do You Know How?

4. You are painting the roof of a shed. You are going to place the base of a ladder 12 feet from the shed. How long does the ladder need to be to reach the roof of the shed?

35 ft

12 ft

5. A box shaped like a right rectangular prism measures 5 centimeters by 3 centimeters by 2 centimeters. What is the length of the interior diagonal of the prism to the nearest hundredth?

6. A wall 12 feet long makes a corner with a wall that is 14 feet long. The other ends of the walls are about 18.44 feet apart. Do the walls form a right angle? Explain.

Go Online | PearsonRealize.com

Name: _____

Practice & Problem Solving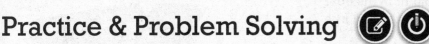

Scan for Multimedia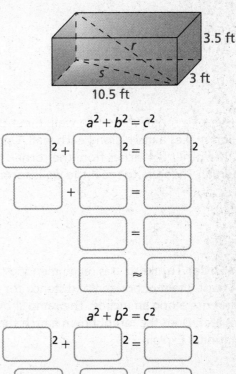

Leveled Practice In **7** and **8**, use the Pythagorean Theorem to solve.

7. You are going to use an inclined plane to lift a heavy object to the top of a shelving unit with a height of 6 feet. The base of the inclined plane is 16 feet from the shelving unit. What is the length of the inclined plane? Round to the nearest tenth of a foot.

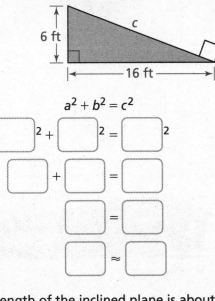

6 ft   c   16 ft

$$a^2 + b^2 = c^2$$

$$\boxed{}^2 + \boxed{}^2 = \boxed{}^2$$

$$\boxed{} + \boxed{} = \boxed{}$$

$$\boxed{} = \boxed{}$$

$$\boxed{} \approx \boxed{}$$

The length of the inclined plane is about $\boxed{}$ feet.

8. Find the missing lengths in the rectangular prism.

3.5 ft   r   s   3 ft   10.5 ft

$$a^2 + b^2 = c^2$$

$$\boxed{}^2 + \boxed{}^2 = \boxed{}^2$$

$$\boxed{} + \boxed{} = \boxed{}$$

$$\boxed{} = \boxed{}$$

$$\boxed{} \approx \boxed{}$$

$$a^2 + b^2 = c^2$$

$$\boxed{}^2 + \boxed{}^2 = \boxed{}^2$$

$$\boxed{} + \boxed{} = \boxed{}$$

$$\boxed{} = \boxed{}$$

$$\boxed{} \approx \boxed{}$$

9. A stainless steel patio heater is shaped like a square pyramid. The length of one side of the base is 19.8 inches. The slant height is 92.8 inches. What is the height of the heater? Round to the nearest tenth of an inch.

10. Reasoning What is the measurement of the longest line segment in a right rectangular prism that is 16 centimeters long, 9 centimeters wide, and 7 centimeters tall? Round to the nearest tenth of a centimeter. © MP.2

11. Felipe is making triangles for a stained glass window. He made the design shown, but wants to change it. Felipe wants to move the purple triangle to the corner. The purple piece has side lengths of 4.5 inches, 6 inches, and 7 inches. Can the purple piece be moved to the corner? Explain.

12. a. What is the longest poster you could fit in the box? Express your answer to the nearest tenth of an inch.

b. Explain why you can fit only one maximum-length poster in the box, but you can fit multiple 21.5-inch posters in the same box.

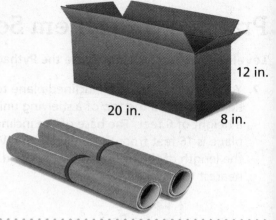

20 in.

12 in.

8 in.

13. The corner of a room where two walls meet the floor should be a right angle. Jeff makes a mark along each wall. One mark is 3 inches from the corner. The other is 4 inches from the corner. How can Jeff use the Pythagorean Theorem to see if the walls form a right angle?

14. Higher Order Thinking It is recommended that a ramp have at least 6 feet of horizontal distance for every 1 foot of vertical rise along an incline. The ramp shown has a vertical rise of 2 feet. Does the ramp shown match the recommended specifications? Explain.

21 ft

©️ Assessment Practice

15. A machine in a factory cuts out triangular sheets of metal. Which of the triangles are right triangles? Select all that apply.

☐ Triangle 1

☐ Triangle 2

☐ Triangle 3

☐ Triangle 4

Triangle Side Lengths

Triangle	Side Lengths (in.)		
1	12	19	$\sqrt{505}$
2	16	19	$\sqrt{467}$
3	14	20	$\sqrt{596}$
4	11	23	$\sqrt{421}$

16. What is the length of the rectangular plot of land shown?

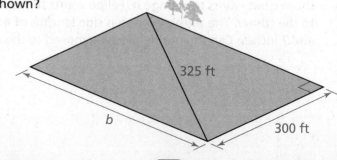

325 ft

b

300 ft

Go Online | PearsonRealize.com

Explore It!

ACTIVITY

Thomas and Jim are outside the haunted castle ride and want to get to the clown tent in time for the next show.

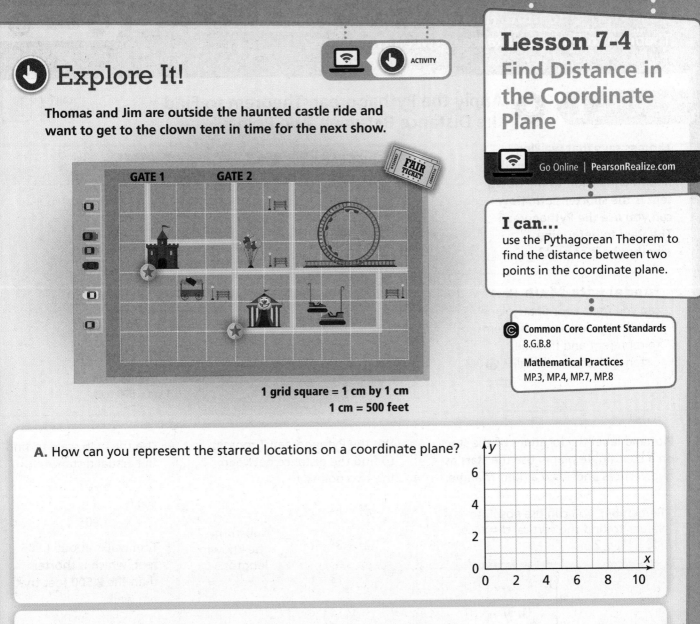

FAIR TICKET

GATE 1   GATE 2

1 grid square = 1 cm by 1 cm
1 cm = 500 feet

I can...
use the Pythagorean Theorem to find the distance between two points in the coordinate plane.

© **Common Core Content Standards**
8.G.B.8

Mathematical Practices
MP.3, MP.4, MP.7, MP.8

A. How can you represent the starred locations on a coordinate plane?

B. Jim says that the marked yellow paths show the shortest path to the tent. Write an expression to represent this and find the distance Jim walks from the haunted mansion to the clown tent.

Focus on math practices

Construct Arguments Why is the distance between two nonhorizontal and nonvertical points always greater than the horizontal or vertical distance? © MP.3

INTERACTIVE ANIMATION

EXAMPLE 1 ◉ **Apply the Pythagorean Theorem to Find the Distance Between Two Points**

Scan for Multimedia

Thomas says that walking along a straight path from the haunted mansion to the clown tent is the shorter path. How can you use the Pythagorean Theorem to determine whether he is correct?

Model with Math How can you use a coordinate plane and the Pythagorean Theorem to represent and find the distance Thomas will walk? © MP.4

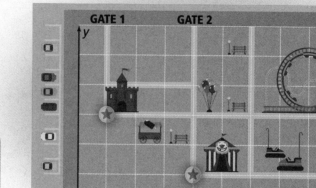

GATE 1   GATE 2

FAIR TICKET

1 grid square = 1 cm by 1 cm
1 cm = 500 feet

Plot and label the locations of the stars on a coordinate plane. Use the stars as two vertices and draw a right triangle.

Remember, you can use absolute values to find the vertical distance. $|1| + |1| = 2$

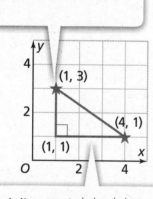

The horizontal distance is $|4| - |1| = 3$.

Use the Pythagorean Theorem to find the distance between the two points.

$$a^2 + b^2 = c^2$$

$$2^2 + 3^2 = c^2$$ — Substitute the known lengths.

$$13 = c^2$$

$$\sqrt{13} = c$$

$$3.61 \approx c$$

Use the map scale to find the actual distance.

$$\frac{1 \text{ cm}}{500 \text{ ft}} = \frac{3.61 \text{ cm}}{x \text{ ft}}$$

$$x = 1,805$$

Tom walks about 1,805 feet, which is shorter than the 2,500 feet that Jim walks.

✓ **Try It!**

What is the distance between points A and B?

The distance between point A and point B is about ☐ units.

Convince Me! Why do you need to use the Pythagorean Theorem to find the distance between points A and B?

 Go Online | PearsonRealize.com

Find the perimeter of △ABC.

STEP 1 Use absolute value to find the lengths of side AC and side BC.

STEP 2 Find the length of the hypotenuse AB.

$c^2 = 5^2 + 3^2$

$c^2 = 25 + 9$

$c^2 = 34$

$\sqrt{c^2} = \sqrt{34}$

$c \approx 5.83$

> Substitute the known side lengths into the Pythagorean Theorem.

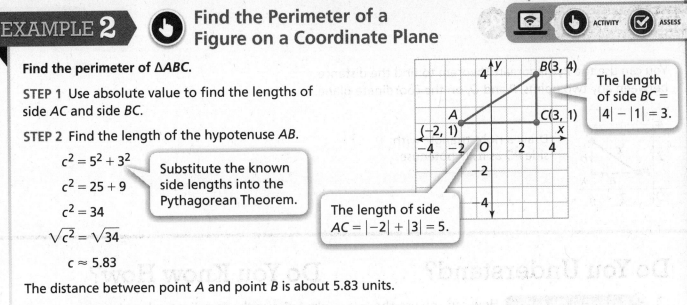

The length of side BC = $|4| - |1| = 3$.

The length of side AC = $|-2| + |3| = 5$.

The distance between point A and point B is about 5.83 units.

STEP 3 Add the lengths of all three sides to find the perimeter.

$5 + 3 + 5.83 = 13.83$

The perimeter of △ABC is about 13.83 units.

✅ Try It!

Find the perimeter of △ABC with vertices (2, 5), (5, −1), and (2, −1).

EXAMPLE **3** 🖑 Use the Pythagorean Theorem to Solve Problems on the Coordinate Plane

Li draws one side of an equilateral triangle with vertices (−1, 1) and (3, 1) on the coordinate plane. The third vertex is in the first quadrant. What are the coordinates of the third vertex of Li's triangle?

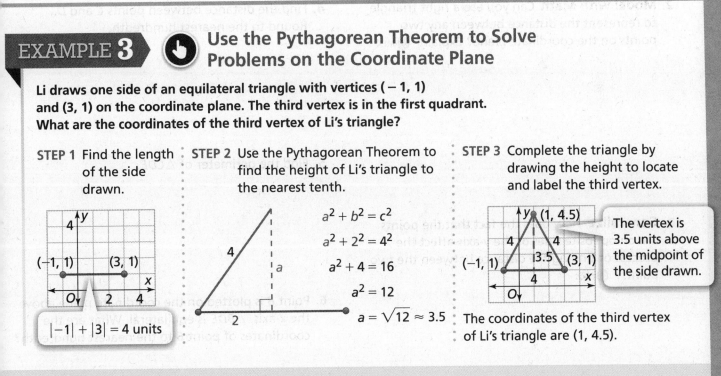

STEP 1 Find the length of the side drawn.

$|-1| + |3| = 4$ units

STEP 2 Use the Pythagorean Theorem to find the height of Li's triangle to the nearest tenth.

$a^2 + b^2 = c^2$

$a^2 + 2^2 = 4^2$

$a^2 + 4 = 16$

$a^2 = 12$

$a = \sqrt{12} \approx 3.5$

STEP 3 Complete the triangle by drawing the height to locate and label the third vertex.

The vertex is 3.5 units above the midpoint of the side drawn.

The coordinates of the third vertex of Li's triangle are (1, 4.5).

✅ Try It!

What are the coordinates, to the nearest tenth, of the third vertex in an isosceles triangle that has one side length of 2 and two side lengths of 5, with vertices at (1, 0) and (1, 2)? The third vertex is in the first quadrant.

You can use the Pythagorean Theorem to find the distance between any two points, P and Q, on the coordinate plane.

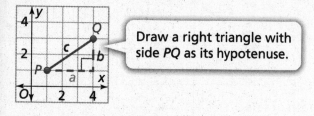

Draw a right triangle with side PQ as its hypotenuse.

Do You Understand?

1. **? Essential Question** How can you use the Pythagorean Theorem to find the distance between two points?

2. **Model with Math** Can you use a right triangle to represent the distance between any two points on the coordinate plane? Explain. Ⓒ MP.4

3. **Generalize** How does the fact that the points are on opposite sides of the y-axis affect the process of finding the distance between the two points? Ⓒ MP.8

Do You Know How?

In **4–6**, use the coordinate plane below.

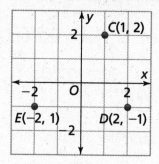

4. Find the distance between points C and D. Round to the nearest hundredth.

5. Find the perimeter of △CDE.

6. Point B is plotted on the coordinate plane above the x-axis. △BDE is equilateral. What are the coordinates of point B to the nearest hundredth?

Go Online | PearsonRealize.com

Name: _____

Practice & Problem Solving

7. Leveled Practice Use the Pythagorean Theorem
to find the distance between points P and Q.

Label the length, in units, of each leg of the right triangle.

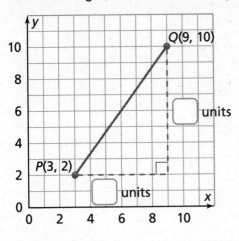

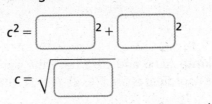

$$c^2 = \boxed{}^2 + \boxed{}^2$$

$$c = \sqrt{\boxed{}}$$

The distance between point P and point Q is
$\boxed{}$ units.

---

8. Find the perimeter of triangle PQR. Round
to the nearest hundredth.

9. Determine whether the triangle is equilateral,
isosceles, or scalene.

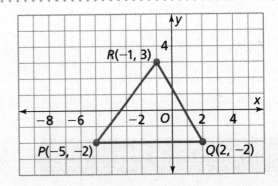

---

10. You walk along the outside of a park starting at point P.
Then you take a shortcut represented by $\overline{PQ}$ on the graph.

  a. What is the length of the shortcut in meters?
  Round to the nearest tenth of a meter.

  b. What is the total length of your walk in the park?
  Round to the nearest tenth of a meter.

Walking Through the Park

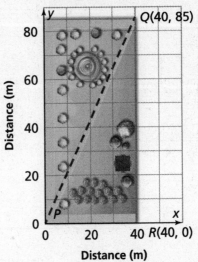

---

11. Suppose a park is located 3.6 miles east of your home. The library is 4.8 miles north of the park. What is the shortest distance between your home and the library?

12. Use Structure Point B has coordinates (2, 1). The x-coordinate of point A is −10. The distance between point A and point B is 15 units. What are the possible coordinates of point A? © MP.7

13. Higher Order Thinking △EFG and △HIJ have the same perimeter and side lengths. The coordinates are E(6, 2), F(9, 2), G(8, 7), H(0, 0), and I(0, 3).

a. What are possible coordinates of point J?

b. Explain why there can be different possibilities for the coordinates for point J.

© **Assessment Practice**

14. Find the distance between P and R. Round to the nearest tenth.

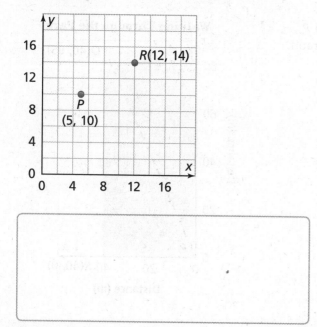

15. Find the distance between A(1, 5) and B(5.5, 9.25). Round to the nearest tenth.

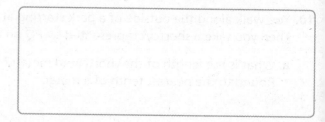 Go Online | PearsonRealize.com

? Topic Essential Question

How can you use the Pythagorean Theorem to solve problems?

Vocabulary Review

Complete each definition and then provide an example of each vocabulary word.

Vocabulary   Converse of the Pythagorean Theorem
hypotenuse   leg   proof   Pythagorean Theorem

Definition	Example
1. A [____] is a logical argument in which every statement of fact is supported by a reason.	
2. The [____] states that if $a^2 + b^2 = c^2$ for side lengths a, b, and c of a triangle, then the triangle is a right triangle.	
3. The [____] states that in a right triangle the sum of the squares of the lengths of the legs is equal to the square of the length of the hypotenuse.	

Use Vocabulary in Writing

All faces of the figure are rectangles. Explain how to find the length of d. Use vocabulary terms in your description.

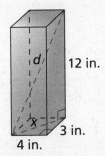

d   12 in.

x   3 in.

4 in.

Concepts and Skills Review

LESSON **7-1** **Understand the Pythagorean Theorem**

Quick Review

The **Pythagorean Theorem** states that, in a right triangle, the sum of the squares of the lengths of the legs, *a* and *b*, is equal to the square of the length of the hypotenuse, *c*. So, $a^2 + b^2 = c^2$.

Example

Find the length of the hypotenuse of a triangle with legs of 7 meters and 24 meters.

Substitute 7 for *a* and 24 for *b*. Then solve for *c*.

$$a^2 + b^2 = c^2$$
$$49 + 576 = c^2$$
$$\sqrt{625} = c$$

The length of the hypotenuse is 25 meters.

Practice

1. Find the length of the hypotenuse.

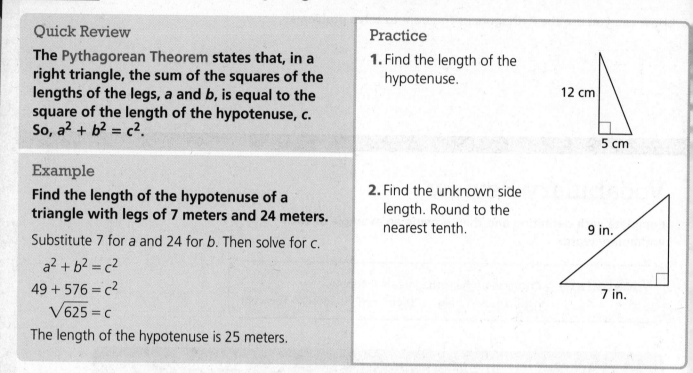

2. Find the unknown side length. Round to the nearest tenth.

LESSON **7-2** **Understand the Converse of the Pythagorean Theorem**

Quick Review

For a triangle with side lengths *a*, *b*, and *c*, if $a^2 + b^2 = c^2$, then the triangle is a right triangle by the **Converse of the Pythagorean Theorem.**

Example

Is a triangle with side lengths of 8 m, 15 m, and 17 m a right triangle? Explain.

Substitute 8 for *a*, 15 for *b*, and 17 for *c*.

$$a^2 + b^2 \stackrel{?}{=} c^2$$
$$8^2 + 15^2 \stackrel{?}{=} 17^2$$
$$289 = 289 \checkmark$$

Because $a^2 + b^2 = c^2$, the triangle is a right triangle.

Practice

1. Is the triangle a right triangle? Explain.

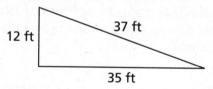

2. A triangle has side lengths 1.5 inches, 2 inches, and 3 inches. Is the triangle a right triangle? Explain.

3. A triangle has side lengths 9 feet, 40 feet, and 41 feet. Is the triangle a right triangle? Explain.

Quick Review

The Pythagorean Theorem can be used to find unknown side lengths of an object that is shaped like a right triangle. It also can be used to find diagonal measures in certain two-dimensional and three-dimensional objects.

Example

A shipping box is 20 inches long along the diagonal of its base. Each diagonal of the box is 29 inches long. How tall is the box?

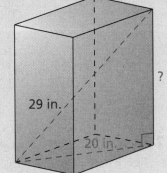

Substitute 20 for a and 29 for c. Then solve for b.

$$a^2 + b^2 = c^2$$
$$20^2 + b^2 = 29^2$$
$$400 + b^2 = 841$$
$$b = \sqrt{441}$$

The height of the shipping box is 21 inches.

Practice

1. A basketball court is in the shape of a rectangle that is 94 feet long and 50 feet wide. What is the length of a diagonal of the court? Round to the nearest tenth.

2. A packaging box for a metal rod is 7.5 inches along a diagonal of the base. The height of the box is 18 inches. What is the length of a diagonal of the box?

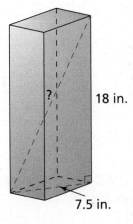

Quick Review

The Pythagorean Theorem can be used to find the distance between any two points on the coordinate plane.

Example

Find the distance between the two points on the coordinate plane. Round to the nearest tenth.

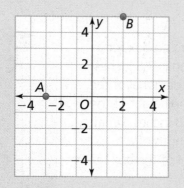

Draw a right triangle. Determine the lengths of its legs.

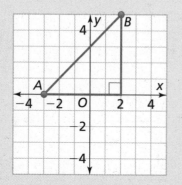

The length of the horizontal leg is 5 units.

The length of the vertical leg is 5 units.

Use the relationship $a^2 + b^2 = c^2$. Substitute 5 for a and 5 for b. Then solve for c.

$$a^2 + b^2 = c^2$$
$$5^2 + 5^2 = c^2$$
$$25 + 25 = c^2$$
$$50 = c^2$$
$$\sqrt{50} = c$$
$$7.1 \approx c$$

The distance between the two points is about 7.1 units.

Practice

1. Points C and D represent the location of two parks on a map. Find the distance between the parks if the length of each unit on the grid is equal to 25 miles. Round to the nearest mile.

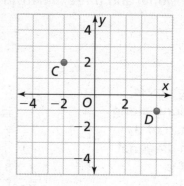

2. Find the perimeter of $\triangle ABC$. Round to the nearest tenth.

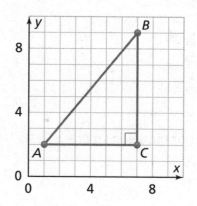

3. Triangle JKL is an equilateral triangle with two of its vertices at points J and K. What are the coordinates of point L? Round to the nearest tenth as needed.

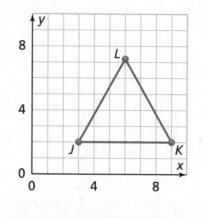

 Go Online | PearsonRealize.com

Riddle Rearranging

Solve each equation. Then arrange the answers in order from least to greatest. The letters will spell out the answer to the riddle below.

I can...
solve multistep equations.
© 8.EE.C.7b

N $6x - 1 = 2(2x - 3)$

R $\frac{1}{5}x - 8 = 2x - 53$

P $4(x + 11) = 56$

S $\frac{3}{2}x + 20 = 2(x - 16)$

A $11 - \frac{5}{2}x = x + 46$

K $\frac{5}{8}x - 9 = 11$

M $3(10 - x) = 60 - x$

Y $1.9 - 7.1x = 1.9$

E $7x - 14 = 5x + 17.2$

Why did the coffee shop server love the job? Because there were so

◯ ◯ ◯ ◯   ◯ ◯ ◯ ◯ ◯ .

TOPIC 8

SOLVE PROBLEMS INVOLVING SURFACE AREA AND VOLUME

? Topic Essential Question

How can you find volumes and surface areas of three-dimensional figures?

Topic Overview

8-1 Find Surface Area of Three-Dimensional Figures

8-2 Find Volume of Cylinders

8-3 Find Volume of Cones

8-4 Find Volume of Spheres

3-Act Mathematical Modeling: Measure Up

Topic Vocabulary

- composite figure
- cone
- cylinder
- sphere

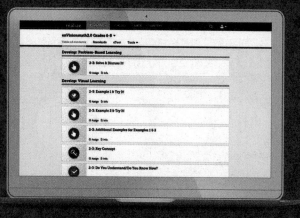

Lesson Digital Resources

INTERACTIVE ANIMATION Interact with visual learning animations.

ACTIVITY Use with *Solve & Discuss It, Explo* and *Explain It* activities, and to explore Exam

VIDEOS Watch clips to support *3-Act Mathe Modeling Lessons* and *STEM Projects*.

PRACTICE Practice what you've learned.

Go online | PearsonRealize.com

Measure Up

▶ Measure Up

Have you ever heard of the terms *griffin beaker*, *Erlenmeyer flask*, or *graduated cylinder*? Maybe you've used them in your science class.

Each piece of equipment in a chemistry lab has a specific purpose, so containers come in many shapes. It's sometimes necessary to pour a solution from one container to another. Think about this during the 3-Act Mathematical Modeling lesson.

Additional Digital Resources

 TUTORIALS Get help from *Virtual Nerd*, right when you need it.

 KEY CONCEPT Review important lesson content.

 GLOSSARY Read and listen to English/Spanish definitions.

 MATH TOOLS Explore math with digital tools.

 GAMES Play Math Games to help you learn.

 ETEXT Interact with your Student's Edition online.

ASSESSMENT Show what you've learned.

STEM Project

📶 ▶ VIDEO

Did You Know?

The production of **packaging is a huge industry** employing over five million people with annual sales of more than 400 billion dollars.

Packaging materials protect and deliver food and products to consumers.

About **30%** of landfills are composed of polystyrene foam.

Polystyrene foam lasts forever!

A plastic bottle takes 450–1,000 years to biodegrade.

Seabirds are dying of starvation with stomachs full of plastic and Styrofoam.

Eco-friendly packaging materials are being **made from mushrooms and bamboo.**

There is even a drink bottle **made from recyclable paper.**

New technology results in packaging materials that are both affordable and biodegradable.

Environmentally friendly companies are producing sustainable packaging. In addition to using recyclable materials, they reduce the water, natural resources, and energy needed for production. They minimize waste when designing products.

Your Task: Wrap it Up! ▶

Engineers consider several factors when designing product packaging. These factors include cost efficiency and eco-friendly design so that materials are disposable, recyclable, biodegradable, and not wasted. Suppose you are an engineer working for Liquid Assets, an environmentally friendly company that designs, builds, and packages water purifiers. You and your classmates will use your knowledge of volume and surface area to determine an environmentally sound way to package the purifiers.

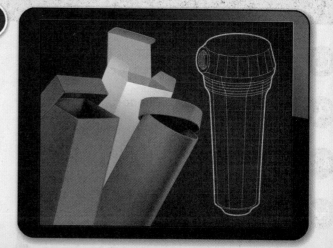

Review What You Know!

Vocabulary

Choose the best term from the box to complete each definition.

> base
> diameter
> radius
> three-dimensional
> two-dimensional

1. The _____ is the distance from the center to the edge of a circle.

2. A shape that has length, width, and height is _____ .

3. Any side of a cube can be considered a _____ .

4. A shape that has length and width, but not height, is _____ .

5. The _____ of a circle is a line segment that passes through its center and has endpoints on the circle.

Multiplying with Decimals

Find the product.

6. $14 \cdot 3.5 =$ [____]

7. $9 \cdot 3.14 =$ [____]

8. $4.2 \cdot 10.5 =$ [____]

Areas of Circles

Find the area of each circle. Use 3.14 for π.

9.

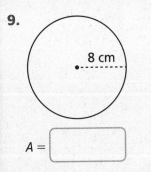

8 cm

$A =$ [____]

10.

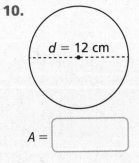

$d = 12$ cm

$A =$ [____]

Use the Pythagorean Theorem

Find the missing side length of the triangle.

11.

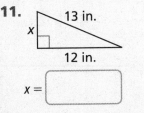

13 in.

x

12 in.

$x =$ [____]

12.

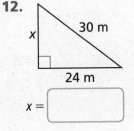

30 m

x

24 m

$x =$ [____]

Prepare for Reading Success

Before beginning each lessons, preview its content. Write what you already know about the lesson in the second column. Then write a question that you want answered about the lesson in the third column. After the lesson, complete the fourth column with the answer to your question.

Lesson	What I Know	Questions I Have	Answer
8-1			
8-2			
8-3			
8-4			

Explore It!

🔊 ⏱ ACTIVITY

Andrea is designing the packaging for a tube-shaped container.

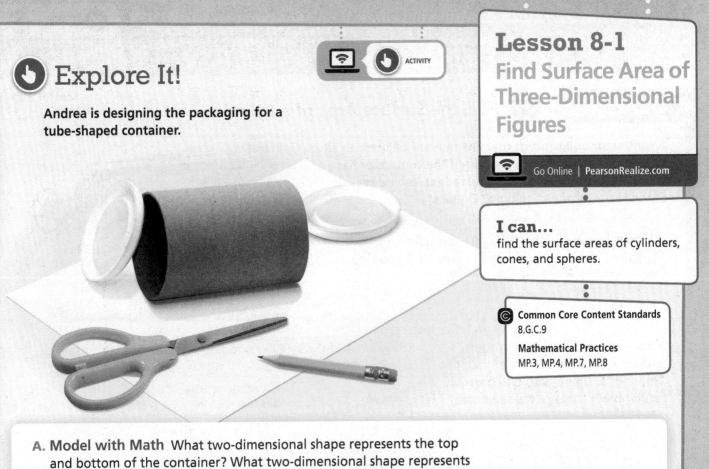

I can...
find the surface areas of cylinders, cones, and spheres.

Common Core Content Standards
8.G.C.9

Mathematical Practices
MP.3, MP.4, MP.7, MP.8

A. Model with Math What two-dimensional shape represents the top and bottom of the container? What two-dimensional shape represents the tube? Draw a net of the tube-shaped container. © MP.4

B. Look for Relationships The circular top and bottom fit perfectly on the ends of the container. How are the measures of the circles and the rectangle related? © MP.7

Focus on math practices

Model with Math How can you check whether the net that you drew accurately represents the tube-shaped container? © MP.8

? Essential Question How are the areas of polygons used to find the surface area formulas for three-dimensional figures?

INTERACTIVE ANIMATION

EXAMPLE 1 ▶ 👁 Find the Surface Area of a Cylinder

Scan for Multimedia

A contractor builds porch columns that are painted on all surfaces with a protective sealant. If the contractor has enough sealant to cover 150 square feet, can he seal all of the surfaces of one column? Explain.

Look for Relationships How does knowing the area of a two-dimensional figure help you find the surface area of the column? © MP.7

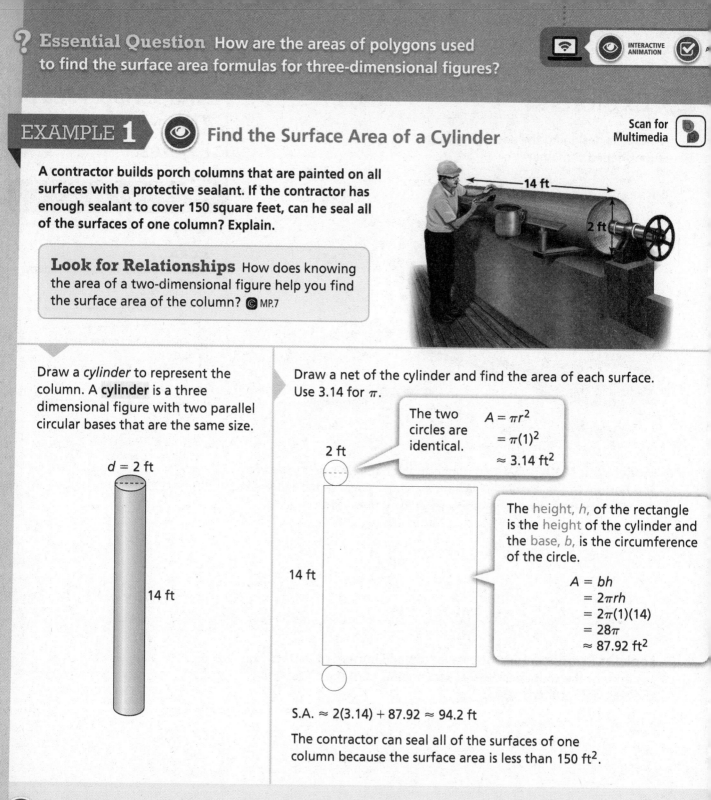

Draw a *cylinder* to represent the column. A **cylinder** is a three dimensional figure with two parallel circular bases that are the same size.

d = 2 ft

14 ft

Draw a net of the cylinder and find the area of each surface. Use 3.14 for π.

2 ft

14 ft

The two circles are identical.

$A = \pi r^2$
$= \pi(1)^2$
$\approx 3.14 \text{ ft}^2$

The height, *h*, of the rectangle is the height of the cylinder and the base, *b*, is the circumference of the circle.

$A = bh$
$= 2\pi rh$
$= 2\pi(1)(14)$
$= 28\pi$
$\approx 87.92 \text{ ft}^2$

S.A. $\approx 2(3.14) + 87.92 \approx 94.2$ ft

The contractor can seal all of the surfaces of one column because the surface area is less than 150 ft².

✓ Try It!

What is the surface area of a cylinder with a height of 9.5 inches and a radius of 2.5 inches?

The surface area of the cylinder is ☐ square inches.

Convince Me! How can you find the surface area of a cylinder if you only know its height and the circumference of its base?

S.A. $= 2(\pi r^2) + (2\pi r)h$

$= 2\pi\left(^2\right) + 2\pi\left(\right)\left(\right)$

$= \pi + \pi$

$= \pi$

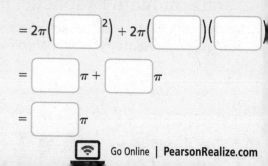

EXAMPLE **2** ▶ 👆 Find the Surface Area of a Cone 🛜 👆 ACTIVITY ☑ ASSESS

A manufacturer packages ice cream cones in paper. How much paper is needed to package one ice cream cone? Use 3.14 for π.

Draw the net of the *cone* to represent the packaging and find the area of each surface. A **cone** is a three-dimensional figure with one circular base and one vertex.

radius 1.5 in.

Ice cream

6 in.

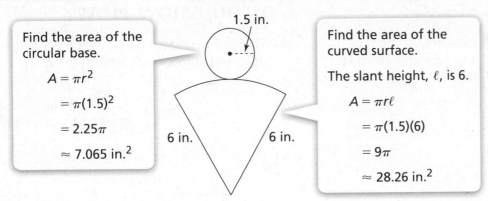

1.5 in.

Find the area of the circular base.

$A = \pi r^2$

$= \pi(1.5)^2$

$= 2.25\pi$

≈ 7.065 in.^{2}

6 in.   6 in.

Find the area of the curved surface.

The slant height, ℓ, is 6.

$A = \pi r \ell$

$= \pi(1.5)(6)$

$= 9\pi$

≈ 28.26 in.^{2}

S.A. $\approx 7.065 + 28.26 = 35.325$ in.^{2}

About 35.325 in.^{2} of paper are needed to package each ice cream cone.

EXAMPLE **3** ▶ 👆 Find the Surface Area of a Sphere

James is making a model of Earth. He has enough blue paint to cover 500 in.^{2}. How can James determine whether he can paint the entire sphere blue?

12 in.

Draw a *sphere* to represent the model of Earth. A **sphere** is the set of all points in space that are the same distance from a center point.

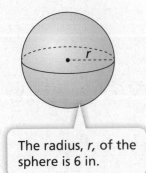

The radius, r, of the sphere is 6 in.

An open cylinder with the same radius as the sphere and a height of $2r$ has the same surface area as the sphere.

An open cylinder has no top or bottom surfaces.

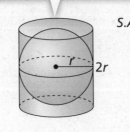

r | $2r$

S.A. $= 2\pi r h$

$= 2\pi r(2r)$

$= 2 \cdot 2 \cdot \pi \cdot r \cdot r$

$= 4\pi r^2$

Use the formula to find the surface area of the model. Use 3.14 for π.

S.A. $= 4\pi r^2$

$= 4\pi(6)^2$

$= 4\pi(36)$

$= 144\pi$

≈ 452.16 in.^{2}

James can paint the entire surface of his model blue.

Generalize The formula to find the surface area of a sphere with radius r is S.A. $= 4\pi r^2$.

☑ **Try It!**

a. What is the surface area of a cone with a radius of 7 feet and a slant height of 9 feet? Use $\frac{22}{7}$ for π.

b. What is the surface area of a sphere with a diameter of 2.7 inches? Use 3.14 for π.

Formulas for finding the area of polygons can be used to find the surface areas of cylinders, cones, and spheres.

Do You Understand?

1. **? Essential Question** How are the areas of polygons used to find the surface area formulas for three-dimensional figures?

2. **Reasoning** Why is the length of the base of the rectangle the same as the circumference of the circles in the net of a cylinder? © MP.2

3. **Construct Arguments** Aaron says that all cones with a base circumference of 8π inches will have the same surface area. Is Aaron correct? Explain. © MP.3

Do You Know How?

4. What is the surface area of the cylinder? Use 3.14 for π, and round to the nearest tenth.

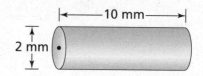

5. What is the surface area of the cone to the nearest tenth? Use 3.14 for π.

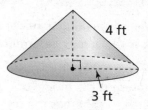

6. What is the surface area of the sphere in terms of π?

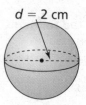

Go Online | PearsonRealize.com

Name: _____

Practice & Problem Solving

Leveled Practice In 7–8, find the surface area.

7. What is the surface area of the cylinder? Use 3.14 for π, and round to the nearest tenth.

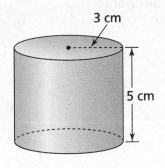

3 cm

5 cm

$S.A. = 2(\pi r^2) + (2\pi r)h$

$= 2\pi\left(\boxed{}^2\right) + 2\pi\left(\boxed{}\right)\left(\boxed{}\right)$

$= 2\pi\left(\boxed{}\right) + 2\pi\left(\boxed{}\right)$

$= \boxed{}\ \pi + \boxed{}\ \pi$

$= \boxed{}\ \pi$

$\approx \boxed{}\ cm^2$

8. What is the surface area of the cone? Use $\frac{22}{7}$ for π.

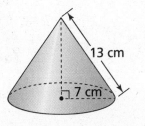

13 cm

7 cm

$S.A. = \pi r^2 + \pi \ell r$

$= \pi\left(\boxed{}^2\right) + \pi\left(\boxed{}\right)\left(\boxed{}\right)$

$= \boxed{}\ \pi + \boxed{}\ \pi$

$= \boxed{}\ \pi$

$\approx \boxed{}\ cm^2$

9. **Construct Arguments** Sasha incorrectly claimed that the surface area of the cylinder is about 76.9 square inches. Explain her likely error and find the correct surface area of the cylinder. © MP.3

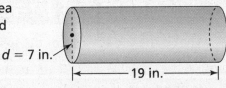

$d = 7$ in.

19 in.

10. A theme park has a ride that is located in half a sphere. The ride goes around the widest part of the sphere, which has a circumference of 514.96 yards. What is the surface area of the sphere? Estimate to the nearest hundredth using 3.14 for π.

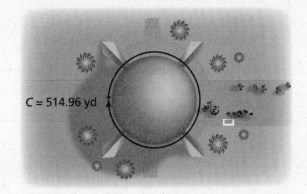

C = 514.96 yd

11. Find the amount of wrapping paper you need to wrap a gift in the cylindrical box shown. You need to cover the top, the bottom, and all the way around the box. Use 3.14 for π, and round to the nearest tenth.

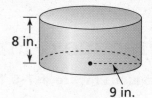

8 in.

9 in.

12. Donna paints ornaments for a school play. Each ornament is made up of two identical cones, as shown. How many bottles of paint does she need to paint 70 ornaments?

She uses one bottle of paint to cover 2,000 cm².

4.1 cm   8.9 cm

13. **Higher Order Thinking**

a. What is the surface area of the cone? Use 3.14 for π, and round to the nearest whole number.

b. **Reasoning** Suppose the diameter and the slant height of the cone are cut in half. How does this affect the surface area of the cone? Explain. © MP.2

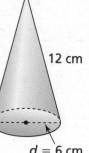

12 cm

$d = 6$ cm

14. What is the surface area of the sphere? Use 3.14 for π, and round to the nearest tenth.

Ⓐ 254.5 cm²

Ⓑ 56.55 cm²

Ⓒ 1,017.4 cm²

Ⓓ 4,071.5 cm²

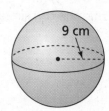

9 cm

15. What is the approximate surface area of the cone? Use 3.14 for π, and round to the nearest whole number.

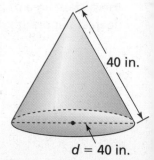

40 in.

$d = 40$ in.

 Go Online | PearsonRealize.com

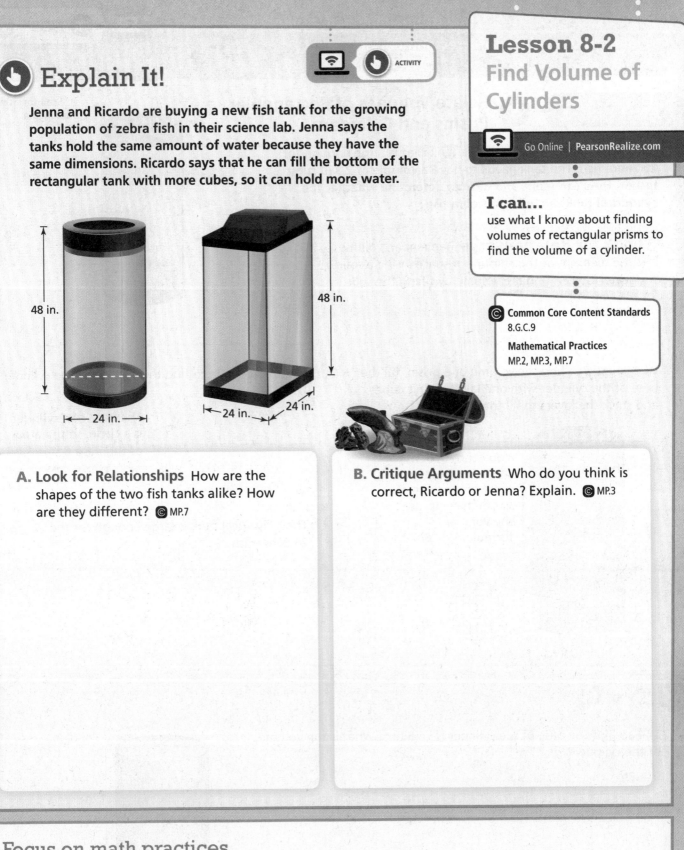

Explain It! 🖱

🖥 ⏱ ACTIVITY

Jenna and Ricardo are buying a new fish tank for the growing population of zebra fish in their science lab. Jenna says the tanks hold the same amount of water because they have the same dimensions. Ricardo says that he can fill the bottom of the rectangular tank with more cubes, so it can hold more water.

48 in.

⊢— 24 in. —⊣

48 in.

⊢—24 in.—⊦ 24 in.

Lesson 8-2
Find Volume of Cylinders

🖥 Go Online | PearsonRealize.com

I can...
use what I know about finding volumes of rectangular prisms to find the volume of a cylinder.

ⓒ **Common Core Content Standards**
8.G.C.9

Mathematical Practices
MP.2, MP.3, MP.7

A. Look for Relationships How are the shapes of the two fish tanks alike? How are they different? ⓒ MP.7

B. Critique Arguments Who do you think is correct, Ricardo or Jenna? Explain. ⓒ MP.3

Focus on math practices

Use Structure How can you use what you know about areas of two-dimensional figures and volumes of prisms to compare the volumes of the fish tanks? ⓒ MP.7

? Essential Question How is the volume of a cylinder related to the volume of a rectangular prism?

INTERACTIVE ANIMATION

EXAMPLE 1 ◉ **Relate Volumes of Rectangular Prisms and Cylinders**

Scan for Multimedia

Jenna and Ricardo need to buy a tank that is large enough for 25 zebra fish. The tank needs to have a volume of 2,310 cubic inches. How can Jenna and Ricardo determine whether the cylindrical tank can hold the zebra fish?

Look for Relationships Remember, volume is the measure of the amount of space inside a solid figure. You can find the volume by filling the solid with unit cubes. ©MP.7

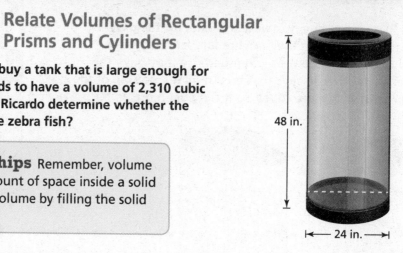
48 in.

24 in.

Like you did to find the volume of a prism, fill the base of the cylinder with one layer of unit cubes and stack the layers to fill the cylinder.

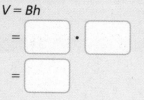
24 in.

48 in.

You cannot count the cubes because some are incomplete, so you have to use the volume formula, $V = Bh$.

Use the formula to find the volume of the cylinder. Use 3.14 for π.

$V = Bh$

$= \pi r^2 \cdot h$

$\approx 3.14 \cdot (12)^2 \cdot 48$

$= 21{,}703.68$ in.^{3}

The base of a cylinder is a circle, so the area of the base $B = \pi r^2$.

The cylindrical tank is large enough for the 25 zebra fish.

☑ Try It!

The area of the base of the cylinder is 78.5 in.^{2}. What is the volume of the cylinder?

$V = Bh$

$= \boxed{} \cdot \boxed{}$

$= \boxed{}$

The volume of the cylinder is $\boxed{}$ cubic inches.

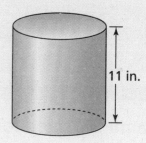
11 in.

Convince Me! Why can you use the formula $V = Bh$ to find the volume of a cylinder?

EXAMPLE **2** ☞ Find an Unknown Measure

ACTIVITY ✓ ASSESS

The volume of the apple juice can is 300 milliliters, which is equal to 300 cubic centimeters. What is the radius of the can? Use 3.14 for π, and round your answer to the nearest tenth.

Use the formula $V = Bh$ to find the radius of the base of the can.

$$V = Bh$$
$$300 = \pi r^2 \cdot 14$$
$$300 = 43.96 r^2$$
$$6.82 \approx r^2$$
$$2.6 \approx r$$

The radius of the can is about 2.6 centimeters.

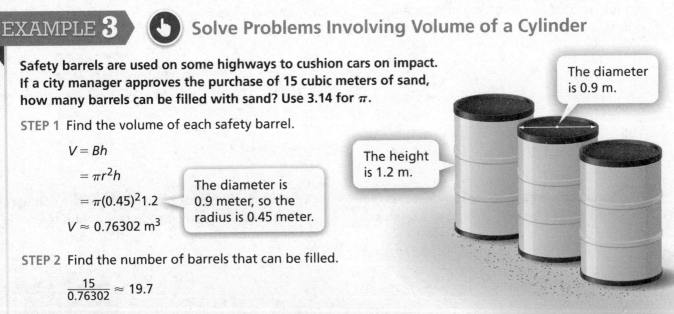

Apple Juice

14 cm

EXAMPLE **3** ☞ Solve Problems Involving Volume of a Cylinder

Safety barrels are used on some highways to cushion cars on impact. If a city manager approves the purchase of 15 cubic meters of sand, how many barrels can be filled with sand? Use 3.14 for π.

STEP 1 Find the volume of each safety barrel.

$$V = Bh$$
$$= \pi r^2 h$$
$$= \pi(0.45)^2 1.2$$
$$V \approx 0.76302 \text{ m}^3$$

The diameter is 0.9 meter, so the radius is 0.45 meter.

The diameter is 0.9 m.

The height is 1.2 m.

STEP 2 Find the number of barrels that can be filled.

$$\frac{15}{0.76302} \approx 19.7$$

The city manager purchased enough sand to fill 19 safety barrels.

✓ Try It!

Lin is building a cylindrical planter with a base diameter of 15 inches. She has 5,000 cubic inches of soil to fill her planter. What is the height of the largest planter Lin can build? Use 3.14 for π, and round to the nearest inch.

The formula for the volume of a cylinder is the same as the formula for the volume of a prism. The formula for volume of a cylinder is $V = Bh$, where B is the area of the circular base and h is the height of the cylinder.

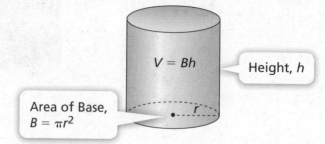

$V = Bh$

Height, h

Area of Base, $B = \pi r^2$

r

Do You Understand?

1. **Essential Question** How is the volume of a cylinder related to the volume of a rectangular prism?

2. Use Structure What two measurements do you need to know to find the volume of a cylinder?
© MP.7

3. Reasoning Cylinder A has a greater radius than Cylinder B. Does Cylinder A necessarily have a greater volume than Cylinder B? Explain. © MP.2

Do You Know How?

4. What is the volume of the cylinder? Express your answer in terms of π.

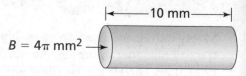

├── 10 mm ──┤

$B = 4\pi$ mm^2

5. What is the approximate height of the cylinder? Use 3.14 for π, and if necessary, round to the nearest tenth.

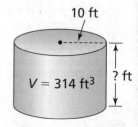

10 ft

$V = 314$ ft^3

? ft

6. What is the volume of the cylinder? Use 3.14 for π, and if necessary, round to the nearest tenth.

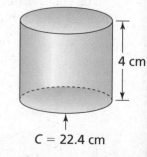

4 cm

$C = 22.4$ cm

 Go Online | PearsonRealize.com

Name: _____

Practice & Problem Solving

7. Leveled Practice What is the volume of a cylinder with a radius of 5 centimeters and height of 2.5 centimeters? Use 3.14 for π.

$V = \pi \cdot \boxed{}^2 \cdot \boxed{}$

$ = \pi \cdot \boxed{} \cdot \boxed{}$

$ = \boxed{}\,\pi$

The volume of the cylinder is about $\boxed{}$ cubic centimeters.

8. Find the volume of each cylinder in terms of π. Which cylinder has the greater volume?

Cylinder A: Area of Base = 6π ft^2, height = 10 ft
Cylinder B: Circumference = 6π ft, height = 6 ft

9. The volume of a cylinder is 225π cubic inches, and the height of the cylinder is 1 inch. What is the radius of the cylinder?

10. A company is designing a new cylindrical water bottle. The volume of the bottle is 103 cubic centimeters. What is the radius of the water bottle? Estimate using 3.14 for π, and round to the nearest hundredth.

8.1 cm

11. Use the figure at the right.

a. Find the volume of the cylinder in terms of π.

b. Is the volume of a cylinder, which has the same radius but twice the height, greater or less than the original cylinder? Explain.

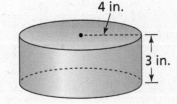
4 in.
3 in.

12. Reasoning A rectangular piece of cardboard with dimensions 6 inches by 8 inches is used to make the curved side of a cylinder-shaped container. Using this cardboard, what is the greatest volume the cylinder can hold? Explain. © MP.2

13. The cylinder shown has a volume of 885 cubic inches.

   a. What is the radius of the cylinder? Use 3.14 for π.

   b. **Reasoning** If the height of the cylinder is changed, but the volume stays the same, then how will the radius change? Explain. © MP.2

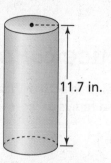

11.7 in.

14. Toy rubber balls are packaged in a cylinder that holds 3 balls. Find the volume of the cylinder. Use 3.14 for π, and round to the nearest tenth.

6.9 cm

20.7 cm

15. **Higher Order Thinking** An insulated collar is made to cover a pipe. Find the volume of the material used to make the collar. Let $r = 3$ inches, $R = 5$ inches, and $h = 21$ inches. Use 3.14 for π, and round to the nearest hundredth.

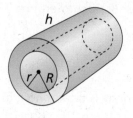

h

r R

Assessment Practice

16. The volume of a cylinder is $1,029\pi$ cubic centimeters. The height of the cylinder is 21 centimeters. What is the radius of the cylinder?

17. The diameter of a cylinder is 7 yards. The height is 12 yards. What is the volume of the cylinder?

 Go Online | PearsonRealize.com

Name: _____

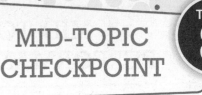
1. **Vocabulary** What is the difference between surface area and volume? *Lesson 8-1 and Lesson 8-2*

In **2–4**, use the figure at the right. Sallie packed a cone-shaped cup inside of a cylindrical package.

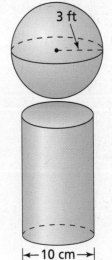

2. The cone-shaped cup is made out of paper. How much paper was used to make the cup, excluding the opening at the top of the cup? Write your answer in terms of π, and round to the nearest tenth. *Lesson 8-1*

3. The cylindrical package is made out of cardboard. In terms of π, how much cardboard was used to make the package? *Lesson 8-1*

4. How much space does the package occupy in terms of π? *Lesson 8-2*

5. What is the surface area of the sphere in terms of π? *Lesson 8-1*

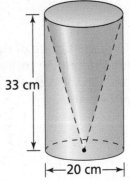

6. The volume of the cylinder is 400π cm³. What is the height of the cylinder? *Lesson 8-2*

Ⓐ 5 cm

Ⓑ 16 cm

Ⓒ 25 cm

Ⓓ 80 cm

How well did you do on the mid-topic checkpoint? Fill in the stars.

☆☆☆

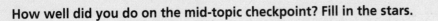

MID-TOPIC PERFORMANCE TASK

Melissa designed a sculpture in which a cylinder-shaped section was removed from a cube.

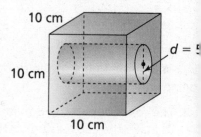

10 cm

10 cm

$d = 5$

10 cm

PART A

Before painting the surface of the sculpture, Melissa wants to sand the surface where the cylinder section was removed. What is the surface area of the section she will sand? Use 3.14 for π. Explain how you found the surface area.

PART B

Melissa has a can of spray paint that covers about 6,500 square centimeters. Can Melissa apply two coats of paint to the entire sculpture? Explain. Use 3.14 for π.

PART C

What is the volume of the sculpture? Use 3.14 for π.

 Go Online | PearsonRealize.com

👆 Solve & Discuss It!

ACTIVITY

A landscape architect uses molds for casting rectangular pyramids and rectangular prisms to make garden statues. He plans to place each finished pyramid on top of a prism. If one batch of concrete mix makes one prism or three pyramids, how does the volume of one pyramid compare to the volume of one prism? Explain.

I can...
find the volume of cones.

© **Common Core Content Standards**
8.G.C.9

Mathematical Practices
MP.1, MP.2, MP.7

Look for Relationships What do you notice about the dimensions of the bases of the pyramid and prism? How are the heights of the two solids related? © MP.7

Focus on math practices

Make Sense and Persevere If the architect mixes 10 batches of concrete, how many sculptures combining 1 prism and 1 pyramid could he make? Explain. © MP.1

INTERACTIVE ANIMATION

EXAMPLE 1 👁 Find the Volume of a Cone

Scan for Multimedia

Kiara is filling a cone-shaped pastry bag with frosting from a cylinder-shaped container. How much frosting can the pastry bag hold? How can Kiara determine how many times she can fill the pastry bag?

Look for Relationships How are a pyramid and a cone alike? How are they different? © MP.7

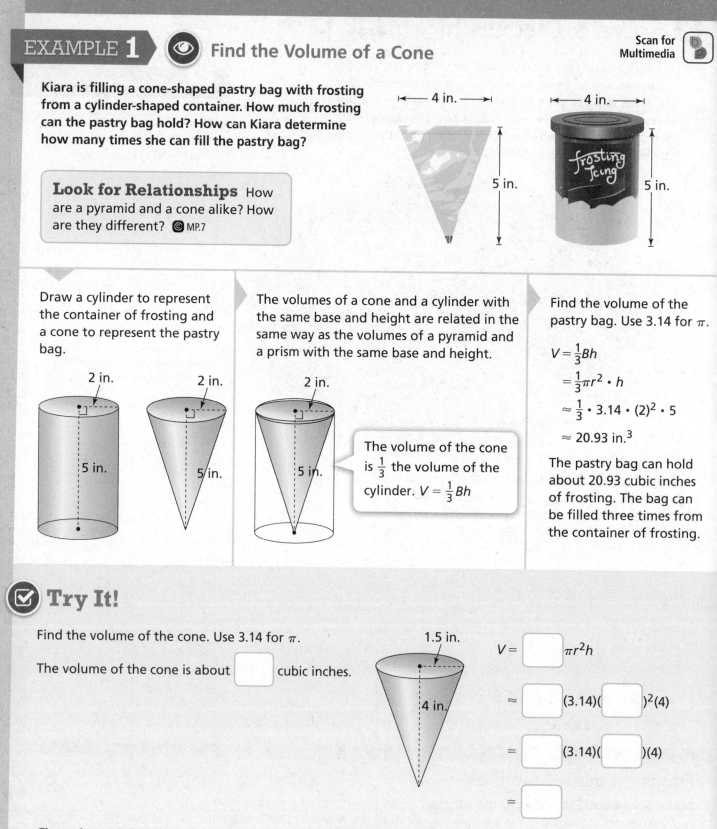

Draw a cylinder to represent the container of frosting and a cone to represent the pastry bag.

2 in.   2 in.

5 in.   5 in.

The volumes of a cone and a cylinder with the same base and height are related in the same way as the volumes of a pyramid and a prism with the same base and height.

2 in.

5 in.

The volume of the cone is $\frac{1}{3}$ the volume of the cylinder. $V = \frac{1}{3}Bh$

Find the volume of the pastry bag. Use 3.14 for π.

$V = \frac{1}{3}Bh$

$= \frac{1}{3}\pi r^2 \cdot h$

$\approx \frac{1}{3} \cdot 3.14 \cdot (2)^2 \cdot 5$

≈ 20.93 in.^{3}

The pastry bag can hold about 20.93 cubic inches of frosting. The bag can be filled three times from the container of frosting.

☑ **Try It!**

Find the volume of the cone. Use 3.14 for π.

The volume of the cone is about [ ] cubic inches.

1.5 in.

4 in.

$V = [\quad] \pi r^2 h$

$\approx [\quad] (3.14)([\quad])^2(4)$

$= [\quad] (3.14)([\quad])(4)$

$= [\quad]$

Convince Me! If you know the volume of a cone, how can you find the volume of a cylinder that has the same height and radius as the cone?

Go Online | PearsonRealize.com

EXAMPLE 2

Apply the Pythagorean Theorem to Solve Volume Problems

ACTIVITY   ASSESS

Midori has a cone full of birdseed to feed the birds at the park. What is the volume of the birdseed in the cone?

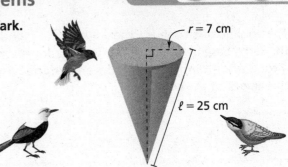

$r = 7$ cm

$\ell = 25$ cm

Look for Relationships How can you use the Pythagorean Theorem to find the height of the cone? © MP.7

STEP 1 Use the Pythagorean Theorem to find the height of the cone.

$$r^2 + h^2 = \ell^2$$
$$7^2 + h^2 = 25^2$$
$$49 + h^2 = 625$$
$$h^2 = 576$$
$$h = 24$$

The height of the cone is 24 centimeters.

STEP 2 Find the volume of the cone. Use $\frac{22}{7}$ for π.

$$V = \frac{1}{3}\pi r^2 h$$
$$= \frac{1}{3}\pi(7)^2(24)$$
$$\approx \frac{1}{3}\left(\frac{22}{7}\right)(49)(24)$$
$$= 1{,}232$$

Substitute the height of the cone from STEP 1.

The cone holds about 1,232 cubic centimeters of birdseed.

EXAMPLE 3

Find the Volume of a Cone Given the Circumference of the Base

The circumference of the base of a cone is 6π inches. What is the volume of the cone in terms of π?

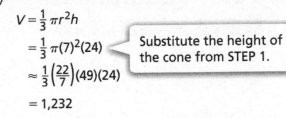

13 in.

STEP 1 Use the circumference to find the radius of the base of the cone.

$$C = 2\pi r$$
$$6\pi = 2\pi r$$
$$\frac{6\pi}{2\pi} = r$$
$$3 = r$$

Substitute 6π for the circumference C.

The radius of the cone is 3 inches.

STEP 2 Find the volume of the cone.

$$V = \frac{1}{3}\pi(3)^2(13)$$
$$= \frac{1}{3}\pi(9)(13)$$
$$= 39\pi$$

Substitute the radius of the cone from STEP 1.

The volume of the cone is 39π inches.

✓ Try It!

Find the volume of each cone.

a. Use $\frac{22}{7}$ for π. Express the answer as a fraction.

b. Express the volume in terms of π.

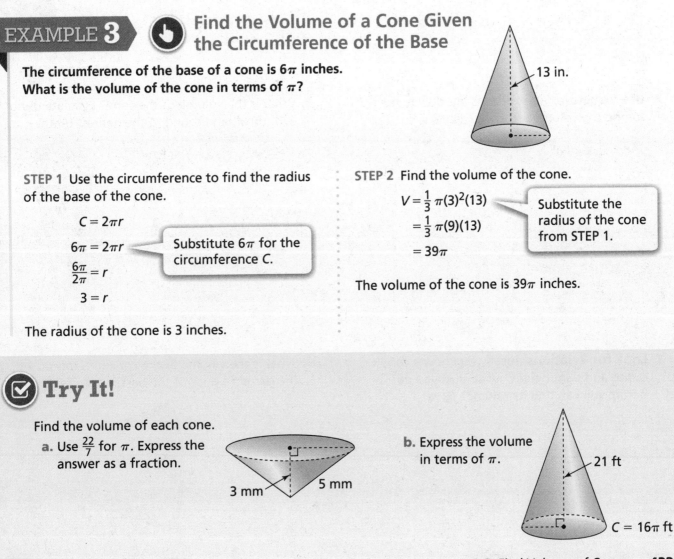

3 mm   5 mm

21 ft

$C = 16\pi$ ft

The volume of a cone is $\frac{1}{3}$ the volume of a cylinder with the same base and height. The formula for the volume of a cone is $V = \frac{1}{3}Bh$, where B is the area of the base and h is the height of the cone.

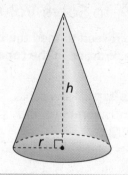

Do You Understand?

1. **Essential Question** How is the volume of a cone related to the volume of a cylinder?

2. **Use Structure** What dimensions do you need to find the volume of a cone? © MP.7

3. **Look for Relationships** If you know a cone's radius and slant height, what must you do before you can find its volume? © MP.7

Do You Know How?

4. Wanda found a cone-shaped seashell on the beach. The shell has a height of 63 millimeters and a base radius of 8 millimeters. What is the volume of the seashell? Estimate using $\frac{22}{7}$ for π.

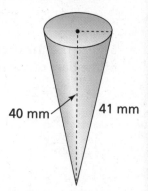

63 mm

8 mm

5. What is the volume of the cone? Estimate using 3.14 for π, and round to the nearest tenth.

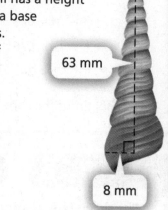

40 mm   41 mm

6. What is the volume of the cone in terms of π if the circumference of the base is 1.4π feet?

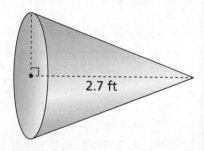

2.7 ft

Practice & Problem Solving

Leveled Practice In **7** and **8**, find the volumes of the cones.

7. What is the volume of the cone? Write your answer in terms of π.

$V = \frac{1}{3}\pi(\boxed{})^2(\boxed{})$

$V = \frac{1}{3}\pi(\boxed{})(\boxed{})$ 3 cm

$V = \frac{1}{3}\pi(\boxed{})$

$V = \boxed{}\pi$ cubic meters

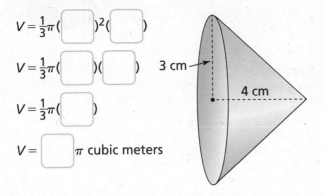

3 cm
4 cm

8. What is the volume of the cone to the nearest hundredth? Use 3.14 for π.

$V \approx \frac{1}{3}(3.14)(\boxed{})^2(\boxed{})$

$V = \frac{1}{3}(3.14)(\boxed{})(\boxed{})$

$V = \frac{1}{3}(\boxed{})$

$V = \boxed{}$ units^3

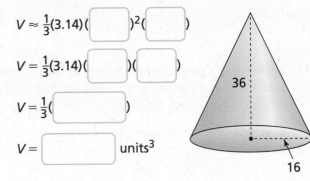

36
16

9. If a cone-shaped hole is 3 feet deep and the circumference of the base of the hole is 44 feet, what is the volume of the hole? Use $\frac{22}{7}$ for π.

10. The volume of the cone is 462 cubic yards. What is the radius of the cone? Use $\frac{22}{7}$ for π.

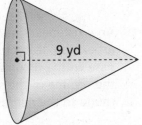

9 yd

11. A city engineer determines that 5,500 cubic meters of sand will be needed to treat the roadways this winter. Does the city have enough sand to treat the roadways? Use $\frac{22}{7}$ for π. Explain.

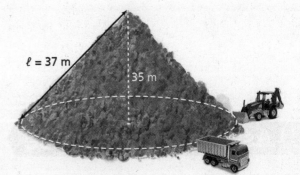

$\ell = 37$ m

35 m

12. A water tank is shaped like the cone shown.

a. How much water can the tank hold? Use 3.14 for π, and round to the nearest tenth.

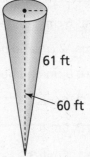

61 ft
60 ft

b. If water is drained from the tank to fill smaller tanks that each hold 500 cubic feet of water, how many smaller tanks can be filled?

13. An ice cream cone is filled exactly level with the top of a cone. The cone has a 9-centimeter depth and a base with a circumference of 9π centimeters. How much ice cream is in the cone in terms of π?

14. In the scale model of a park, small green cones represent trees. What is the volume of one green cone? Use $\frac{22}{7}$ for π.

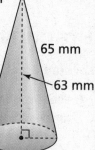

65 mm

63 mm

15. Reasoning Compare the volumes of two cones. One has a radius of 5 feet and a slant height of 13 feet. The other one has a height of 5 feet and a slant height of 13 feet. ⓒ MP.2

a. Which cone has the greater volume?

b. What is the volume of the larger cone in terms of π?

16. An artist makes a cone-shaped sculpture for an art exhibit. If the sculpture is 7 feet tall and has a base with a circumference of 24.492 feet, what is the volume of the sculpture? Use 3.14 for π, and round to the nearest hundredth.

17. Higher Order Thinking A cone has a radius of 3 and a height of 11.

a. Suppose the radius is increased by 4 times its original measure. How many times greater is the volume of the larger cone than the smaller cone?

b. How would the volume of the cone change if the radius were divided by four?

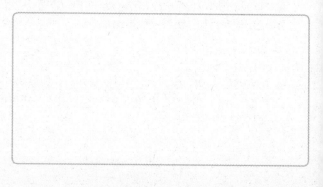

ⓒ Assessment Practice

18. List the cones described below in order from least volume to greatest volume.

- Cone 1: radius 6 cm and height 12 cm

- Cone 2: radius 12 cm and height 6 cm

- Cone 3: radius 9 cm and height 8 cm

Ⓐ Cone 2, Cone 3, Cone 1

Ⓑ Cone 1, Cone 3, Cone 2

Ⓒ Cone 2, Cone 1, Cone 3

Ⓓ Cone 1, Cone 2, Cone 3

19. What is the volume of a cone that has a radius of 8 inches and a height of 12 inches? Use 3.14 for π.

 Go Online | PearsonRealize.com

👆 Explore It!

Marshall uses the beaker to fill the bowl with water.

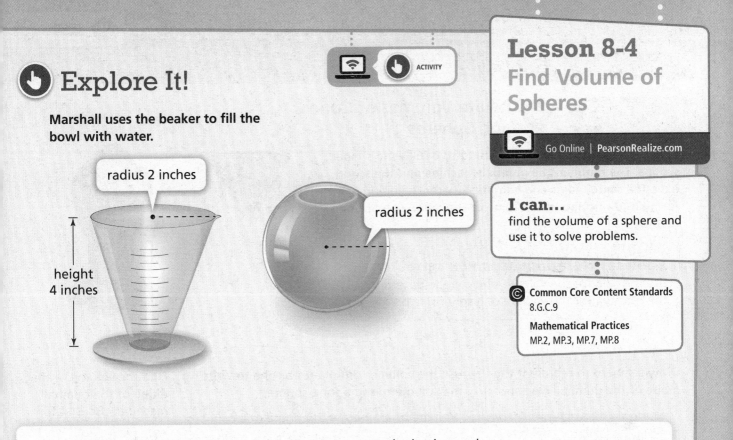

radius 2 inches

height 4 inches

radius 2 inches

I can...
find the volume of a sphere and use it to solve problems.

© **Common Core Content Standards**
8.G.C.9

Mathematical Practices
MP.2, MP.3, MP.7, MP.8

A. Draw and label three-dimensional figures to represent the beaker and the bowl.

B. Marshall has to fill the beaker twice to completely fill the bowl with water. How can you use an equation to represent the volume of the bowl?

Focus on math practices

Reasoning How are the volume of a sphere and the volume of a cone related? What must be true about the radius and height measurements for this relationships to be valid? © MP.2

? **Essential Question** How is the volume of a sphere related to the volume of a cone?

INTERACTIVE ANIMATION

EXAMPLE 1 👁 Relate Volumes of Cones and Spheres

Scan for Multimedia

Taye fills the gumball machine using two full cone-shaped scoops. The globe of the gumball machine and the scoop have the same radius and height. How can Taye find a formula to calculate the volume of the gumball machine globe?

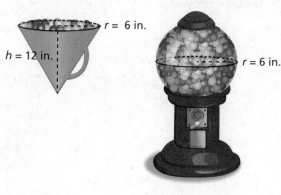
$r = 6$ in.
$h = 12$ in.
$r = 6$ in.

Look for Relationships How can you use the formula for the volume of a cone to determine the formula for the volume of a sphere? © MP.7

Draw a sphere to represent the globe of the gumball machine.

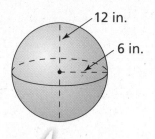
12 in.
6 in.

The volume of a sphere is the same as twice the volume of a cone with the same circular base and height.

Use the volume formula for a cone to write the volume formula for a sphere.

Volume of a sphere = 2(Volume of a cone)

$$V = 2\left(\tfrac{1}{3}Bh\right)$$

$$= 2\left(\tfrac{1}{3}\pi r^2 h\right)$$

$$= 2\left(\tfrac{1}{3}\pi r^2 \cdot 2r\right)$$

The height of a sphere is twice its radius.

$$= \tfrac{4}{3}\pi r^3$$

Generalize The formula for the volume of a sphere is $V = \tfrac{4}{3}\pi r^3$. © MP.8

Find the volume of the globe of the gumball machine. Use 3.14 for π.

$$V = \tfrac{4}{3}\pi r^3$$

$$= \tfrac{4}{3}\pi (6)^3$$

$$= \tfrac{4}{3}\pi (216)$$

$$= 288\pi$$

$$\approx 904.32$$

The volume of the globe is about 904.32 cubic inches.

☑ **Try It!**

What is the volume of a ball with a diameter of 6 centimeters? Use 3.14 for π.

Convince Me! How is the volume of a sphere related to the volume of a cone that has the same circular base and height?

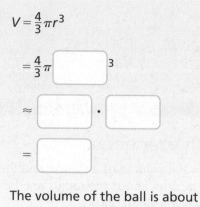

$$V = \tfrac{4}{3}\pi r^3$$

$$= \tfrac{4}{3}\pi \,\boxed{}^3$$

$$\approx \boxed{} \cdot \boxed{}$$

$$= \boxed{}$$

The volume of the ball is about $\boxed{}$ cm³.

EXAMPLE **2** 👆 **Find the Volume of a Sphere Given the Surface Area**

ACTIVITY   ASSESS

What is the volume of the soccer ball, rounded to the nearest whole number? Use 3.14 for π.

S.A. ≈ 1,519.76 cm²

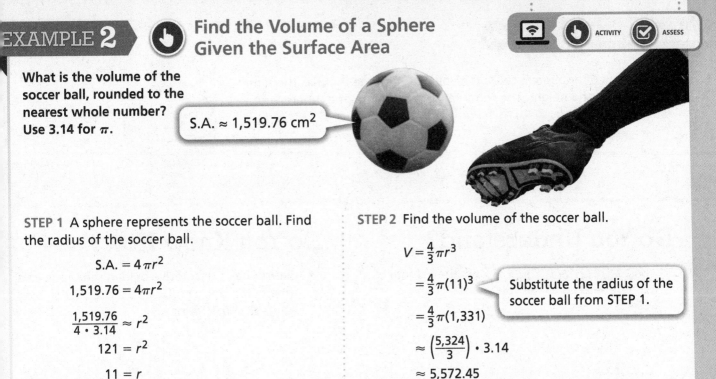

STEP 1 A sphere represents the soccer ball. Find the radius of the soccer ball.

$$S.A. = 4\pi r^2$$

$$1{,}519.76 = 4\pi r^2$$

$$\frac{1{,}519.76}{4 \cdot 3.14} \approx r^2$$

$$121 = r^2$$

$$11 = r$$

The radius is about 11 centimeters.

STEP 2 Find the volume of the soccer ball.

$$V = \frac{4}{3}\pi r^3$$

$$= \frac{4}{3}\pi(11)^3$$

Substitute the radius of the soccer ball from STEP 1.

$$= \frac{4}{3}\pi(1{,}331)$$

$$\approx \left(\frac{5{,}324}{3}\right) \cdot 3.14$$

$$\approx 5{,}572.45$$

The volume of the soccer ball is approximately 5,572 cubic centimeters.

EXAMPLE **3** 👆 **Find the Volume of a Composite Figure**

A composite figure is the combination of two or more figures into one object. A corn silo is an example of a composite figure in the shape of a cylinder with a hemisphere of the same diameter on top. The diameter of this silo is 4 meters. How many cubic meters of corn can be stored in the silo? Use 3.14 for π.

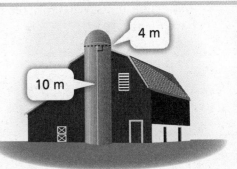

4 m

10 m

STEP 1 Find the volume of the hemisphere.

$$V = \frac{1}{2} \cdot \frac{4}{3}\pi r^3$$

A hemisphere is half of a sphere.

$$= \frac{1}{2} \cdot \frac{4}{3}\pi(2)^3$$

$$= \frac{1}{2} \cdot \frac{4}{3}(8)\pi$$

$$= \frac{16}{3}\pi$$

The volume of the hemisphere is $\frac{16}{3}\pi$ cubic meters.

STEP 2 Find the volume of the cylinder.

$$V = \pi r^2 h$$

$$= \pi(2)^2(10)$$

$$= \pi(4)(10)$$

$$= 40\pi$$

The volume of the cylinder is 40π m³.

STEP 3 Add the volumes.

$$\frac{16}{3}\pi + 40\pi = \frac{136}{3}\pi \approx 142.3$$

The volume of the silo is about 142.3 cubic meters.

✅ **Try It!**

What is the volume of the composite figure shown? Use 3.14 for π.

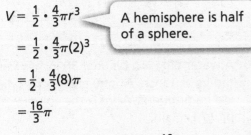

2 in.

6 in.

The volume of a sphere is twice the volume of a cone that has the same circular base and height. The formula for the volume of a sphere with radius r is $V = \frac{4}{3}\pi r^3$.

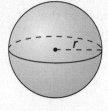

Do You Understand?

1. ⬤ **Essential Question** How is the volume of a sphere related to the volume of a cone?

2. Critique Reasoning Kristy incorrectly says that the volume of the sphere below is 144π cubic units. What mistake might Kristy have made? © MP.3

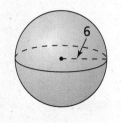

3. Generalize Mehnaj has a set of blocks that are all the same height. The cone-shaped block has a volume of 125 cubic inches. The sphere-shaped block has a volume of 250 cubic inches. What do you know about the radius of the base of the cone-shaped block? Explain. © MP.8

Do You Know How?

4. Clarissa has a decorative bulb in the shape of a sphere. If it has a radius of 3 inches, what is its volume? Use 3.14 for π.

5. A sphere has a surface area of about 803.84 square centimeters. What is the volume of the sphere? Use 3.14 for π and round to the nearest whole number.

6. A water pipe is a cylinder 30 inches long, with a radius of 1 inch. At one end of the cylinder there is a hemisphere. What is the volume of the water pipe? Explain.

Name: _____

7. **Leveled Practice** What is the amount of air, in cubic centimeters, needed to fill the stability ball? Use 3.14 for π, and round to the nearest whole number.

Use the formula $V = \frac{4}{3}\pi r^3$.

$$V = \frac{4}{3}\pi\left(\right)^3$$

$$V = \frac{4}{3}\pi\left(\right)$$

$$V \approx \frac{4}{3}\left(\right)\left(\right)$$

$$V \approx $$

55 cm

The volume of the stability ball is approximately [ ] cubic centimeters.

8. A spherical balloon has a 22-inch. diameter when it is fully inflated. Half of the air is let out of the balloon. Assume that the balloon remains a sphere. Keep all answers in terms of π.

   a. Find the volume of the fully-inflated balloon.

   b. Find the volume of the half-inflated balloon.

   c. What is the radius of the half-inflated balloon? Round to the nearest tenth.

9. Find the volume of the figure. Use 3.14 for π, and round to the nearest whole number.

|← 14 cm →|

17 cm

10. The surface area of a sphere is about 2,826 square millimeters. What is the volume of the sphere? Use 3.14 for π, and round to the nearest whole number.

11. A sphere has a volume of 1,837.35 cubic centimeters. What is the radius of the sphere? Use 3.14 for π, and round to the nearest tenth.

12. Find the volume of the solid. Use 3.14 for π, and round to the nearest whole number.

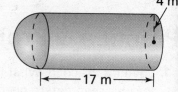

4 m

17 m

13. Your friend says that the volume of a sphere with a diameter of 3.4 meters is 164.55 cubic meters. What mistake might your friend have made? Find the correct volume. Use 3.14 for π and round to the nearest hundredth. © MP.3

14. A solid figure has a cone and hemisphere hollowed out of it. What is the volume of the remaining part of the solid? Use 3.14 for π, and round to the nearest whole number.

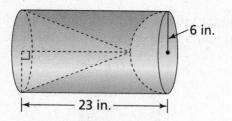

6 in.

23 in.

15. Higher Order Thinking A student was asked to find the volume of a solid where the inner cylinder is hollow. She incorrectly said the volume is 2,034.72 cubic inches.

a. Find the volume of the solid. Use 3.14 for π. Round to the nearest whole number.

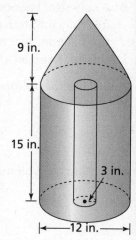

9 in.

15 in.

3 in.

12 in.

b. What mistake might the student have made?

© **Assessment Practice**

16. A spherical boulder is 20 feet in diameter and weighs almost 8 tons. Find its volume. Use 3.14 for π. Round to the nearest whole number.

17. A bowl is in the shape of a hemisphere (half a sphere) with a diameter of 13 inches. Find the volume of the bowl. Use 3.14 for π, and round to the nearest whole number.

Measure Up

3-Act Mathematical Modeling:
Measure Up

🛜 Go Online | PearsonRealize.com

ⓒ **Common Core Content Standards**
8.G.C.9

Mathematical Practices
MP.4

ACT 1

1. After watching the video, what is the first question that comes to mind?

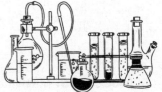

2. Write the Main Question you will answer.

3. Construct Arguments Predict an answer to this Main Question. Explain your prediction. ⓒ MP.3

4. On the number line below, write a number that is too small to be the answer. Write a number that is too large.

Too small   Too large

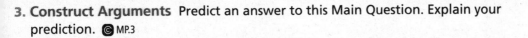

5. Plot your prediction on the same number line.

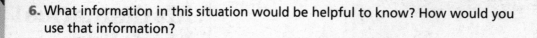

6. What information in this situation would be helpful to know? How would you use that information?

7. Use Appropriate Tools What tools can you use to get the information you need? Record the information as you find it. © MP.5

8. Model with Math Represent the situation using the mathematical content, concepts, and skills from this topic. Use your representation to answer the Main Question. © MP.4

9. What is your answer to the Main Question? Is it higher or lower than your prediction? Explain why.

Go Online | **PearsonRealize.com**

10. Write the answer you saw in the video.

11. Reasoning Does your answer match the answer in the video? If not, what are some reasons that would explain the difference? © MP.2

12. Make Sense and Persevere Would you change your model now that you know the answer? Explain. © MP.1

Reflect

13. Model with Math Explain how you used a mathematical model to represent the situation. How did the model help you answer the Main Question? © MP.4

14. Make Sense and Persevere When did you struggle most while solving the problem? How did you overcome that obstacle? © MP.1

15. Generalize Suppose you have a graduated cylinder half the height of the one in the video. How wide does the cylinder need to be to hold the liquid in the flask? © MP.8

? Topic Essential Question

How can you find volumes and surface areas of three-dimensional figures?

Vocabulary Review

Complete each definition and then provide an example of each vocabulary word.

Vocabulary   composite figure   cone   cylinder   sphere

Definition	Example
1. A three-dimensional figure with two identical circular bases is a [ ].	
2. A three-dimensional figure with one circular base and one vertex is a [ ].	
3. A [ ] is the set of all points in space that are the same distance from a center point.	
4. A [ ] is the combination of two or more figures into one object.	

Use Vocabulary in Writing

Draw a composite figure that includes any two of the following: a cylinder, a cone, a sphere, and a hemisphere. Label each part of your drawing. Then describe each part of your composite figure. Use vocabulary terms in your description.

Concepts and Skills Review

Quick Review

Surface area is the total area of the surfaces of a three-dimensional figure. The chart gives formulas for finding the surface area of a cylinder, a cone, and a sphere.

Shape	3-D Model	Surface Area Formula
cylinder		$S.A. = 2\pi r^2 + 2\pi rh$
cone		$S.A. = \pi r\ell + \pi r^2$
sphere		$S.A. = 4\pi r^2$

Example

What is the surface area of the cylinder? Use 3.14 for π.

> Radius, $r = \frac{10}{2} = 5$. Substitute 5 for r and 15 for h.

$S.A. = 2\pi r^2 + 2\pi rh$

$= 2\pi(5)^2 + 2\pi(5)(15)$

$= 50\pi + 150\pi$

$= 200\pi \approx 628 \text{ cm}^2$

15 cm

← 10 cm →

Practice

1. What is the surface area of the cone? Use 3.14 for π.

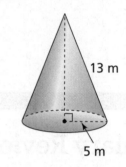

13 m

5 m

2. What is the surface area of the sphere in terms of π?

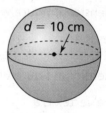

$d = 10$ cm

3. What is the surface area of the cylinder in terms of π?

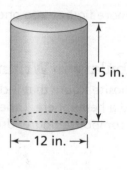

15 in.

← 12 in. →

 Go Online | PearsonRealize.com

Quick Review

The volume of a cylinder is equal to the area of its base times its height.

V = area of base • height, or $V = \pi r^2 h$

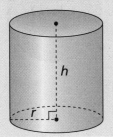

Example

What is the volume of the cylinder? Use 3.14 for π.

> Radius, $r = \frac{40}{2} = 20$. Substitute 20 for r and 60 for h.

$V = \pi r^2 h$

$= \pi(20)^2(60)$

$= 24{,}000\pi \approx 75{,}360$ cm^3

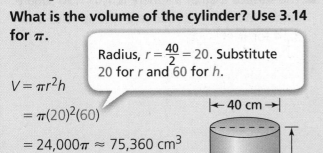

|← 40 cm →|

60 cm

Practice

1. What is the volume of the cylinder in terms of π?

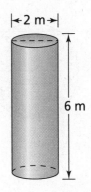

|← 2 m →|

6 m

2. The volume of the cylinder is 141.3 cubic centimeters. What is the radius of the cylinder? Use 3.14 for π.

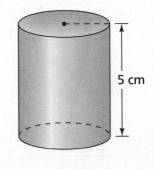

5 cm

Quick Review

To find the volume of a cone, use the formula $V = \frac{1}{3}\pi r^2 h$.

Example

What is the volume of the cone? Use 3.14 for π.

> Substitute 6 for r and 9 for h.

$V = \frac{1}{3}\pi r^2 h$

$= \frac{1}{3}\pi(6)^2(9)$

$= 108\pi \approx 339.12$ in.^{3}

9 in.

6 in.

Practice

1. What is the volume of the cone in terms of π?

8 in.

3 in.

2. What is the volume of the cone? Use 3.14 for π.

5 cm

4 cm

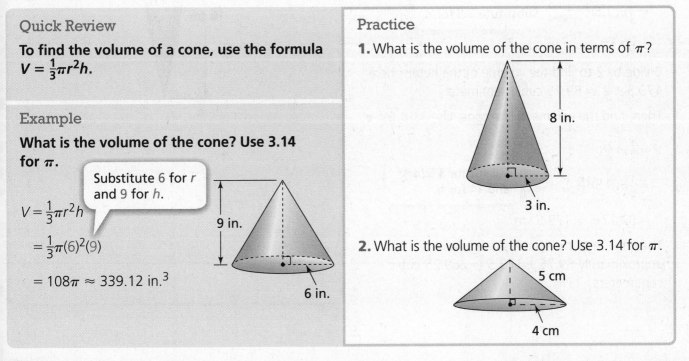

**Find Volume of Spheres**

Quick Review

To find the volume of a sphere, use the formula $V = \frac{4}{3}\pi r^3$.

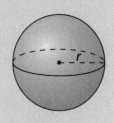

Example

Find the volume of the composite figure. Use 3.14 for π.

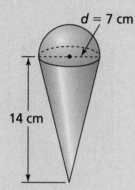

$d = 7$ cm

14 cm

First, find the volume of the sphere. Use 3.14 for π.

$V = \frac{4}{3}\pi r^3$

$= \frac{4}{3}\pi (3.5)^3$ ← Substitute 3.5 for r.

$= 57.17\pi \approx 179.5$ cm^3

Divide by 2 to find the volume of the hemisphere: $179.5 \div 2 \approx 89.75$ cubic centimeters.

Then, find the volume of the cone. Use 3.14 for π.

$V = \frac{1}{3}\pi r^2 h$

$= \frac{1}{3}\pi (3.5)^2 (14)$ ← Substitute 3.5 for r and 14 for h.

$= 57.17\pi \approx 179.5$ cm^3

The volume of the composite figure is approximately $89.75 + 179.5 \approx 269.25$ cubic centimeters.

Practice

1. What is the volume of the sphere? Use $\frac{22}{7}$ for π.

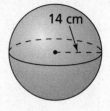

14 cm

2. The surface area of a sphere is 1,017.36 square inches. What is the volume of the sphere? Use 3.14 for π.

3. What is the volume of the composite figure? Use 3.14 for π.

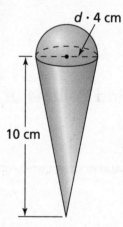

$d \cdot 4$ cm

10 cm

Go Online | PearsonRealize.com

Hidden Clue

For each ordered pair, solve the equation to find the unknown coordinate. Then locate and label the corresponding point on the graph. Draw line segments to connect the points in alphabetical order. Use the completed picture to help answer the riddle below.

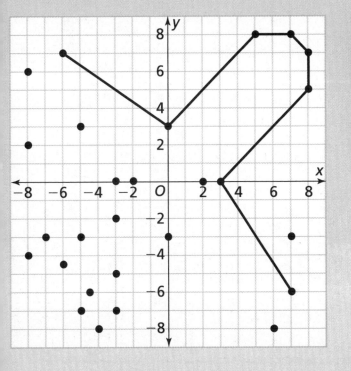

What do squares, triangles, pentagons, and octagons have in common?

A $(-13 + 6x = -x + 36, -6)$ ☐, −6

B $(\frac{2}{3}x + 1 = 5, -8)$ ☐, −8

C $(0, 2.5y - 2.3 = -9.8)$ 0, ☐

D $(-3, 1.4 - 0.7y = -1.2y - 1.1)$ −3, ☐

E $(3(x + 5) = 6, -7)$ ☐, −7

F $(23 - \frac{1}{2}x = 25, -8)$ ☐, −8

G $(-4.5, 6y + 1 - 3y = -17)$ −4.5, ☐

H $(-6, y + 6 - 3y = 15)$ −6, ☐

I $(-8, -6y - y = -2(y - 10))$ −8, ☐

J $(-7, \frac{1}{2}y + 11 + \frac{1}{6}y = 9)$ −7, ☐

K $(4x + 7 - x = -8, -3)$ ☐, −3

L $(-3, 7y + 11 = 4y + 11)$ −3, ☐

M $(1.5x + 6.8 = -5.2, 6)$ ☐, 6

N $(-2(3x + 4) = -5x - 2, 7)$ ☐, 7

GLOSSARY

ENGLISH

A

alternate interior angles Alternate interior angles lie within a pair of lines and on opposite sides of a transversal.

Example ∠1 and ∠4 are alternate interior angles. ∠2 and ∠3 are also alternate interior angles.

angle of rotation The angle of rotation is the number of degrees a figure is rotated.

Example The angle of rotation is 180°.

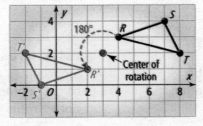

C

categorical data Categorical data consist of data that fall into categories.

Example Data collected about gender is an example of categorical data because the data have values that fall into the categories "male" and "female."

center of rotation The center of rotation is a fixed point about which a figure is rotated.

Example *O* is the center of rotation.

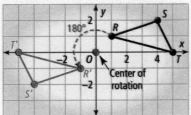

SPANISH

ángulos alternos internos Los ángulos alternos internos están ubicados dentro de un par de rectas y a lados opuestos de una secante.

ángulo de rotación El ángulo de rotación es el número de grados que se rota una figura.

datos por categorías Los datos por categorías son datos que se pueden clasificar en categorías.

centro de rotación El centro de rotación es el punto fijo alrededor del cual se rota una figura.

ENGLISH

SPANISH

cluster A cluster is a group of points that lie close together on a scatter plot.

grupo Un grupo es un conjunto de puntos que están agrupados en un diagrama de dispersión.

Example This graph shows two clusters.

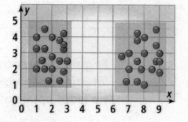

composite figure A composite figure is the combination of two or more figures into one object.

figura compuesta Una figura compuesta es la combinación de dos o más figuras en un objeto.

cone A cone is a three-dimensional figure with one circular base and one vertex.

cono Un cono es una figura tridimensional con una base circular y un vértice.

Example

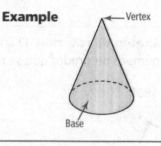

congruent figures Two two-dimensional figures are congruent (≅) if the second can be obtained from the first by a sequence of rotations, reflections, and translations.

figuras congruentes Dos figuras bidimensionales son congruentes ≅ si la segunda puede obtenerse a partir de la primera mediante una secuencia de rotaciones, reflexiones y traslaciones.

Example △SRQ ≅ △ABC

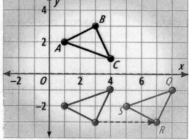

ENGLISH	SPANISH
converse of the Pythagorean Theorem If the sum of the squares of the lengths of two sides of a triangle equals the square of the length of the third side, then the triangle is a right triangle. If $a^2 + b^2 = c^2$, then the triangle is a right triangle.	**expresión recíproca del Teorema de Pitágoras** Si la suma del cuadrado de la longitud de dos lados de un triángulo es igual al cuadrado de la longitud del tercer lado, entonces el triángulo es un triángulo rectángulo. Si $a^2 + b^2 = c^2$, entonces el triángulo es un triángulo rectángulo.

Example Since $3^2 + 4^2 = 25$, or 5^2, the triangle is a right triangle.

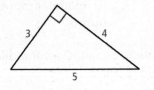

| **corresponding angles** Corresponding angles lie on the same side of a transversal and in corresponding positions. | **ángulos correspondientes** Los ángulos correspondientes se ubican al mismo lado de una secante y en posiciones correspondientes. |

Example $\angle 1$ and $\angle 3$ are corresponding angles. $\angle 2$ and $\angle 4$ are also corresponding angles.

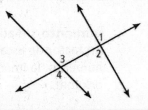

| **cube root** The cube root of a number, n, is a number whose cube equals n. | **raíz cúbica** La raíz cúbica de un número, n, es un número que elevado al cubo es igual a n. |

Example The cube root of 27 is 3 because $3 \cdot 3 \cdot 3 = 27$. The cube root of -27 is -3 because $(-3) \cdot (-3) \cdot (-3) = -27$.

| **cylinder** A cylinder is a three-dimensional figure with two parallel circular bases that are the same size. | **cilindro** Un cilindro es una figura tridimensional con dos bases circulares paralelas que tienen el mismo tamaño. |

Example

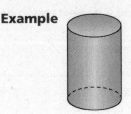

ENGLISH

SPANISH

D

dilation A dilation is a transformation that moves each point along the ray through the point, starting from a fixed center, and multiplies distances from the center by a common scale factor. If a vertex of a figure is the center of dilation, then the vertex and its image after the dilation are the same point.

dilatación Una dilatación es una transformación que mueve cada punto a lo largo de la semirrecta a través del punto, a partir de un centro fijo, y multiplica las distancias desde el centro por un factor de escala común. Si un vértice de una figura es el centro de dilatación, entonces el vértice y su imagen después de la dilatación son el mismo punto.

Example △$A'B'C'$ is the image of △ABC after a dilation with center A and scale factor 2.

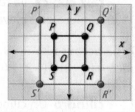

E

enlargement An enlargement is a dilation with a scale factor greater than 1. After an enlargement, the image is bigger than the original figure.

aumento Un aumento es una dilatación con un factor de escala mayor que 1. Después de un aumento, la imagen es más grande que la figura original.

Example The dilation is an enlargement with scale factor 2.

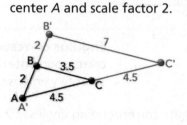

exterior angle of a triangle An exterior angle of a triangle is an angle formed by a side and an extension of an adjacent side.

ángulo externo de un triángulo Un ángulo externo de un triángulo es un ángulo formado por un lado y una extensión de un lado adyacente.

Example ∠1 is an exterior angle of △ABC.

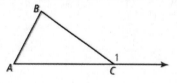

ENGLISH

SPANISH

(F)

function A function is a rule for taking each input value and producing exactly one output value.

función Una función es una regla por la cual se toma cada valor de entrada y se produce exactamente un valor de salida.

(G)

gap A gap is an area of a graph that contains no data points.

espacio vacío o brecha Un espacio vacío o brecha es un área de una gráfica que no contiene ningún valor.

Example This graph shows one gap.

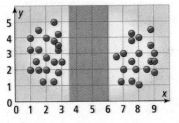

(H)

hypotenuse In a right triangle, the longest side, which is opposite the right angle, is the hypotenuse.

hipotenusa En un triángulo rectángulo, el lado más largo, que es opuesto al ángulo recto, es la hipotenusa.

Example

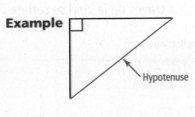

(I)

image An image is the result of a transformation of a point, line, or figure.

imagen Una imagen es el resultado de una transformación de un punto, una recta o una figura.

Example

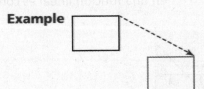

The blue figure is the image of the black figure.

initial value The initial value of a linear function is the value of the output when the input is 0.

valor inicial El valor inicial de una función lineal es el valor de salida cuando el valor de entrada es 0.

Example The initial value of the function $y = 2x + 4$ is 4 because when $x = 0$, $y = 2(0) + 4 = 4$.

ENGLISH	SPANISH
interval An interval is a period of time between two points of time or events.	**intervalo** Un intervalo es un período de tiempo entre dos puntos en el tiempo o entre dos sucesos.

Example A 3-hour interval is between 2:00 PM and 5:00 PM.

irrational numbers An irrational number is a number that cannot be written in the form $\frac{a}{b}$, where a and b are integers and $b \neq 0$. In decimal form, an irrational number cannot be written as a terminating or repeating decimal.	**números irracionales** Un número irracional es un número que no se puede escribir en la forma $\frac{a}{b}$ donde a y b, son enteros y $b \neq 0$. Los números racionales en forma decimal no son finitos y no son periódicos.

Example The numbers π and $\sqrt{2}$ are irrational numbers.

L

leg of a right triangle In a right triangle, the two shortest sides are legs.	**cateto de un triángulo rectángulo** En un triángulo rectángulo, los dos lados más cortos son los catetos.

Example

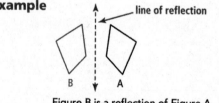

line of reflection A line of reflection is a line across which a figure is reflected.	**eje de reflexión** Un eje de reflexión es una línea a través de la cual se refleja una figura.

Example

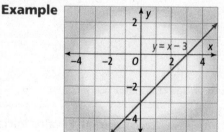

Figure B is a reflection of Figure A.

linear function A linear function is a function whose graph is a straight line. The rate of change for a linear function is constant.	**función lineal** Una función lineal es una función cuya gráfica es una línea recta. La tasa de cambio en una función lineal es constante.

Example

Go Online | PearsonRealize.com

ENGLISH	SPANISH

measurement data Measurement data consist of data that are measures.

datos de mediciones Los datos de mediciones son datos que son medidas.

Example Data collected about heights are an example of measurement data because the data are measures, such as 62 inches or 5 ft 2 inches.

N

negative association There is a negative association between two data sets if the *y*-values tend to decrease as the *x*-values increase.

asociación negativa Existe una asociación negativa entre dos conjuntos de datos si los valores de *y* tienden a disminuir mientras de los valores de *x* a aumentar.

Example

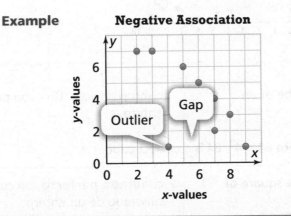

Negative Association

negative exponent property For every nonzero number *a* and integer *n*, $a^{-n} = \frac{1}{a^n}$.

propiedad del exponente negativo Para todo número distinto de cero *a* y entero *n*, $a^{-n} = \frac{1}{a^n}$.

Example $8^{-5} = \frac{1}{8^5}$

nonlinear function A nonlinear function is a function that does not have a constant rate of change.

función no lineal Una función no lineal es una función que no tiene una tasa de cambio constante.

Example

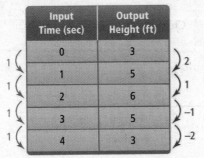

ENGLISH

O

outlier An outlier is a piece of data that doesn't seem to fit with the rest of a data set.

Example This data set has two outliers.

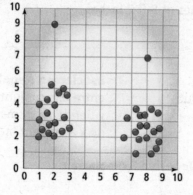

SPANISH

valor extremo Un valor extremo es un valor que parece no ajustarse al resto de los datos de un conjunto.

P

perfect cube A perfect cube is the cube of an integer.

Example Since $64 = 4^3$, 64 is a perfect cube.

cubo perfecto Un cubo perfecto es el cubo de un entero.

---

perfect square A perfect square is the square of an integer.

Example Since $25 = 5^2$, 25 is a perfect square.

cuadrado perfecto Un cuadrado perfecto es el cuadrado de un entero.

---

positive association There is a positive association between two data sets if the y-values tend to increase as the x-values increase.

asociación positiva Existe una asociación positiva entre dos conjuntos de datos si los valores de y tienden a aumentar mientras de los valores de x a aumentar.

Example

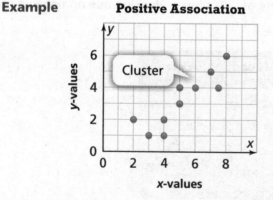

---

power of powers property To find the power of a power, keep the base and multiply the exponents.

propiedad de la potencia de una potencia Para hallar la potencia de una potencia, se deja la misma base y se multiplican los exponentes.

ENGLISH	SPANISH
power of products property To multiply two powers with the same exponent and different bases, multiply the bases and keep the exponent.	**propiedad de la potencia de productos** Para multiplicar dos potencias que tienen el mismo exponente y bases diferentes, se multiplican las bases y se deja el mismo exponente.
product of powers property To multiply two powers with the same base, keep the common base and add the exponents.	**propiedad del producto de potencias** Para multiplicar dos potencias con la misma base, se deja la misma base y se suman los exponentes.
proof A proof is a logical, deductive argument in which every statement of fact is supported by a reason.	**comprobación** Una comprobación es un argumento lógico y deductivo en el que cada enunciado de un hecho está apoyado por una razón.
Pythagorean Theorem In any right triangle, the sum of the squares of the lengths of the legs equals the square of the length of the hypotenuse. If a triangle is a right triangle, then $a^2 + b^2 = c^2$, where a and b represent the lengths of the legs, and c represents the length of the hypotenuse.	**Teorema de Pitágoras** En cualquier triángulo rectángulo, la suma del cuadrado de la longitud de los catetos es igual al cuadrado de la longitud de la hipotenusa. Si un triángulo es un triángulo rectángulo, entonces $a^2 + b^2 = c^2$, donde a y b representan la longitud de los catetos, y c representa la longitud de la hipotenusa.

Example $6^2 + 8^2 = 10^2$

Q

qualitative graph A qualitative graph is a graph that represents important qualities or features of situations without using quantities, or numbers.	**gráfica cualitativa** Gráfica que representa cualidades o atributos importantes de una situación sin usar cantidades o números.
quotient of powers property To divide two powers with the same base, keep the common base and subtract the exponents.	**propiedad del cociente de potencias** Para dividir dos potencias con la misma base, se deja la misma base y se restan los exponentes.

R

rate of change The rate of change of a linear function is the ratio $\frac{\text{vertical change}}{\text{horizontal change}}$ between any two points on the graph of the function.	**tasa de cambio** La tasa de cambio de una función lineal es la razón del $\frac{\text{cambio vertical}}{\text{cambio horizontal}}$ que existe entre dos puntos cualesquiera de la gráfica de la función.

Example The rate of change of the function $y = \frac{2}{3}x + 5$ is $\frac{2}{3}$.

ENGLISH

reduction A reduction is a dilation with a scale factor less than 1. After a reduction, the image is smaller than the original figure.

Example The dilation is a reduction with scale factor $\frac{1}{2}$.

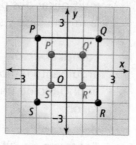

reflection A reflection, or flip, is a transformation that flips a figure across a line of reflection.

Example

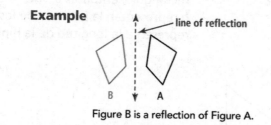

Figure B is a reflection of Figure A.

relation Any set of ordered pairs is called a relation.

Example {(0, 0), (1, 8), (2, 16), (3, 24), (4, 32)}

relative frequency table A relative frequency table shows the ratio of the number of data in each category to the total number of data items. The ratio can be expressed as a fraction, decimal, or percent.

Example

Cars in Parking Lot

Color	Relative Frequency
Red	45%
Blue	25%
Silver	30%
Total	100%

SPANISH

reducción Una reducción es una dilatación con un factor de escala menor que 1. Después de una reducción, la imagen es más pequeña que la figura original.

reflexión Una reflexión, o inversión, es una transformación que invierte una figura a través de un eje de reflexión.

relación Todo conjunto de pares ordenados se llama relación.

mesa relativa de frecuencia Una mesa relativa de la frecuencia muestra la proporción del número de datos en cada categoría al número total de artículos de datos. La proporción puede ser expresada como una fracción, el decimal, o el por ciento.

ENGLISH

SPANISH

remote interior angles Remote interior angles are the two nonadjacent interior angles corresponding to each exterior angle of a triangle.

ángulos internos no adyacentes Los ángulos internos no adyacentes son los dos ángulos internos de un triángulo que se corresponden con el ángulo externo que está más alejado de ellos.

Example ∠1 and ∠2 are remote interior angles of ∠3.

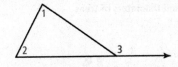

rotation A rotation is a rigid motion that turns a figure around a fixed point, called the center of rotation.

rotación Una rotación es un movimiento rígido que hace girar una figura alrededor de un punto fijo, llamado centro de rotación.

Example A rotation about the origin maps triangle *RST* to triangle *R'S'T'*.

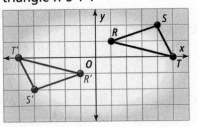

same-side interior angles Same-side interior angles are in the interior of two lines on the same side of a transversal.

ángulos internos del mismo lado Los ángulos internos del mismo lado se ubican dentro de dos rectas que están del mismo lado de una secante.

scale factor The scale factor is the ratio of a length in the image to the corresponding length in the original figure.

factor de escala El factor de escala es la razón de una longitud de la imagen a la longitud correspondiente en la figura original.

Example △*A'B'C'* is a dilation of △*ABC* with center *A*. The scale factor is 4.

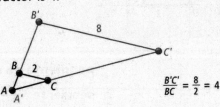

$$\frac{B'C'}{BC} = \frac{8}{2} = 4$$

ENGLISH

SPANISH

scatter plot A scatter plot is a graph that uses points to display the relationship between two different sets of data. Each point can be represented by an ordered pair.

diagrama de dispersión Un diagrama de dispersión es una gráfica que usa puntos para mostrar la relación entre dos conjuntos de datos diferentes. Cada punto se puede representar con un par ordenado.

Example

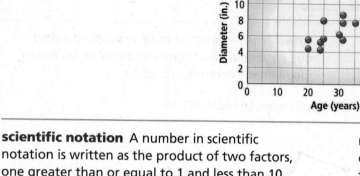

Ages and Diameters of Trees

scientific notation A number in scientific notation is written as the product of two factors, one greater than or equal to 1 and less than 10, and the other a power of 10.

notación científica Un número en notación científica está escrito como el producto de dos factores, uno mayor que o igual a 1 y menor que 10, y el otro una potencia de 10.

Example 37,000,000 is $3.7 \cdot 10^7$ in scientific notation.

similar figures A two-dimensional figure is similar (~) to another two-dimensional figure if you can map one figure to the other by a sequence of rotations, reflections, translations, and dilations.

figuras semejantes Una figura bidimensional es semejante (~) a otra figura bidimensional si puedes hacer corresponder una figura con otra mediante una secuencia de rotaciones, reflexiones, traslaciones y dilataciones.

Example Rectangle *ABCD* ~ Rectangle *EFGH*

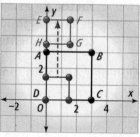

slope of a line

$$\text{slope} = \frac{\text{change in } y\text{-coordinates}}{\text{change in } x\text{-coordinates}} = \frac{\text{rise}}{\text{run}}$$

pendiente de una recta

$$\text{pendiente} = \frac{\text{cambio en las coordenadas } y}{\text{cambio en las coordenadas } x}$$
$$= \frac{\text{distancia vertical}}{\text{distancia horizontal}}$$

Example The slope of the line is $\frac{2}{4} = \frac{1}{2}$.

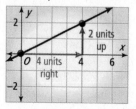

 Go Online | PearsonRealize.com

ENGLISH	SPANISH

slope-intercept form An equation written in the form $y = mx + b$ is in slope-intercept form. The graph is a line with slope m and y-intercept b.

forma pendiente-intercepto Una ecuación escrita en la forma $y = mx + b$ está en forma de pendiente-intercepto. La gráfica es una línea recta con pendiente m e intercepto en y b.

Example The equation $y = 2x + 1$ is written in slope-intercept form with slope 2 and y-intercept 1.

---

solution of a system of linear equations A solution of a system of linear equations is any ordered pair that makes all the equations of that system true.

solución de un sistema de ecuaciones lineales Una solución de un sistema de ecuaciones lineales es cualquier par ordenado que hace que todas las ecuaciones de ese sistema sean verdaderas.

Example $(-4, -11)$ is the solution of $y = 3x + 1$ and $y = 2x - 3$ because it makes both equations true.

---

sphere A sphere is the set of all points in space that are the same distance from a center point.

esfera Una esfera es el conjunto de todos los puntos en el espacio que están a la misma distancia de un punto central.

Example

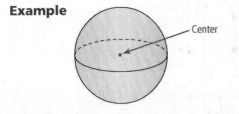

Center

---

square root A square root of a number is a number that, when multiplied by itself, equals the original number.

raíz cuadrada La raíz cuadrada de un número es un número que, cuando se multiplica por sí mismo, es igual al número original.

Example $\sqrt{9} = 3$, because $3^2 = 9$.

---

system of linear equations A system of linear equations is formed by two or more linear equations that use the same variables.

sistema de ecuaciones lineales Un sistema de ecuaciones lineales está formado por dos o más ecuaciones lineales que usan las mismas variables.

Example $y = 3x + 1$ and $y = 2x - 3$ form a system of linear equations.

T

theorem A theorem is a conjecture that is proven.

teorema Un teorema es una conjetura que se ha comprobado.

Example The Pythagorean Theorem states that in any right triangle, the sum of the squares of the lengths of the legs equals the square of the length of the hypotenuse.

ENGLISH

transformation A transformation is a change in position, shape, or size of a figure. Three types of transformations that change position only are translations, reflections, and rotations.

Example

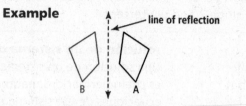

Figure B is a reflection, or flip, of Figure A.

translation A translation, or slide, is a rigid motion that moves every point of a figure the same distance and in the same direction.

Example A translation 5 units down and 3 units to the right maps square *ABCD* to square *A'B'C'D*.

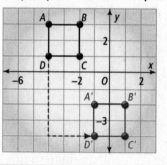

transversal A transversal is a line that intersects two or more lines at different points.

Example

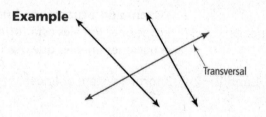

Transversal

SPANISH

transformación Una transformación es un cambio en la posición, la forma o el tamaño de una figura. Tres tipos de transformaciones que cambian sólo la posición son las traslaciones, las reflexiones y las rotaciones.

traslación Una traslación, o deslizamiento, es un movimiento rígido que mueve cada punto de una figura a la misma distancia y en la misma dirección.

transversal o secante Una transversal o secante es una línea que interseca dos o más líneas en distintos puntos.

ENGLISH

trend line A trend line is a line on a scatter plot, drawn near the points, that approximates the association between the data sets.

Example

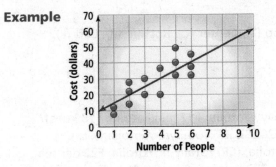

SPANISH

línea de tendencia Una línea de tendencia es una línea en un diagrama de dispersión, trazada cerca de los puntos, que se aproxima a la relación entre los conjuntos de datos.

Y

y-intercept The y-intercept of a line is the y-coordinate of the point where the line crosses the y-axis.

intercepto en y El intercepto en y de una recta es la coordenada y del punto por donde la recta cruza el eje de las y.

Example The y-intercept of the line is 4.

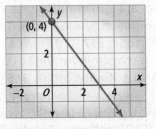

Z

zero exponent property For any nonzero number a, $a^0 = 1$.

propiedad del exponente cero Para cualquier número distinto de cero a, $a^0 = 1$.

Example
$$4^0 = 1$$
$$(-3)^0 = 1$$
$$x^0 = 1$$

ACKNOWLEDGEMENTS

Photographs

Photo locators denoted as follows: Top (T), Center (C), Bottom (B), Left (L), Right (R), Background (Bkgd)

Cover klagyivik/Fotolia.

F16 (CL) Aurielaki/Fotolia, (TR) Taras Livyy/Fotolia; **F17** piai/Fotolia; **F18** kues1/Fotolia; **F19** FedotovAnatoly/Fotolia; **F20** (Bkgrd) totallypic/Fotolia, (CL, CR) abert84/Fotolia; **F21** (CL) Eyematrix/Fotolia, (CR) totallypic/Fotolia; **F22** darnell_vfx/Fotolia; **F23** blueringmedia/Fotolia; **253** kalafoto/Fotolia; **254** (C) vicgmyr/Fotolia, (TR) vikpit74/Fotolia, (CL) akepong/Fotolia, (CR) travelphotos/Fotolia, (TL) patrimonio designs/Fotolia, (BR) makieni/Fotolia, (BCR) yossarian6/Fotolia; **257** Bedrin/Fotolia; **262** iadams/Shutterstock; **263** (CL) Elnur/Fotolia, (CR) Alliance/Fotolia, (T) cfarmer/Fotolia; **271** Rawpixel.com/Fotolia; **273** anton_lunkov/Fotolia; **275** (TCR) Richard Kane/Fotolia, (TR) Paul Yates/Fotolia, (T) Tolgatezcan/Fotolia; **276** Monkey Business/Fotolia; **278** Ant Clausen/Shutterstock; **283** kalafoto/Fotolia; **293** keytoken/Fotolia; **294** (TC) Kletr/Fotolia, (TCR) sveta/Fotolia, (TR) volff/Fotolia, (CL) andreusK/Fotolia, (C) murgvi/Fotolia, (CR) Alexander Potapov/Fotolia, (BCR) sapgreen/Fotolia, (BR) yossarian6/Fotolia; **297** (CR) Photka/Fotolia,(C) Goir/Fotolia, (CL) Photka/Fotolia; **309** Tarchyshnik Andrei/Fotolia; **321** keytoken/Fotolia; **339** (TC) Goir/Fotolia,(C) Africa Studio/Fotolia; **345** (C) Veniamin Kraskov/Fotolia, (TR) Goir/Fotolia, (CR) Ruslan Ivantsov/Fotolia, (CL) Studio KIWI/Shutterstock; **371** Stockphoto/Getty Images; **373** Marek/Fotolia; **374** (CL) kub_21212/Fotolia, (CR) kubais/Fotolia, (C) BirgitKorber/Fotolia, (TR, TCR) andrew_rybalko/Fotolia, (BR) Evgeny Korshenkov/Fotolia, (BCR) yossarian6/Fotolia; **377** tab62/Fotolia; **383** Marek/Fotolia; **387** (C) goodween123/Fotolia, (CL) Renewer/Fotolia; **394** (C) vladimirfloyd/Fotolia, (R) Big Face/Fotolia; **400** 3dmavr/Fotolia; **413** Pinkomelet/Shutterstock; **414** (CL) Subbotina Anna/Fotolia, (TCR) Bill/Fotolia, (TR) Yeko Photo Studio/Fotolia, (TC) Maxal Tamor/Fotolia, (BR) Natbasil/Fotolia, (BC) Natis/Fotolia, (BCR) Zonda/Fotolia, (B) yossarian6/Fotolia; **417** (C) Silkstock/Fotolia, (TC) Nagel's Blickwinkel/Fotolia, (CL) Ekarin/Fotolia; **439** Anekoho/Fotolia; **443** Pinkomelet/Shutterstock.